WRITING SYSTEMS OF THE WOR
AS USED IN MAJOR NEWSPAPERS

This map shows the official or native script of each region, but within each re minority-group newspapers published in many different languages. See th The names of countries are given on the back endpapers.

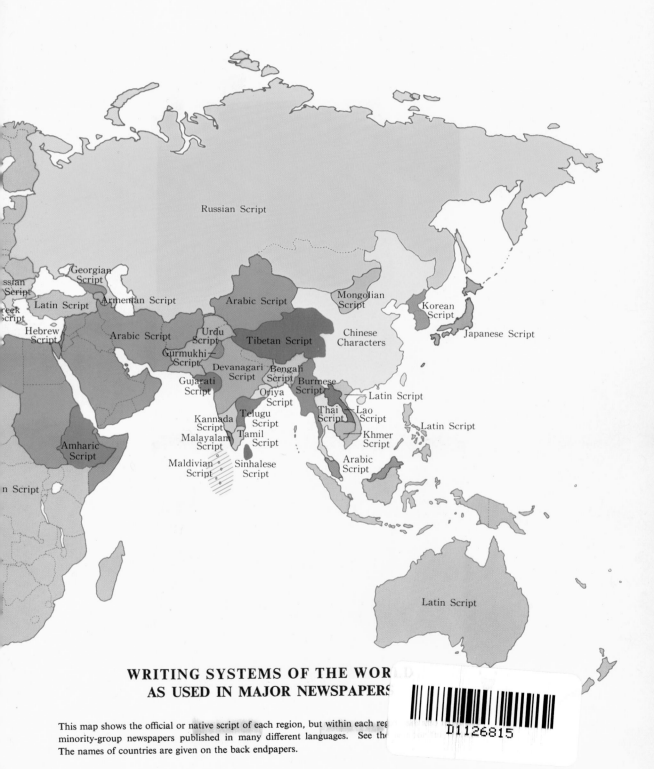

Nakanishi, Akira
Writing systems of the world.

WRITING SYSTEMS OF THE WORLD

WRITING SYSTEMS OF THE WORLD

—ALPHABETS • SYLLABARIES • PICTOGRAMS—

by AKIRA NAKANISHI

CHARLES E. TUTTLE COMPANY
Rutland · Vermont : Tokyo · Japan

Representatives

For Continental Europe:
BOXERBOOKS, INC., *Zurich*

For the British Isles:
PRENTICE-HALL INTERNATIONAL, INC., *London*

For Australasia:
BOOK WISE (AUSTRALIA) PTY. LTD.
104–108 Sussex Street, Sydney 2000

This is an English-language edition of *Sekai no Moji* (Kyoto: Shōkadō, 1975). New illustrations and newspaper samples have been added, and the text has been revised to make the information in this book current as of the date of publication.

Published by the Charles E. Tuttle Company, Inc.
of Rutland, Vermont & Tokyo, Japan
with editorial offices at
Suido 1-chome, 2–6, Bunkyo-ku, Tokyo

Library of Congress Catalog Card No. 79–64826
International Standard Book No. 0–8048 1293–4

First printing, 1980

Printed in Japan

TABLE OF CONTENTS

Acknowledgment is made to the following for permission to reproduce script samples: to Chuo Koronsha Publishing for I. Sugi, *Kekkei-moji Nyumon* (Tokyo, 1968) on pages 40, 41, and 42; to the Hutchinson Publishing Group for D. Diringer, *The Alphabet: A Key to the History of Mankind* (London, 1968) on pages 26, 27, 41, 43, 44, 68, 69, 104, 109, 110, and 114; to the Japan Bible Society for E. A. Nida, *The Book of a Thousand Tongues* (New York, 1972) on pages 22, 28, 42, 43, 69, 80, 97, 98, 105, 109, and 110; to Kenkyusha Publishing Co. for S. Ichikawa, H. Kozu, and S. Hattori, *Sekai Gengo Gaisetsu* (Tokyo, 1971) on page 41; to Motilal Banarsidass for B. A. Grierson, *Linguistic Survey of India* (Delhi, 1963–) on pages 44, 68, and 69; to Routledge and Kegan Paul for E. A. Wallis Budge, *Egyptian Language* (London, 1966) on page 104; to the University of Chicago Press for I. J. Gelb, *A Study of Writing* (Revised edition. Chicago and London, 1963) on pages 26, 40, 41, 43, and 109; and to Veb Deutscher Verlag der Wissenschaften for H. Jensen, *Die Schrift in Vergangenheit und Gegenwart* (Berlin, 1969) on pages 27, 28, 40, 42, 43, 44, 68, 104, and 105.

INTRODUCTION

Ever since my student days in Kyoto University, I have been fascinated by scripts or written characters, which I consider the most important product of human culture. My interest has been deepened by my work as a printer, and my collection of script samples now includes books, manuscripts, pictures of inscriptions, and movable type, as well as newspapers gathered during my travels. This collection has gradually taught me that scripts or written characters not only represent spoken languages but also reflect historical, political, and cultural developments.

As a collector, I discovered books about each language and about the dramatic deciphering of various ancient inscriptions. But I could not find a relatively simple survey of scripts for collectors and general readers rather than specialists. I therefore wrote a short book on this subject in Japanese.

Because of the popularity of this book in my country I am now able, with the help of the Charles E. Tuttle Company, to translate and adapt my survey into English. In this version, various scripts in common use throughout the world are explained for English-speaking people. The phrase "in common use" means here that the scripts are those used in daily newspapers. For the convenience of the reader, the phonetic value of each letter in the various scripts is represented as simply as possible by Latin letters (that is, letters of the English alphabet) in italic type.

The resultant pronunciation will, of course, only approximate the phonetic system of each language. Nevertheless, I hope that travelers, using this book, will attempt to read scripts that would otherwise be as meaningless to them as bird tracks or worm squiggles in the sand. Though they will not necessarily be able to understand what they read, they will in many cases be able to recognize borrowed words and the names of people and places, to find restaurants, hotels, and small shops. If one knows a little Russian script, for example, one can recognize PECTOPAH as "restaurant" and one may even be able to have a meal. I hope, too, that by familiarizing the reader with the appearance and approximate pronunciation of foreign scripts, this book will encourage international understanding. And I am sure it will be helpful to stamp collectors and other hobbyists in many ways.

Upon the publication of this book, I would like to express my deepest gratitude to Dr. Tatsuo Nishida, Professor of the Faculty of Letters of Kyoto University, who has deciphered Hsihsia characters and who kindly assisted me in my collection and study of written characters. I would also like to express my appreciation to the staff of the Charles E. Tuttle Company, who provided the opportunity to write this book in English. Furthermore, I would like to thank the foreign embassies in Japan and Japanese embassies in foreign countries that helped me obtain samples of various newspapers and some information about them.

—Akira Nakanishi

Kyoto, Japan

HOW TO USE THIS BOOK

This book describes twenty-nine scripts in common use throughout the world. General readers can of course look through the various sections at their leisure. Those who need to study the script of a particular country —travelers or stamp collectors— should look at the world script map on the endpapers, find the name of the script used in the country, and then use the Table of Contents or Index to find where in this book the discussion of that script appears.

To identify an unfamiliar script on a postage stamp, go to the beginning of each chapter and scan the scripts that appear in brackets after the countries' names until you find the script that matches the one on your stamp. For other materials written in unfamiliar scripts, look carefully through the newspaper samples that appear in the script sections. If you can't find the script in this way, look at the ends of Chapters 2, 3, 4, 5, 6, 7, and 9, where other scripts not used in daily newspapers as well as interesting samples of extinct scripts are given.

Nations are listed at the beginning of each chapter by their common names. Other names used are given in parentheses after the common name. The names of nations and states are given in their official scripts in brackets; italic letters for pronunciation follow the official script if it is written with non-Latin letters. For example, "[မြန်မာ *myanmā*]" shows that the official name of Burma written in Burmese script is မြန်မာ, which is pronounced *myanmā* (see the note on pronunciation, below). Such names in vernacular scripts are often seen on postage stamps. Some nations include dependencies, and a few nations have been omitted because of their size and the relative unimportance of their scripts, or because of recent political changes.

These nation sections also contain general information about the scripts to be discussed in the chapter and notes on the various languages and scripts used in each country. Every language mentioned has been assigned a group within one of the following thirteen language families.

- Indo-European
- Semitic-Hamitic
- Caucasian (including Basque)
- Uralic (comprising the Finno-Ugric and Samoyed languages)
- Altaic (including Japanese and Korean)
- Sino-Tibetan (including Vietnamese)
- Austroasiatic
- Malayo-Polynesian (also called Austronesian)
- Dravidian
- African (comprising the Bantu, Sudanic, and Khoisan languages)
- Australian (including the Papuan and Tasmanian languages)
- Paleo-Asiatic (including the Eskimo languages)
- Languages of the Indians in North and South America

The presentation "(Slavic/Indo-European)" for Bulgarian, for example, shows that the Bulgarian language belongs to the Slavic group within the family of Indo-European languages.

Each of the twenty-nine scripts in common use appears in a separate script section. The content of each section varies according to the script discussed, but generally it includes: a chart of the symbols or letters used, with pronunciation readings; a list of the most important signs and diacritical marks; a discussion of the mechanics of script writing—style of letter, shape transformation, tone and vowel indication, joining of letters, etc.; notes on reading and script direction; and the figures used for numerals. In addition, a recent newspaper sample is given as an example of the script in daily use.

The pronunciation, or phonetic value, of each letter is shown by Latin letters in italic type (*a*, *b*, *c*, etc.). Accurately transcribing sounds is a complex matter, even if one ignores the regional differences of a single language, and since this is a book primarily about the mechanics of script writing I have thought it better to offer only approximate readings. Almost all the italic letters used should be pronounced as they are in English, within the following guidelines.

Consonants

- *b* as in "bird"
- *bh* aspirate *b*, that is, *b* pronounced with breath, as in "Bob Hope" read quickly
- *ch* as in "cheese"
- *chh* aspirate *ch*
- *d* as in "dog"
- *dh* aspirate *d*
- *ḍ* cerebral *d*, that is, *d* pronounced under the tongue, which is curled up backward; used especially in Asiatic and Indian languages
- *ḍh* aspirate *ḍ*
- *f* as in "fan"
- *g* as in "gold," never as in "gem"
- *gh* aspirate *g*
- *h* as in "horn"; but see also *bh*, *ch*, *chh*, *dh*, *ḍh*, *gh*, *jh*, *kh*, *ph*, *sh*, *th*, *ṭh*
- *j* as in "jam"
- *jh* aspirate *j*
- *k* as in "key"
- *kh* aspirate *k*
- *l* as in "lamp"
- *m* as in "map"
- *n* as in "name"; also used to show a nasal sound
- *ṇ* cerebral *n*
- *ng* as in "king" or "Bengal"
- *ṅ* same as *ng*; used only when followed by *g*, *h*, *k*, or *y*
- *ny* as in "Nyasaland"
- *ñ* same as *ny*; used only when followed by *y*
- *p* as in "pen"
- *ph* aspirate *p*, never as in "photo"
- *q* light *k* as in "Iraq"
- *r* as in "rat"
- *s* as in "sand"; but see also *ts*
- *sh* as in "shell"
- *t* as in "tank"
- *th* aspirate *t*, never as in "this" or "think"
- *ṭ* cerebral *t*
- *ṭh* aspirate *ṭ*
- *ts* as in "rats"
- *v* as in "valley"
- *w* as in "wing"
- *x* "ch" sound as in Scottish "loch" or German "Bach"; never *ks* or *z*
- *y* as in "yacht"; but see also *ny*
- *z* as in "zoo"
- *'* glottal stop, that is, a stop made by a brief closure of the glottis

Conjunct consonants (consonants pronounced together) are indicated by the juxtaposition of the consonants in the above list. For example, *ks*, *ty*, *pr*, *kt*, *ml*, *str*, and so on.

Vowels

- *a* as in "alms"
- *ā* long or extended *a* (that is, normal *a* lasting two counts, as in "Aah")
- *e* as in "echo"

- *ē* long *e*
- *i* as in "chief"
- *ī* long *i*
- *o* as in "orient"
- *ō* long *o*
- *u* as in "rule"
- *ū* long *u*

When diacritical signs and other appendages on letters are discussed, ◌ shows the position of the base letter. For example, the umlaut in German is shown as ◌̈.

Numerals are given for each script even if they are no longer used. The signs 1, 2, 3, 4, 5, 6, 7, 8, 9, and 0 are called Arabic figures, though the Arabic numerals used in Arabic script have different shapes.

There are two appendixes. Appendix 1 is a short discussion of the differences between the two basic kinds of script systems that have been developed by human cultures throughout the ages. Appendix 2 is a discussion of the various directions in which scripts can be written and read.

In the Glossary appear explanations of the less-common terms used in the script discussions. I have, however, tried to keep this book as nontechnical as possible.

1. SCRIPTS OF EUROPE

In Europe, generally speaking, Latin script is used in the areas of Roman Catholicism and Protestantism; in areas of Greek Orthodoxy Cyrillic script is used. In Greece, Greek script is used in a revival of its classical writing. Latin script is explained on page 14, Cyrillic (or Russian) script on page 20, and Greek script on page 16.

Each nation in Europe has its own language; for that reason, each adds letters to or deletes letters from Latin or Cyrillic script as necessary. The scripts used in newspapers are given here with the languages of each nation.

ALBANIA [SHQIPERIA]

Albanian (Albanian/Indo-European) is written in Latin script with the additional letters ç and ë, and without the letter w.

A postage stamp of Albania.

AUSTRIA [REPUBLIK ÖSTERREICH]

Newspapers are in German, which is written in Latin script with the additional letters ä, ö, ü, and ß. ß is the ligature of sz or ss.

BELGIUM [BELGIQUE; BELGIE]

The official languages of Belgium are French and Flemish, the latter being the same as Dutch with but slight differences. Newspapers are published in these two languages.

BULGARIA [БЪЛГАРИЯ *bulgariya*]

Newspapers are published in Bulgarian (Slavic/Indo-European), which is written in Russian script without the letters ë, ы, and э. German newspapers are also published.

CZECHOSLOVAKIA
[ČESKOSLOVENSKO]

In Czechoslovakia, Czech (or Bohemian) and Slovak are the official languages, and both are used in newspapers. Czech (Slavic/Indo-European) is written in Latin script with the additional letters á, č, ď, é, ě, í, ň, ó, ř, š, ť, ú, ů, ý, and ž and without the letters q, w, and x. Slovak (Slavic/Indo-European) also uses Latin script but with the additional letters ä, á, č, ď, é, í, ľ, ň, ó, ô, ŕ, š, ť, ú, ý, and ž, and without the letters q, w, and x.

DENMARK [DANMARK]

Newspapers are published in Danish (Germanic/Indo-European), which is written in Latin script with the additional letters å, æ, ö, and ø. The letter å is the same as aa.

FINLAND [SUOMI]

Newspapers are published in Swedish and in Finnish (Finnic/Uralic), also called Suomian, which is written in Latin script with the additional letters ä and ö, and without b, c, f, q, w, x, and z.

FRANCE [REPUBLIQUE FRANÇAISE]

In France, in addition to French (Italic/Indo-European), there are the Basque (Basque/Caucasian) and Provençal (Italic/Indo-European) languages. However, these languages are not used in daily newspapers. All newspapers are published in French, which is written in Latin script with the additional letters à, â, ç, ë, é, è, ê, ï, î, ô, œ, ü, ù, and û. The letters k and w are only used for borrowed words.

GERMANY, EAST
[DDR; Deutsche Demokratische Republik]
Newspapers are published in German (Germanic/Indo-European).

GERMANY, WEST (Federal Republic of Germany) [Deutsche Bundes]
Newspapers are in German. In both Germanies and in Scandinavian nations, the Gothic letters shown on page 14 are also used ornamentally.

GREECE [*ΕΛΛΑΣ hellas*]
Newspapers are published in Greek (Hellenic/Indo-European), in English, and in French. Greek is the official language, and though it differs somewhat from ancient Greek, it is written in the same Greek script.

HUNGARY [MAGYAR]
Newspapers are published in Hungarian (Ugric/Uralic), which is written in Latin script with the additional letters á, é, í, ó, ő, ö, ű, ü, and ú, but without q, w, and x.

ICELAND [ÍSLAND]
Newspapers are published in Icelandic (Germanic/Indo-European), which is written in Latin script with the additional letters á, æ, é, í, ó, ö, ú, ý, ð, and þ, but without c, q, and w. The letter þ indicates a "th" sound as in "think" in English, and ð indicates a "th" sound as in "the".

IRELAND (Eire) [éıre]
Newspapers are published in English and in Irish (Celtic/Indo-European), which is written in Latin script with the additional letters á, é, í, ó, and ú. It contains no j, k, q, v, w, x, y, or z.

A postage stamp of Ireland.

Irish is also written in Gaelic script, which consists of eighteen letters as follows (see also page 28).

GAELIC	ᴀ	ᴅ	c	ᴅ	e	ꝼ	ᵹ	h	ı
LATIN	a	b	c	d	e	f	g	h	i
	l	m	n	o	p	ꞃ	ꞅ	ꞇ	u
	l	m	n	o	p	r	s	t	u

ITALY [ITALIA]
Most newspapers are published in Italian (Italic/Indo-European), which is written in Latin script with the additional letters à, è, ì, ò, and ù. The letters j, k, w, x, and y are only used in borrowed words. Besides Italian newspapers, there are also English, German, and Slovene newspapers published.

LUXEMBOURG
Newspapers are published in French and in German.

THE NETHERLANDS (Holland) [NEDERLAND]
Newspapers are published in Dutch (Germanic/Indo-European), which is written in Latin script consisting of the same twenty-six letters used in English.

NORWAY [NORGE]
Newspapers are published in Norwegian (Germanic/Indo-European), which is written in Latin script with the additional letters å, æ, and ø.

POLAND [POLSKA]
Newspapers are published in Polish (Slavic/Indo-European), which is written in

Latin script with the additional letters ą, ć, ę, ł, ń, ó, ś, ź, and ż, and without j, q, v, and x.

PORTUGAL

Newspapers are published in Portuguese (Italic/Indo-European), which is written in Latin script with the additional letters ã, á, à, â, ç, ë, é, è, ê, ï, í, ó, ò, ô, õ, ü, and ú. The letters k, w, and y are used only in borrowed words.

ROMANIA (Rumania)

Newspapers are published in Romanian (Italic/Indo-European), which is written in Latin script with the additional letters ă, î, ş, and ţ, but without k, q, w, x, and y.

SPAIN [ESPAÑA]

Newspapers are published in Spanish (Italic/Indo-European), which is written in Latin script with the additional letters á, é, í, ñ, ó, ü, and ú. The letters k and w are only used in borrowed words. The Basque language in northern Spain does not seem to be used in any newspaper.

SWEDEN [SVERIGE]

Newspapers are published in Swedish (Germanic/Indo-European), which is written in Latin script with the additional letters å, ä, and ö.

SWITZERLAND [HELVETIA; SCHWEIZ; SUISSE; SVIZZERA]

The official languages of Switzerland are German, French, Italian, and Rhaeto-Romanic (Italic/Indo-European). Newspapers are published in these languages as well as in English for tourists.

UNITED KINGDOM (Great Britain)

Newspapers are published in English (Germanic/Indo-European), which is written in Latin script (twenty-six letters).

YUGOSLAVIA [JUGOSLAVIJA; ЈУГОСЛАВИЈА *yugoslabiya*]

Yugoslavia is a union of six republics; the language and script situation there is quite intricate. In Slovenia in the north, newspapers are published in Slovene (Slavic/Indo-European), which is written in Latin script with the additional letters č, š, and ž, and without the letters q, w, x, and y.

A postage stamp of Yugoslavia.

In the other republics newspapers are published in Serbo-Croatian (Slavic/Indo-European), which in Croatia is written in Latin script but which in the other republics is written in Serbian script. Broadly speaking, the Serbian alphabet belongs to Cyrillic script, though it differs a little from the Russian alphabet. Serbian and Latin alphabets used in Serbo-Croatian are contrasted in the table below.

SERBIAN	А	Б	В	Г	Д	Ђ	Е	Ж	З	И	Ј	К	Л	Љ
LATIN	A	B	V	G	D	Đ	E	Ž	Z	I	J	K	L	Lj
PHON.	*a*	*b*	*v*	*g*	*d*	*j*	*e*	*j*	*z*	*i*	*y*	*k*	*l*	*ly*

М	Н	Њ	О	П	Р	С	Т	Ћ	У	Ф	Х	Ц	Ч	Џ	Ш
M	N	Nj	O	P	R	S	T	Ć	U	F	H	C	Č	Dž	Š
m	*n*	*ny*	*o*	*p*	*r*	*s*	*t*	*ty*	*u*	*f*	*h*	*ts*	*ch*	*j*	*sh*

Latin Script

Latin script, which is the most widely used in the world today, was originally the writing of the ancient Roman Empire. In the Middle Ages it became the writing of Roman Catholicism and spread with this doctrine through western Europe. At present, most European nations, some nations in Asia, almost all the countries in Africa, and all the nations of the Americas and Oceania use Latin script to write their languages.

Alphabet Though the original Latin alphabet consisted of the twenty-four letters A, B, C, D, E, F, G, H, I, K, L, M, N, O, P, Q, R, S, T, U, V, X, Y, and Z, in this book the twenty-six-letter alphabet with J and W is called Latin script. For English and for Dutch these twenty-six letters are used intact, but for other languages additional letters and diacritical signs are used. In some nations, a few of the twenty-six letters are used only for borrowed words.

There are capital (majuscule) and small (minuscule) letters and roman (standing) and italic (oblique) styles. The capital letters are generally used for the beginning letter of a sentence and for the first letter of a proper noun, though this varies according to the language. In Germany and the surrounding areas, Gothic or German letters are customarily used in captions and in classic books.

The styles of these letters are contrasted in the table at the right. Approximate phonetic values are also given because of the differences in each language.

Ligatures Many ligatures were used in Medieval Latin script, but nowadays only the ampersand [&] remains; it means "and" and is pronounced differently in each language, for example, *e'* in French.

ROMAN:	CAPITAL	A	B	C	D	E	F
	SMALL	a	b	c	d	e	f
ITALIC:	CAPITAL	*A*	*B*	*C*	*D*	*E*	*F*
	SMALL	*a*	*b*	*c*	*d*	*e*	*f*
GOTHIC:	CAPITAL	𝔄	𝔅	ℭ	𝔇	𝔈	𝔉
	SMALL	𝔞	𝔟	𝔠	𝔡	𝔢	𝔣
PHONETIC VALUE		*a*	*b,p*	*s,k,ch*	*d,t*	*e*	*f*

G	H	I	J	K	L	M	N	O	P
g	h	i	j	k	l	m	n	o	p
G	*H*	*I*	*J*	*K*	*L*	*M*	*N*	*O*	*P*
g	*h*	*i*	*j*	*k*	*l*	*m*	*n*	*o*	*p*
𝔊	ℌ	ℑ	𝔍	𝔎	𝔏	𝔐	𝔑	𝔒	𝔓
𝔤	𝔥	𝔦	𝔧	𝔨	𝔩	𝔪	𝔫	𝔬	𝔭
g,k	*h*	*i*	*j,y*	*k*	*l*	*m*	*n*	*o*	*p*

Q	R	S	T	U	V	W	X	Y	Z
q	r	s	t	u	v	w	x	y	z
Q	*R*	*S*	*T*	*U*	*V*	*W*	*X*	*Y*	*Z*
q	*r*	*s*	*t*	*u*	*v*	*w*	*x*	*y*	*z*
𝔔	ℜ	𝔖	𝔗	𝔘	𝔙	𝔚	𝔛	𝔜	ℨ
𝔮	𝔯	ſ,𝔰	𝔱	𝔲	𝔳	𝔴	𝔵	𝔶	𝔷
q,k	*r*	*s,z*	*t*	*u*	*v,f*	*w*	*ks,z,x*	*y*	*z,ts*

Reading and Punctuation Latin script always runs from left to right on a horizontal line. Punctuation (period, comma, colon, question mark, and so on) is in each language the same as in English, though [¿] is used in Spanish.

Numerals

I	II	III	IV	V	VI	VII	VIII	IX	X
1	2	3	4	5	6	7	8	9	10

L	C	D	M,ↀ	ↁ	ↂ
50	100	500	1,000	5,000	10,000

Arabic figures (1, 2, 3 . . .) are most commonly used.

Schranz bei den Superstars in USA Letzter — Rom: Italien gegen BRD 0 : 0 / S. 13

𝔄𝔯𝔟𝔢𝔦𝔱𝔢𝔯=𝔍𝔢𝔦𝔱𝔲𝔫𝔤

GEGRÜNDET 1889

S 2.50 / Lire 250 / Din 4.50

AZ

Nr. 49 P. b. b.
WIEN, MITTWOCH
27. FEBRUAR 1974

Steirische VP stellt nun auch Schleinzer in Frage

„Als Kanzlerkandidat für 1975 keineswegs sicher"

GRAZ (AZ). Die Vermutungen, mit der Kritik an VP-Generalsekretär Kohlmaier meinte man eigentlich ÖVP-Obmann Schleinzer, wurden von den Spitzenfunktionären der steirischen ÖVP in Hörfunkinterviews massiv bestätigt. Zwar sprachen sich alle noch für eine Wiederwahl Schleinzers am kommenden Parteitag aus. Mit brutaler Offenheit wurde allerdings eine Reihe von Vorbehalten gegen Schleinzer vorgebracht.

So meinte Landeshauptmann Niederl, man sei für die Wiederwahl Schleinzers, „weil sich keine Alternativen bieten", obwohl er Schleinzer nicht für den idealen Obmann hält. Der steirische Wirtschaftsbundobmann und Landesrat Peltzmann stellte gar in Frage, ob Schleinzer 1975 Spitzenkadidat für das Amt des Bundeskanzlers sein werde.

Die Interviews wurden vom ORF-Studio Steiermark über den steirischen Regionalsender ausgestrahlt. Dabei versuchte Niederl erstmals, seine Kritik an Kohlmaier zu artikulieren. Kohlmaier sei nicht jener Managertyp, der die Organisation voll in der Hand habe, meinte Niederl.

Im Verlauf der Interviews kam dann allerdings immer stärker ÖVP-Obmann Schleinzer ins Schußfeld. Zwar betonte Niederl, man sei für die Wiederwahl Schleinzers, meinte

FORTSETZUNG AUF SEITE 2

Gespräche Israel-Syrien in Wien?

Gerüchte aus Damaskus — Außenministerium: Grundsätzliche Bereitschaft

LONDON/DAMASKUS/WIEN (ap, apa, afp, upi, AZ). Wenn die derzeitige Nahostmission des amerikanischen Außenministers Kissinger tatsächlich zu syrisch-israelischen Truppenentflechtungsgesprächen führen, dann werden diese, wie es in syrischen Kreisen heißt, wahrscheinlich in Wien stattfinden. Ein Sprecher des Außenministeriums in Wien teilte zu diesem Gerücht mit, daß bisher noch niemand offiziell an Wien herangetreten sei. Grundsätzlich hat Österreich wiederholt zu erkennen gegeben, daß es seine Dienste als Gastland für internationale Gespräche und Konferenzen zur Verfügung stellt, wenn beide Seiten dies wünschen.

Es gibt keine syrische Botschaft in Wien, sondern der syrische Botschafter in Budapest ist in Wien mitakkreditiert. In Wien befindet sich lediglich der syrische Kulturattaché. Dieser erklärte auf AZ-Anfrage, er habe über diese Angelegenheit auch nur aus Presseberichten gehört, wisse aber offiziell noch nichts über sie.

Außenminister Kissinger ist Dienstag von London nach Syrien abgeflogen, mit der Hoffnung, Syriens Präsidenten Assad zu einer Aufnahme von Friedensverhandlungen mit Israel zu bewegen. Er wurde am A[illegible]n Damaskus erwartet. Kissingers Zusammentreffen mit dem 43jährigen syrischen Luftwaffengeneral wird darüber Aufschluß geben, ob der Außenminister durch seine Reisediplomatie nach Unterzeichnung des ägyptisch-israelischen Entflechtungsvertrages auch die Schwierigkeiten bei den Verhandlungen Israels mit seinem nördlichen Nachbarstaat beseitigen kann.

Mit der Erklärung der israelischen Regierungschefin Golda Meir, die Golanhöhen seien ein Teil Israels, sind die USA nicht einverstanden. Dies erklärte Thomas Scotes, Leiter der amerikanischen Interessenvertretung in der italienischen Botschaft in Damaskus, in einem Dienstag veröffentlichten Interview mit der libanesischen Tageszeitung „Daily Star".

Ein israelischer Autobus mit amerikanischen Juden ist auf einer Tour durch Sinai in der Nähe von Ismailia versehentlich auf ägyptisches Territorium gelangt. Israel verlangte die Rückgabe des Fahrzeuges sowie die Auslieferung der US-Touristen.

Militärrevolte in Äthiopien

Soldaten können mit ihrem Sold nicht leben

ADDIS ABEBA (reuter, dpa). Militäreinheiten unter dem Kommando junger Offiziere haben die Stadt Asmara im Norden von Äthiopien besetzt, weil sie mit ihrer Besoldung unzufrieden sind.

Nach den in Addis Abeba einlaufenden spärlichen Berichten wurden in Asmara mehrere hohe Offiziere überwältigt und unter Bewachung gestellt. Ein Reisender berichtete, die Soldaten hätten ihm erklärt, sie seien nicht gegen die Regierung an sich. Aber sie könnten von dem ihnen gegenwärtig gezahlten Sold einfach nicht leben. Steigende Lebenshaltungskosten hatten in Äthiopien in jüngster Zeit wiederholt zu Ausschreitungen geführt.

Ärzte verzögern Gesundenuntersuchung

Verhandlungen festgefahren — Ärztekammer verlangt höhere Honorare

WIEN (SK). Die Durchführung der Gesundenuntersuchungen dürfte noch eine geraume Weile auf sich warten lassen, weil die Verhandlungen mit der Ärztekammer festgefahren sind. Die größte Schwierigkeit bei den Verhandlungen bereitet die Höhe der Ärztehonorare. Die Ärztekammer fordert um 80 Prozent mehr, als die Kassen bieten.

Die einfachste Variante — man geht mit dem Krankenschein zum Arzt und läßt die Untersuchungen führt. In Österreich gibt es 17 derartige Anstalten, die größte davon ist die der Wiener Gemeindebediensteten mit 86.000 Versicherten und Mitversicherten. Mindestens 100.000 Österreicher könnten also die Gesundenuntersuchung nicht in Anspruch nehmen, auch wenn sich Hauptverband und Ärztekammer über die Honorare einigen.

Der Hauptverband regte bereits an, daß die Krankenfürsorgeanstalten den Verhandlungen zugezogen Nichtversicherten lehnt die Ärztekammer jedoch mit dem Argument, „die Frau Mautner Markhof kann sich die Untersuchung selbst zahlen", ab. Der Kreis der Nichtversicherten umfaßt jedoch in Wirklichkeit auch die Fürsorgerentner, also keineswegs nur zahlungskräftige Personen.

EIN EIGENES GESETZ?

Im Hauptverband befürchtet man, daß vor den Ärztekammerwahlen im April eine einvernehmliche Lösung

Liza in Rio

Trotz strömenden Regens ging es beim traditionellen Karneval in Rio wieder hoch her. Auch Showstar Liza Minnelli (Bild) war von den 44.000 Sambatänzern begeistert, die sich vor hunderttausenden Zuschauern um den begehrten Titel der besten Tanzgruppe bewarben. Wieder gab es auch viele Verletzte (upi-Funkbild)

Nixon: „Keine Amtsenthebung"

Präsident glaubt nicht an Verfahren gegen ihn

WASHINGTON (dpa). Präsident Nixon hat in der Nacht zum Dienstag die Überzeugung geäußert, daß der amerikanische Kongreß kein Verfahren zu seiner Amtsenthebung einleitet. In einer von Fernsehen und Rundfunk direkt übertragenen Pressekonferenz wies Nixon darauf hin, daß vor einem formellen „Prozeß" des Senats das Repräsentantenhaus eine „Anklage" erheben müsse. „Nach meiner Auffassung werden sie (das Repräsentantenhaus) eine solche Entscheidung nicht treffen."

Gleichzeitig stellte Nixon fest, daß seiner Auffassung nach ein kriminelles Vergehen nötig sei, um einen Präsidenten anzuklagen und des Amtes zu entheben. Der Präsident widersprach damit dem Expertenstab des Rechtsausschusses im Repräsentantenhaus, der auch nichtkriminelle Vergehen, wie Mißbrauch der Macht oder des Regierungsapparats, als Grundlage für ein Verfahren befürwortete. Der Rechtsausschuß untersucht gegenwärtig, ob Gründe vorliegen, gegen Nixon wegen der Watergateaffäre und damit verbundener Skandale ein Verfahren einzuleiten.

Effekt" in der Frage des arabischen Ölembargos haben. Nixon äußerte auch „Sympathien" mit dem russischen Schriftsteller Alexander Solschenizyn, machte jedoch klar, daß seine Ausweisung den Entspannungsprozeß zwischen Washington und Moskau nicht stoppen dürfte.

15 Millionen Schilling für die Sahelzone

WIEN (SK). Mit rund 15 Millionen Schilling wird Österreich zur Hilfsaktion der UNO für die von der Trockenheit schwer getroffene Sahelzone beitragen, teilte Staatssekretär Veselsky Dienstag anläßlich des Besuches des stellvertretenden UN-Generalsekretärs Morse in Wien mit.

Morse, der direkt aus dem Katastrophengebiet kommt, besucht Österreich als erstes von zehn europäischen Ländern, um die mittel- und langfristige Hilfe für die Sahelstaaten zu koordinieren. Österreichs Beitrag konzentriert sich zunächst

An Austrian newspaper written in German in Latin script. Its title printed in Gothic letters is 𝔄𝔯𝔟𝔢𝔦𝔱𝔢𝔯 𝔍𝔢𝔦𝔱𝔲𝔫𝔤 *arbaiter tsaitung*.

Greek Script

Greek script has a long history. The writing system of ancient Greece remains and is written and read in present-day Greece, though the modern Greek language differs somewhat from ancient Greek.

Alphabet Greek script has distinct capital (majuscule) and small (minuscule) letters and consists of the following twenty-four letters.

CAPITAL	*Α*	*Β*	*Γ*	*Δ*	*Ε*	*Ζ*	*Η*	*Θ*
SMALL	*α*	*β*	*γ*	*δ*	*ε*	*ζ*	*η*	*θ*
PHON.	*a*	*v*	*g,y*	*d*	*e*	*z*	*i*	*s*
	Ι	*Κ*	*Λ*	*Μ*	*Ν*	*Ξ*	*Ο*	*Π*
	ι	*κ*	*λ*	*μ*	*ν*	*ξ*	*ο*	*π*
	i	*k*	*l*	*m*	*n*	*ks*	*o*	*p*
	Ρ	*Σ*	*Τ*	*Υ*	*Φ*	*Χ*	*Ψ*	*Ω*
	ρ	*σ,ς*	*τ*	*υ*	*φ*	*χ*	*ψ*	*ω*
	r	*s,z*	*t*	*i*	*f*	*x*	*ps*	*o*

The small letter of *Σ* is *σ*, but *ς* is the final form, used at the end of a word.
Both *Γ* and *Σ* have two phonetic values; the pronunciation of each is determined by the letter that follows.
Diphthongs and some combinations of letters are pronounced as special sounds:

αι	*αυ*	*ει*	*ευ*	*οι*	*ου*	*ηυ*	*υι*	*γγ*
e	*af,av*	*i*	*ef,ev*	*i*	*u*	*if,iv*	*i*	*ng*

γκ	*γξ*	*γχ*
g,ng	*nks*	*nkh*

A postage stamp of Greece, with the country's name in the lower part, read *hellas*.

Diacritical marks Greek texts use many diacritical marks, some of which are the following. ◌́ (acute), ◌̀ (grave), and ◌͂ (circumflex) are three signs for accents. Greek accents are not stress accents but pitch accents.
In Greek, when a vowel or diphthong, sometimes *ρ*, comes at the beginning of a word, whether it includes an aspirate or not must be indicated on the top of the vowel (or second vowel of the diphthong). Such a sign is called an aspirate or breathing sign: ◌̔ means rough breathing and ◌̓ means smooth breathing. If both the accent and aspirate signs are on one vowel, ◌̀ or ◌́ is placed to the right of ◌̔ or ◌̓, and ◌͂ is placed above: *ἅ*, *ἇ*.
◌ͅ is called iota subscription; it is another form of *ι* (iota). This sign is added below the three vowels *α*, *η*, and *ω*: *ᾳ ā*, *ῃ ē*, and *ῳ ō*.
Sometimes ◌̈ (called a diaeresis) is used on *ι* or *υ* to separate a diphthong: *και* is read *ke* but *καϊ* is read *kai*. Accent signs are placed within this diaeresis: *ΰ*, *ῒ*, but *ῧ*.
◌̄ shows a long vowel and ◌̆ shows a short vowel. These are sometimes used in rhymed verse.
Thus, in Greek, movable types for accents are required as follows for the letter *α*.

ά ὰ ἀ ἁ ἄ ἂ ἅ ἃ ᾶ ἆ ἇ ᾱ ᾰ ᾶ ᾳ ᾴ ᾲ ᾀ ᾁ ᾄ ᾂ ᾅ ᾃ ᾷ ᾆ ᾇ

Reading and punctuation Greek script runs from left to right on a horizontal line. The period and comma are the same as in English; the colon, however, is not 〔:〕 but 〔·〕, and the question mark is not 〔?〕 but 〔;〕.

Numerals Originally Greek numbers were written using letters of the old alphabet with 〔′〕 on the right shoulder.

Α′	*Β′*	*Γ′*	*Δ′*	*Ε′*	*F′*	*Ζ′*	*Η′*	*Θ′*	*Ι′*	*Ρ′*
1	2	3	4	5	6	7	8	9	10	100

Now, however, Arabic figures are used.

ΑΚΡΟΠΟΛΙΣ

ΑΡΙΘ. 14.463 ΤΡΙΤΗ 8 ΟΚΤΩΒΡΙΟΥ 1974 ΕΤΟΣ ΙΔΡΥΣΕΩΣ 1881 ΤΙΜΗ ΔΡΧ. 4

ΤΟ ΚΥΠΡΙΑΚΟ ΘΑ ΛΥΘΗ ΜΕΤΑΞΥ ΚΛΗΡΙΔΗ – ΝΤΕΝΚΤΑΣ ΒΕΒΑΙΩΝΕΙ Ο κ. ΚΙΣΣΙΝΓΚΕΡ

ΣΕΛΙΣ 10

Ὁρκίζεται αὔριον

ΝΕΑ ΥΠΟ ΤΟΝ κ. ΚΑΡΑΜΑΝΛΗΝ ΚΥΒΕΡΝΗΣΙΣ

Στὴν Ἀθήνα ἡ πρώτη ὁμιλία τοῦ Πρωθυπουργοῦ

ΔΕΝ ΕΞΕΛΙΠΑΝ ΟΙ ΚΙΝΔΥΝΟΙ ΥΠΟΝΟΜΕΥΣΕΩΣ ΤΩΝ ΕΚΛΟΓΩΝ

ΕΠΙ ΙΣΟΙΣ ΟΡΟΙΣ

Ἑνοποιοῦνται σὲ κοινὸ κόμμα Ε.Κ. καὶ Κ.Ν.Π.Δ.

ΑΡΧΗΓΟΣ Ο κ. Γ. ΜΑΥΡΟΣ. ΑΠΕΜΟΝΩΘΗ Ο κ. Ι. ΖΙΓΔΗΣ.— ΚΑΙ ΣΥΜΠΡΑΞΙΣ ΕΔΑ – Κ.Κ.Ε.

Ἀπολύονται ὑπάλληλοι ΕΛ.ΤΑ. ποὺ διετέλεσαν λογοκριταὶ τῶν ἐπιστολῶν

ΠΡΟΧΩΡΕΙ ΤΟ ΞΗΛΩΜΑ ΤΟΥ ΜΗΧΑΝΙΣΜΟΥ ΥΠΟΚΛΟΠΗΣ ΤΗΛΕΦΩΝΗΜΑΤΩΝ.— ΔΗΛΩΣΕΙΣ ΤΟΥ ΥΦΥΠΟΥΡΓΟΥ κ. ΕΜΜ. ΚΕΦΑΛΟΓΙΑΝΝΗ

Φοιτητικαὶ ἐκλογαὶ στὶς 9 Νοεμβρίου

ΝΕΑΙ ΠΡΥΤΑΝΙΚΑΙ ΑΡΧΑΙ ΕΞΕΛΕΓΗΣΑΝ.— ΔΗΛΩΣΕΙΣ ΤΟΥ κ. ΔΗΜ. ΤΣΑΤΣΟΥ

Ο κ. ΖΙΓΔΗΣ ΕΠΕΖΗΤΗΣΕ ΝΑ ΕΙΣΕΛΘΗ ΣΤΗΝ ΚΥΒΕΡΝΗΣΙ

ΚΑΙ ΒΑΛΛΕΙ ΚΑΤΑ ΤΟΥ κ. Κ. ΚΑΡΑΜΑΝΛΗ ΔΙΟΤΙ ΔΕΝ ΙΚΑΝΟΠΟΙΗΘΗ.— ΔΗΛΩΣΕΙΣ ΤΟΥ κ. Π. ΛΑΜΠΡΙΑ

«ΕΛΕΥΘΕΡΟΣ ΣΥΝΔΙΚΑΛΙΣΜΟΣ ΔΕΝ ΜΠΟΡΕΙ ΝΑ ΥΠΑΡΞΗ ΧΩΡΙΣ ΔΗΜΟΚΡΑΤΙΑ»

ΔΙΑΨΕΥΔΕΤΑΙ ΟΤΙ ΤΑΝΚΣ ΕΚΙΝΗΘΗΣΑΝ ΤΗΝ ΝΥΚΤΑ ΤΟΥ ΣΑΒΒΑΤΟΥ

Σήμερα

Γουωτεργκαίητ

Ο ΘΑΝΑΤΟΣ ΕΝΟΣ ΠΡΟΕΔΡΟΥ

Δὲν ἀμνηστεύονται τὰ ἐγκλήματα τοῦ Πολυτεχνείου καὶ οἱ βασανισταὶ

ΔΗΛΩΣΕΙΣ ΤΟΥ κ. Κ. ΠΑΠΑΚΩΝΣΤΑΝΤΙΝΟΥ

A Greek newspaper. Its title is *ΑΚΡΟΠΟΛΙΣ akropolis*.

2. SCRIPTS OF THE UNION OF SOVIET SOCIALIST REPUBLICS

The Union of Soviet Socialist Republics [Союз Советских Социалистических Республик *soyuz sovetskix sotsialisticheskix respublik*] consists of fifteen republics, each of which has its own government. Because the country is so vast and multiracial, I have organized the descriptions of the various scripts by republic.

The picture below shows the reverse side of Soviet paper money. The words meaning "one rouble" are written in fifteen languages and in four scripts. On the upper part of the bill the Russian for "one rouble" is written in ornamental style. Below it, Ukrainian and Byelorussian are on the first line; Uzbek, Kazakh, and Georgian are on the second line; Azerbaijani, Lithuanian, and Moldavian are on the third line; Lettish, Kirghiz, and Tajiki are on the fourth line; and Armenian, Turkmen, and Estonian are on the fifth line. These fifteen languages are the official languages of the USSR.

Russian (Slavic/Indo-European) is the state language of the Russian Republic and is the language used by the Soviet government. Russian is written in Cyrillic or Russian script, which is explained on page 20.

The reverse side of Soviet paper money.

Newspapers in Russian are printed throughout the USSR, while in individual republics newspapers are published in the vernacular languages used there. Newspapers in the languages of local minority groups are also published in some areas.

In all, five types of script are used in the newspapers of the USSR: Latin, Russian, Georgian, Armenian, and Hebrew.

Armenia [Հայկական ՍՍՀ *haykakan s s h*] In Armenia, newspapers are published in Armenian (Armenian/Indo-European), which is written in a peculiar script that is explained on page 24.

Azerbaijan [Азәрбајҹан ССР *azerbayjan s s r*] Azerbaijani (Turkish/Altaic) is now written in Russian script with the additional letters ғ, ә, j, ҝ, ө, ү, һ, and ҹ, but without ё, й, ц, щ, ъ, ь, э, ю, and я.

Byelorussia (White Russia) [Белорусская ССР *belorusskaya s s r*] Byelorussian (Slavic/Indo-European) is written in Russian script with the additional letters і and ў, but without и, щ, and ъ.

Estonia [Eesti NSV] Estonian (Finnic/Uralic) is written in Latin script with the additional letters ä, ö, õ, and ü, but without c, f, q, w, x, y, and z.

Georgia [საქართველოს სსრ *sakharthvelos s s r*] Georgian (Kartvelian/Caucasian) is written in a peculiar script that is explained on page 22.

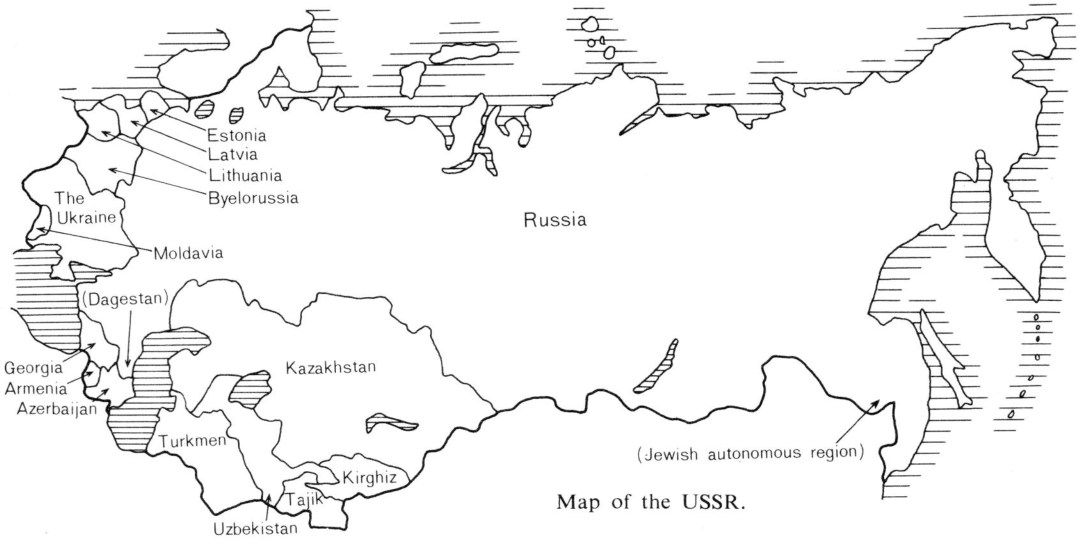

Map of the USSR.

Kazakhstan [Қазақстан ССР *khazakhstan s s r*] The Kazakh language (Turkish/Altaic) is written in Russian script with the additional letters ә, ғ, қ, ң, ө, ұ, ү, һ, and і.

Kirghiz [Кыргыз ССР *kirgiz s s r*] The Kirghiz language (Turkish/Altaic) is written in Russian script with the additional letters ң, ө, and ү.

Latvia [Latvijas PSR] In Latvia, newspapers are published in Lettish (Baltic/Indo-European), which is written in Latin script with the additional letters ā, č, ē, ģ, ī, ķ, ļ, ņ, š, ū, and ž, but without q, w, x, and y.

Lithuania [Lietuvos TSR] Lithuanian (Baltic/Indo-European) is written in Latin script with the additional letters ą, č, ę, ė, į, š, ų, ū, and ž, but without q, w, and x.

Moldavia [РСС Молдова *r s s moldova*] Moldavian (Italic/Indo-European) is the same as Romanian, but it is written in Russian script without ё, щ, and ъ.

Russia (The Russian Soviet Federative Socialist Republic) [Российская СФСР *rossīskaya s f s r*] In Russia, most newspapers are published in Russian. In the Jewish autonomous region, Yiddish newspapers are published in Hebrew script (page 32), though Yiddish is a German dialect.

Tajik [РСС Тоҷикистон *r s s tojikiston*] Tajiki (Iranian/Indo-European) is now written in Russian script with the additional letters ғ, й, қ, ӯ, ҳ, and ҷ.

Turkmen [Туркмен ССР *turkmen s s r*] The Turkmen language (Turkish/Altaic) is written in Russian script with the additional letters җ, ң, ө, ү, and ә.

The Ukraine [Українська РСР *ukrainsika r s r*] Ukrainian (Slavic/Indo-European) is written in Russian script with the additional letters є, і, and ї, but without ё, ъ, ы, and э. On the signs at Kiev Airport, you will find KIEV, Киев, Київ, written respectively in English, Russian, and Ukrainian.

Uzbekistan [Ўзбекистон ССР *uzbekiston s s r*] The Uzbek language (Turkish/Altaic) is written in Russian script with the additional letters ғ, қ, ў, ҳ, and ҷ, but without щ and ы.

Russian Script

Russian script is also called Cyrillic script. In a narrow sense the designation Cyrillic means the script created by St. Cyril for the Slavic languages, but it now signifies all the Russian scripts which have been developed from the original Cyrillic script. In this book the thirty-three-letter alphabet established by the Soviet government is called Russian script.

Russian script and later additional systems spread over eastern Europe with the Greek Orthodox church. Thus, countries now using Cyrillic script can be said to have once had a strong Greek Orthodox church.

Russian script is used to write not only Russian and the related Slavic languages, but also the USSR's more than sixty other languages that belong to the Altaic, Uralic, Caucasian, and Paleo-Asiatic families. Outer Mongolia has also accepted Russian script in place of Mongolian script to write its language.

A postage stamp of the USSR.

Alphabet Russian script consists of thirty-three letters and is always written from left to right, with a space separating each word. It has both the roman (standing) and italic (oblique) styles, and capital and small letters.

ROMAN: CAPITAL	А	Б	В	Г	Д	Е	Ё	Ж	З		
SMALL	а	б	в	г	д	е	ё	ж	з		
ITALIC: CAPITAL	*А*	*Б*	*В*	*Г*	*Д*	*Е*	*Ё*	*Ж*	*З*		
SMALL	*а*	*б*	*в*	*г*	*д*	*е*	*ё*	*ж*	*з*		
PHONETIC VALUE	*a*	*b*	*v*	*g*	*d*	*ye*	*yo*	*j*	*z*		

И	Й	К	Л	М	Н	О	П	Р	С	Т	У
и	й	к	л	м	н	о	п	р	с	т	у
И	*Й*	*К*	*Л*	*М*	*Н*	*О*	*П*	*Р*	*С*	*Т*	*У*
и	*й*	*к*	*л*	*м*	*н*	*о*	*п*	*р*	*с*	*т*	*у*
i	*i*	*k*	*l*	*m*	*n*	*o*	*p*	*r*	*s*	*t*	*u*

Ф	Х	Ц	Ч	Ш	Щ	Ъ	Ы	Ь	Э	Ю	Я
ф	х	ц	ч	ш	щ	ъ	ы	ь	э	ю	я
Ф	*Х*	*Ц*	*Ч*	*Ш*	*Щ*	*Ъ*	*Ы*	*Ь*	*Э*	*Ю*	*Я*
ф	*х*	*ц*	*ч*	*ш*	*щ*	*ъ*	*ы*	*ь*	*э*	*ю*	*я*
f	*x*	*ts*	*ch*	*sh*	*shch*	–	*ui*	–	*e*	*yu*	*ya*

Soft and hard signs In the Russian language soft and hard sounds are used to distinguish the vowels and consonants. The hard vowels are а, о, у, ы, and э; the soft ones are я, е, ё, ю, и, and й. The letters б, в, д, з, л, м, н, п, р, с, т, and ф are the hard consonants. Their corresponding soft consonants are expressed by putting the soft sign ь after the letter, a sign which almost always stands for a soft *i*; thus, мь is read *mi*.
The hard sign ъ shows that consonants and soft vowels must be pronounced discretely; thus, ся is pronounced *sya*, but съя is pronounced *s-ya*.

Numerals The Russian system uses Arabic figures and Latin numerals.

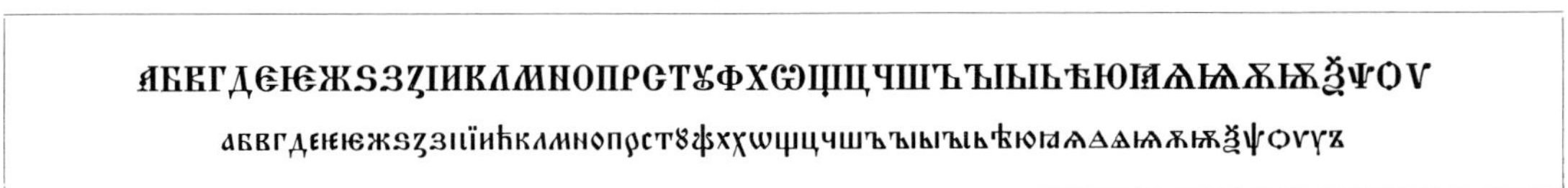

Alphabet of Old Cyrillic script.

Пролетарии всех стран, соединяйтесь!

Коммунистическая партия Советского Союза

ПРАВДА

Орган Центрального Комитета КПСС

Газета основана 5 мая 1912 года В. И. ЛЕНИНЫМ

№ 109 (20348) • Пятница, 19 апреля 1974 г. • Цена 3 коп.

Граждане Советского Союза! Активно участвуйте в предстоящих выборах в Верховный Совет СССР! Изберем в Верховный Совет СССР лучших сынов и дочерей советского народа, достойных представителей нерушимого блока коммунистов и беспартийных! (Из Призывов ЦК КПСС).

ВЫСОКОЕ ДОВЕРИЕ НАРОДА

Началось выдвижение кандидатов в депутаты Верховного Совета СССР

Предвыборное собрание на Московском заводе автотракторной электроаппаратуры № 2. Выступает шлифовщик инструментального цеха Н. В. Кудрявцев. Фото В. Воронина.

A representative newspaper of the USSR. Its title is Правда *pravda.*

Пролетарҳои ҳамаи мамлакатҳо, як шавед!

ҲАҚИҚАТИ ЎЗБЕКИСТОН

Органи КМ ПК Ўзбекистон, Совети Олӣ ва Совети Вазирони РСС Ўзбекистон

НАШРИ СОЛИ 48-УМ | № 89 (8343) | 28 июли соли 1973 | ШАНБЕ | Нархаш 2 тин.

ДАР ЯК САФ—БА СУИ ҒАЛАБАҲОИ НАВ

БА РСС УКРАИНА СУПУРДАНИ ОРДЕНИ ДЎСТИИ ХАЛҚҲО

ШАЪНУ ШАРАФ БА ПАРТИЯИ ЛЕНИНӢ

МАҶЛИСИ ТАНТАНАВӢ ДАР ТОШКЕНТ

ҚАДАМҲОИ БАҲОДУРОНАИ ПАНҶСОЛА

УПРАВЛЕНИЯИ МАРКАЗИИ СТАТИСТИКИИ РСС ЎЗБЕКИСТОН ИҶРОИ ПЛАНИ ДАВЛАТИИ ТАРАҚҚИЁТИ ХОҶАГИИ ХАЛҚИ РЕСПУБЛИКАРО ДАР НИМАИ ЯКУМИ СОЛИ 1973 ҶАМЪБАСТ КАРД

An Uzbek newspaper issued in Tashkent. Its title is Ҳақиқати Ўзбекистон *hakikati uzbekiston.*

Georgian Script

According to one tradition in Georgia, Georgian script was invented by King Parnavas in the 3rd century; but another tradition attributes it to St. Mesrop in the 5th century. In any case, the system of Georgian script was undoubtedly influenced by the Greek writing system. In Georgian script, there are two systems: the ecclesiastical writing called Khutsuri and the warriors' writing called Mkhedruli.

Khutsuri Khutsuri has two forms, capitals called Asomtavruli and small letters called Nuskhuri. Khutsuri was employed exclusively for the church. Bibles were once printed in it, but it is now extinct, being seen only in the Asomtavruli inscriptions on the walls of old churches.

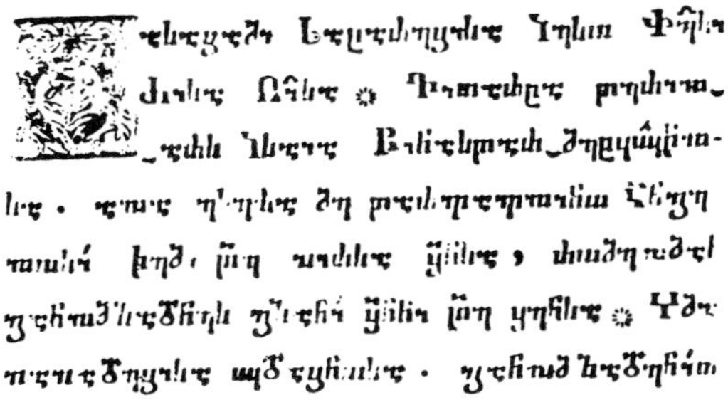

Part of a Bible printed in Khutsuri script.

Mkhedruli Mkhedruli is used in newspapers and other common printed matter. It consists of the forty letters shown in the table below. It makes no distinction between capitals and small letters; all the letters look like the small letters of Latin script with kerns in the upper or lower part.

Though Mkhedruli does not use either capital letters or an italic style, letters somewhat like capitals, all of which have the same height from top to bottom, and oblique letters resembling italic ones have been invented for newspapers and other printing.

A Georgian postage stamp, issued in 1919. On the left, right, and below, Georgian script is used.

Reading and punctuation Georgian script always runs from left to right on a horizontal line, with a space between each word. In Georgian, [,] stands for a comma, [.] for a colon, and [:] for a period. The mark [.] is now also used as a period.

Numerals In Georgian script there are no distinct figures. Georgian letters in alphabetical order were employed for numerals as shown in the table below. Arabic figures are now used in all printed matter.

FORM OF LETTER	ა	ბ	გ	დ	ე	ვ	ზ	ჱ	თ	ი	კ	ლ	მ	ნ	ჲ	ო	პ	ჟ
PHONETIC VALUE	*a*	*b*	*g*	*d*	*e*	*v*	*z*	*h*	*th*	*i*	*k*	*l*	*m*	*n*	*i*	*o*	*p*	*j*
NUMERICAL VALUE	1	2	3	4	5	6	7	8	9	10	20	30	40	50	60	70	80	90

რ	ს	ტ	უ	ჳ	ფ	ქ	ღ	ყ	შ	ჩ	ც	ძ	წ	ჭ	ხ	ჴ	ჯ	ჰ	ჵ	ჶ	ჷ
r	*s*	*t*	*u*	*wi*	*ph*	*kh*	*gh*	*q*	*sh*	*ch*	*ts*	*dz*	*ts*	*chh*	*x*	*xh*	*j*	*h*	*ō*	*f*	*e*
100	200	300	400	—	500	600	700	800	900	1,000	2,000	3,000	4,000	5,000	6,000	7,000	8,000	9,000	10,000	—	—

A Georgian newspaper printed in Georgian script. Its title is ახალგაზრდა კომუნისტი *axalgazrda komunisti.*

Armenian Script

An Armenian tradition tells that Armenian script was invented by St. Mesrop in the 5th century, as was Georgian script. Though the shapes of some Armenian letters are believed to have originated from the Pahlavik script of Persia, it is clear that Armenian script was created under the influence of Greek script because it is written from left to right and the vowel signs are independent of the consonant signs.

An Armenian postage stamp issued in 1921.

Alphabet Armenian script consists of the thirty-eight letters shown in the table below. There are capitals and small letters, and roman and italic forms. The italic form is the original style of Armenian script.

Ligature The letter *և* is the ligature of *ե* and *ւ* , read *ev* and meaning "and." It is also used within words, for example, in *Երևան* *erevan*.

In Erevan, the capital of Armenia, street names are given in three scripts: Armenian, Russian, and Latin.

Numerals Special figures do not exist in Armenian script; letters in alphabetical order are employed as numerals, as in Greek. Recently, Arabic figures have been used in newspapers and other printed matter.

Reading and punctuation Armenian script runs from left to right on a horizontal line with a space between each word. In Armenian (,) is a comma, (:) is the ordinary period, and (.) is used as a period for abbreviations.

ITALIC: CAPITAL	*Ա*	*Բ*	*Գ*	*Դ*	*Ե*	*Զ*	*Է*	*Ը*	*Թ*	*Ժ*	*Ի*	*Լ*	*Խ*	*Ծ*	*Կ*	*Հ*	*Ձ*
SMALL	*ա*	*բ*	*գ*	*դ*	*ե*	*զ*	*է*	*ը*	*թ*	*ժ*	*ի*	*լ*	*խ*	*ծ*	*կ*	*հ*	*ձ*
ROMAN: CAPITAL	Ա	Բ	Գ	Դ	Ե	Զ	Է	Ը	Թ	Ժ	Ի	Լ	Խ	Ծ	Կ	Հ	Ձ
SMALL	ա	բ	գ	դ	ե	զ	է	ը	թ	ժ	ի	լ	խ	ծ	կ	հ	ձ
PHONETIC VALUE	*a*	*p*	*k*	*t*	*e*	*z*	*e*	*a*	*t*	*j*	*i*	*l*	*x*	*z*	*k*	*h*	*ts*
NUMERICAL VALUE	1	2	3	4	5	6	7	8	9	10	20	30	40	50	60	70	80

Ղ	*Ճ*	*Մ*	*Յ*	*Ն*	*Շ*	*Ո*	*Չ*	*Պ*	*Ջ*	*Ռ*	*Ս*	*Վ*	*Տ*	*Ր*	*Ց*	*Ւ*	*Փ*	*Ք*	*Օ*	*Ֆ*
ղ	*ճ*	*մ*	*յ*	*ն*	*շ*	*ո*	*չ*	*պ*	*ջ*	*ռ*	*ս*	*վ*	*տ*	*ր*	*ց*	*ւ*	*փ*	*ք*	*օ*	*ֆ*
Ղ	Ճ	Մ	Յ	Ն	Շ	Ո	Չ	Պ	Ջ	Ռ	Ս	Վ	Տ	Ր	Ց	Ւ	Փ	Ք	Օ	Ֆ
ղ	ճ	մ	յ	ն	շ	ո	չ	պ	ջ	ռ	ս	վ	տ	ր	ց	ւ	փ	ք	օ	ֆ
gh	*j*	*m*	*h,y*	*n*	*sh*	*o*	*ch*	*b*	*ch*	*r*	*s*	*v*	*d*	*r*	*ts*	*u,v*	*p*	*k*	*o*	*f*
90	100	200	300	400	500	600	700	800	900	1,000	2,000	3,000	4,000	5,000	6,000	7,000	8,000	9,000	10,000	20,000

A newspaper published in Armenia. It is printed in the Armenian language and script. Its title is *Երեկոյան Երևան erekoyan erevan.*

Other Scripts in Europe and the USSR

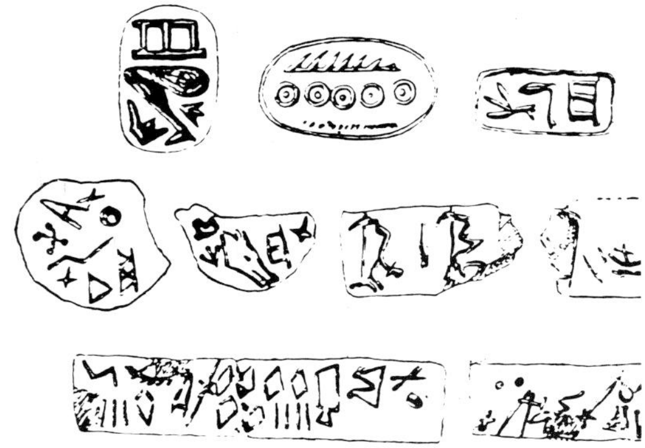

CRETAN (MINOAN) IDEOGRAMS. Pictograms from the island of Crete. From the middle Minoan period. Undeciphered. (Diringer)

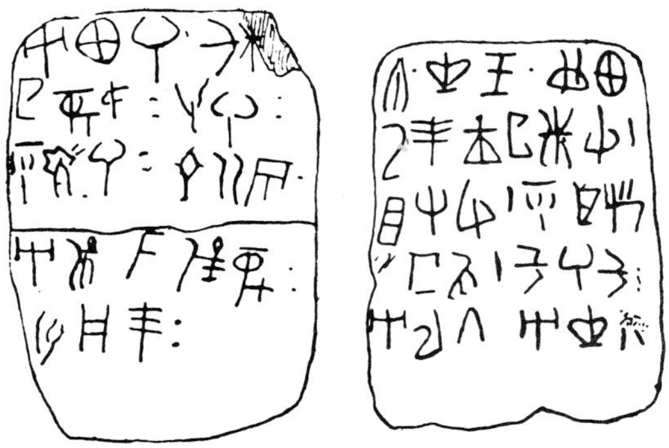

CRETAN LINEAR A SCRIPT. The earlier of the two ancient Cretan linear scripts. Undeciphered, from the 18th–15th century B.C. (Diringer)

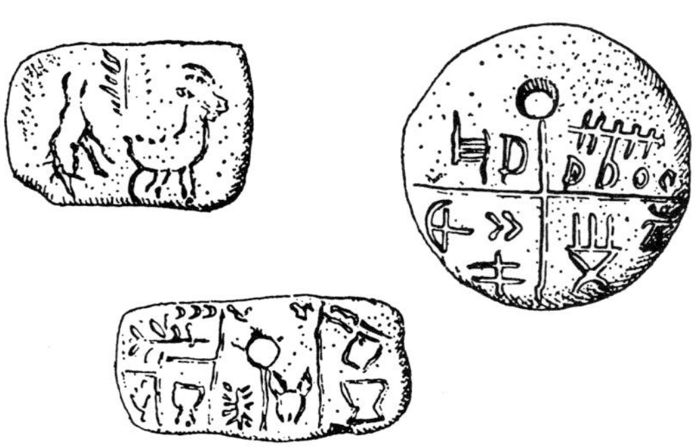

TARTARIA SCRIPT. This script, recently discovered in Romania, may be one of the oldest writing systems in human culture. From the 4th millennium B.C. (Hood)

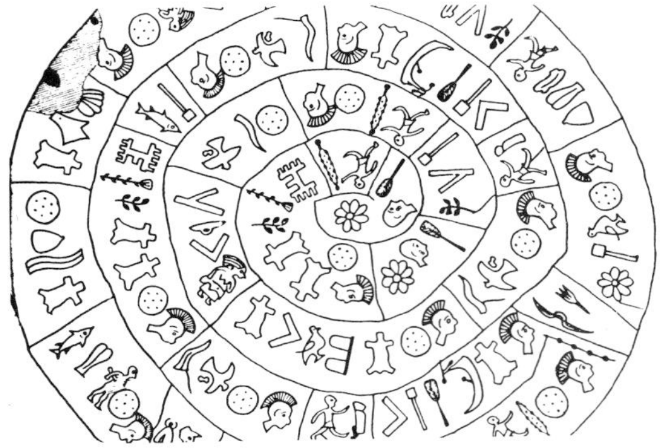

SCRIPT OF THE PHAISTOS DISC. Only one disc impressed with this script has been discovered on Crete. From the 17th century B.C. Undeciphered. (Yajima)

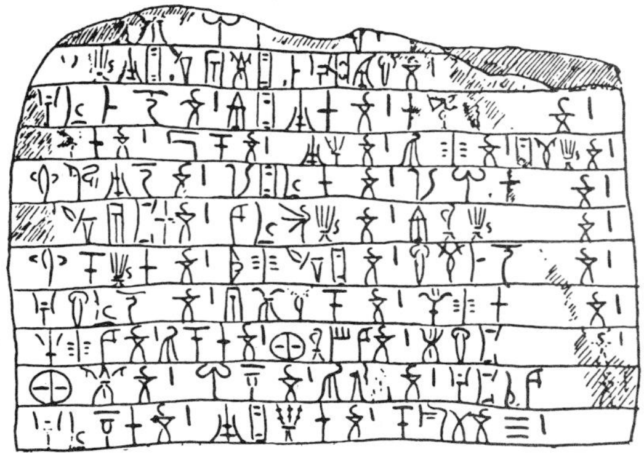

CRETAN LINEAR B SCRIPT. The later of the Cretan linear scripts. It has been deciphered by M. Ventris. (Gelb)

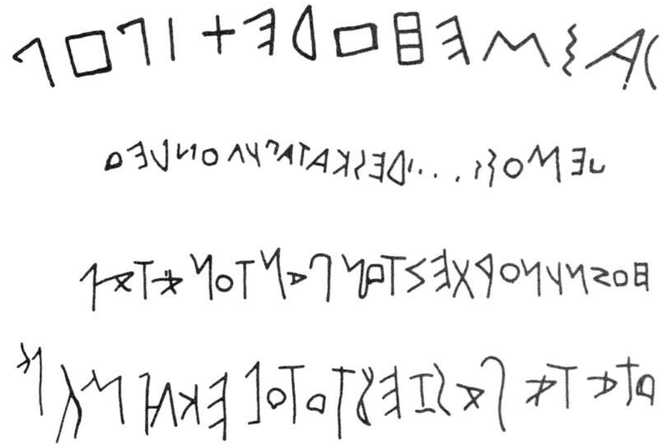

EARLY GREEK SCRIPT. Early Greek script was written from right to left. From the 8th century B.C., Athens. (Diringer)

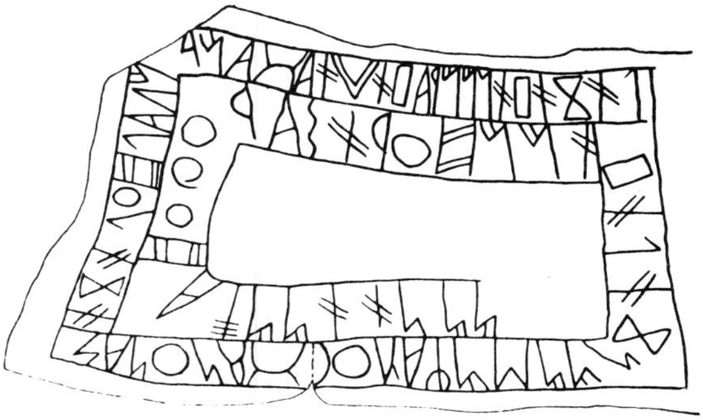

IBERIAN SCRIPT. Used on the Iberian peninsula before it became a territory of the Roman Empire. Currently being deciphered. (Diringer)

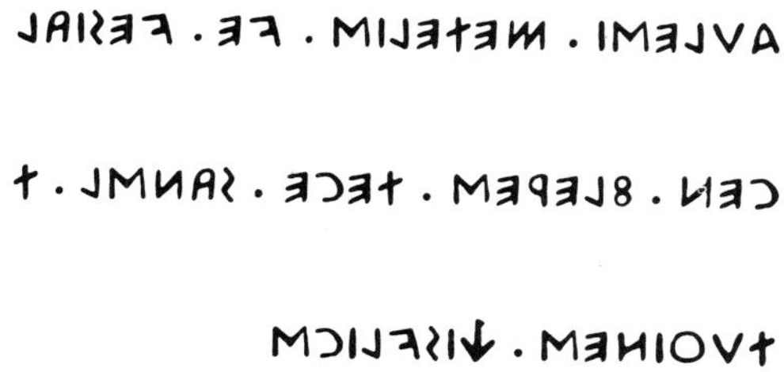

ETRUSCAN SCRIPT. Etruria was a powerful nation on the Italian peninsula before the Roman Republic. (Fossey)

RUNIC SCRIPT. Writings of ancient German tribes from the 3rd–17th century in northern Europe. (Jensen)

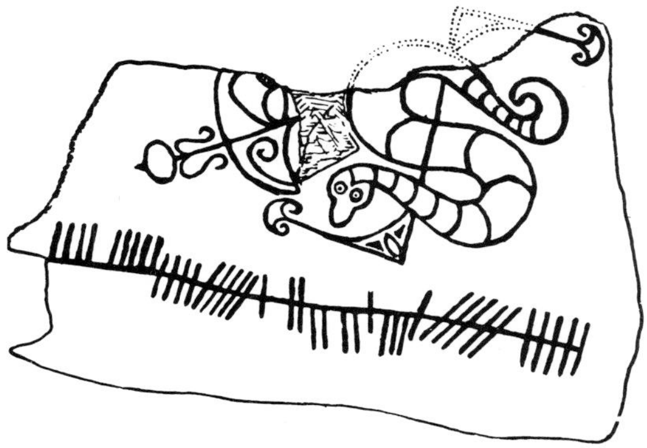

OGHAM SCRIPT. Used in the 5th and 6th centuries in northern Britain and Ireland. Its text consisted of a line crossed with short lines. (Diringer)

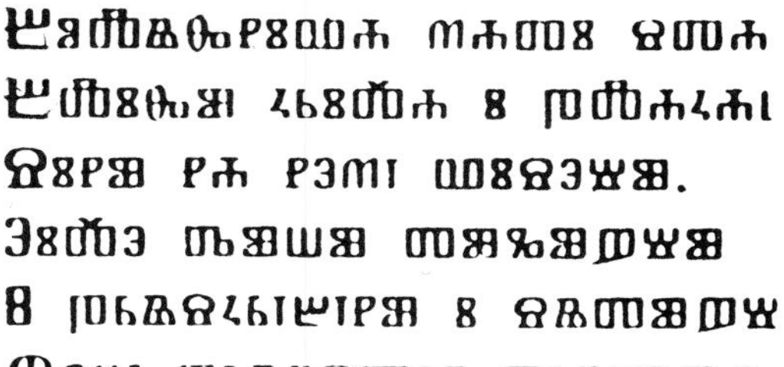

GLAGOLITIC SCRIPT OR GLAGOLITSA. From the 9th century in Croatia and Bulgaria. It is related to Kirillitsa, but is more esthetic. (Gilyarevsky)

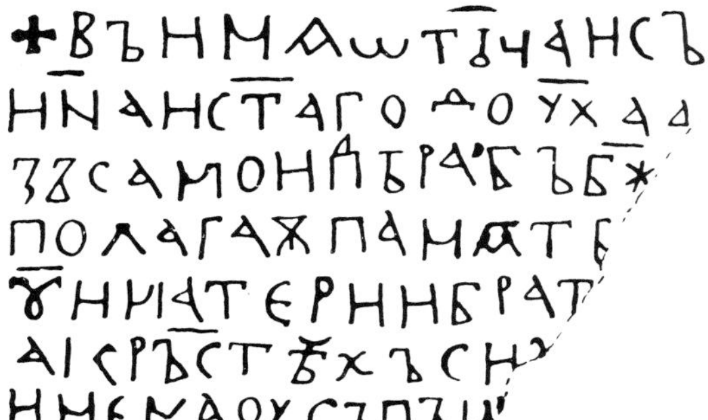

CYRILLIC SCRIPT OR KIRILLITSA. Invented in Bulgaria in the 9th century; based on Greek script. (Ogawa)

Old Hungarian script. This is considered a descendant of Kök Turki script in Europe. From the 16th century. (Doblhofer)

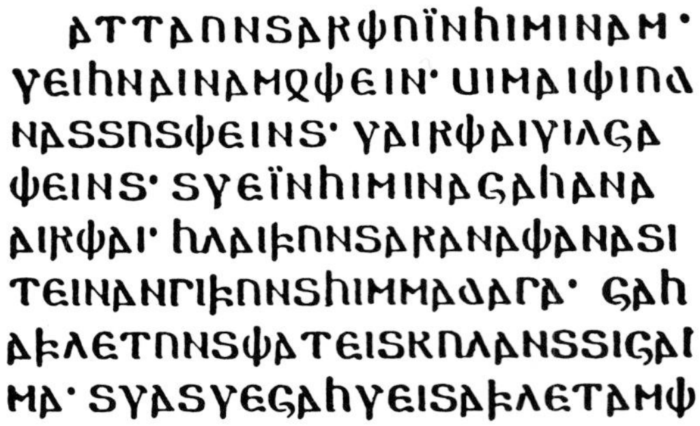

Gothic script. Used by Gothic tribes who lived on the north of the Black Sea before the migration of nations. Sample from a 4th-century codex. (Yajima)

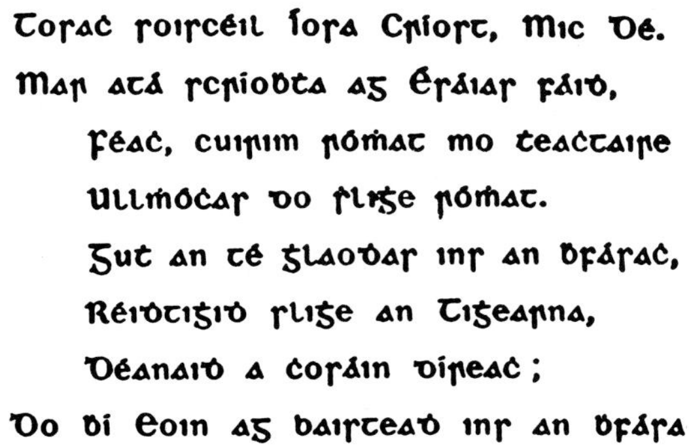

Gaelic (Irish) script. A variety of Latin alphabet from the 6th century A.D. It is used now in Ireland. See also page 12. (Nida)

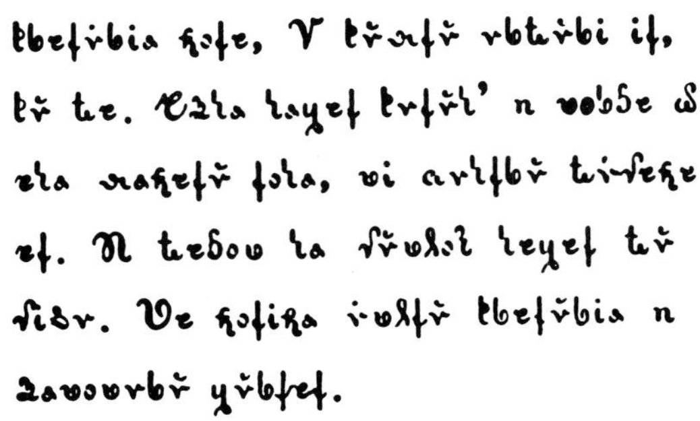

Albanian script. One of the three Albanian scripts developed during the period of Turkish control. It is also called Buthakukye script. (Jensen)

3. SCRIPTS OF WEST ASIA

Asia is immense and cannot be considered a single unit. Its scripts fall into three main zones: (1) the Islamic, or West Asian, writing-zone, (2) the Indian and Southeast Asian writing-zone, and (3) the writing-zone of China and surrounding areas.

The first group of scripts consists of the descendants of the Aramaic script that originated in Syria. It contains the Hebrew, South Arabic, Avesta, Arabic, Syriac, Middle Persian, Sogdian, Kök Turki, Uighur, Mongolian, and Manchu scripts, which are generally used by the nomads in West and North Asia. Scripts of this group are mostly written from right to left on a horizontal line.

The second group consists of the descendants of the Brahmi script that developed in ancient India. It contains many varieties of Indian script as well as Khotanese, Tibetan, Burman, Thai, Shan, Lao, Khmer, Ceylonese, Sumatran, Javanese, Celebes, and Philippine scripts, most of which are used mainly by agricultural peoples in tropical Asia. Scripts of this group are generally written from left to right on a horizontal line.

The third group consists of Chinese ideograms and of characters invented in the areas around China under the influence of Chinese writing. It includes Japanese, Khitan, Nuchen, Hsihsia, Korean, Annanese, Lolo, and Moso characters. Characters of this group are generally written from top to bottom on vertical lines shifting from right to left.

Since the 18th century, Latin and Russian scripts have been introduced into these three zones, and the number of nations which have adopted these scripts to write their own languages has been increasing.

The description of Asian scripts, excluding those of the USSR (page 18), will be divided into four chapters: West Asia, in and around India (page 45), Southeast Asia (page 70), and East Asia (page 82).

West Asia is here defined as those Asian countries lying west of and including Pakistan and the Maldive Islands. Almost all countries in West Asia are Moslem and mainly use Arabic (Southwest Semitic/Semitic-Hamitic). Though Arabic script is also used to write other languages (Persian, Kurdish, Pashto, Sindhi, and others) spoken there, Latin, Greek, Hebrew, Urdu, and Maldivian scripts are also used. Hebrew script is explained on page 32, Urdu on page 36, and Maldivian on page 38. Unless special mention is made, the reader should assume that Arabic script is used to write Arabic in the places where Arabic is spoken. Arabic script is explained on page 34.

AFGHANISTAN [افغانستان *afghānistān*]

Though the linguistic situation in Afghanistan is intricate, the official languages are Pashto or Afghan (Iranian/Indo-European) and Iranian. Pashto is written in Arabic script consisting of the basic twenty-eight Arabic letters plus the additional eleven letters shown below:

پ	ټ	څ	چ	ډ	ړ
p	*ṭ*	*ts*	*ch*	*ḍ*	*r*
ژ	ږ	ښ	گ	ڼ	
z	*g*	*x*	*g*	*ṇ*	

Newspapers are published in Iranian and Pashto, both using Arabic script.

BAHRAIN [البحرين *al-baxrēn*]

The official language is Arabic.

CYPRUS [ΚΥΠΡΟΣ *kipros*; KIBRIS]

In Cyprus, both Greek and Turkish are used. Newspapers are published in these two languages and in English.

A postage stamp of Cyprus.

IRAN (Persia) [ایران *irān*]

The official language of Iran is Iranian or Modern Persian (Iranian/Indo-European), which is written in Arabic script. The Arabic alphabet for Iranian consists of thirty-two letters with four letters, پ *p*, چ *ch*, ژ *z*, and گ *g* added to the twenty-eight letters of the basic Arabic alphabet.

Though Iran is known for its elegant Nastaliq style script, Iranian newspapers are printed in the ordinary Naskhi style because they require movable type. English newspapers are also published in Latin script.

IRAQ [العراق *al-'irāq*]

Iraq was the site of ancient Mesopotamia, which was the cradle of the scripts of the Sumerian culture. Arabic is now the official language, and newspapers are published in it and in English. The formal name of Iraq on postage stamps, الجمهورية العراقية , means Republic of Iraq.

ISRAEL [ישראל *yisrā'ēl*; اسرائيل *isrā'il*]

The official language of Israel is Hebrew (Canaanite/Semitic-Hamitic) but Arabic and English are also public languages. Newspapers are printed in Hebrew, Arabic, and Latin scripts. Hebrew script is explained on page 32.

An Israeli postage stamp printed in Hebrew, Arabic, and Latin scripts.

JORDAN [الأردن *al-'urdun*]

The official language of Jordan is Arabic, which is used in its newspapers. The formal name in Arabic script, المملكة الأردنية الهاشمية, means Hashemite Kingdom of Jordan.

KUWAIT [الكويت *al-kuweyt*]

Newspapers are published in Arabic and English.

LEBANON (LIBAN) [لبنان *lubnān*]

Lebanon was ancient Phoenicia, the cradle of the alphabet. In Lebanon, newspapers are published in Arabic, English, and French.

THE MALDIVES [ދިވެހިރާއްޖެ *divehirā'je*]

Though these islands are situated near India, Maldivian script belongs to the West Asian group. Maldivian is a dialect of Sinhalese (Indic/Indo-European) but has been strongly influenced by Arabic. It is written in a very peculiar script, which is explained on page 38. Daily newspapers, what few there are, are in the Maldivian language and script, and are mimeographed rather than printed.

OMAN [عمان *'omān*]

The official language is Arabic. The formal name on postage stamps, سلطنة عمان , means Sultanate of Oman.

PAKISTAN [پاکستان *pākistān*]

The official language of Pakistan is Urdu (Indic/Indo-European). Though Urdu is written in Arabic script, the newspapers are printed using handwriting in the Nastaliq style, which looks different from Arabic script. Therefore, in this book, Urdu script is treated separately; it is explained on page 36. In Pakistan, newspapers are published in Urdu, English, Sindhi, Punjabi (see page 50), and Gujarati (see page 52). Sindhi (Indic/Indo-European) is written in Arabic script with the additional twenty-four letters below. Thus, the Sindhi alphabet has the most letters of all the languages written in Arabic script.

ٻ	ڀ	ٿ	ٽ	ٺ	پ	ڦ	ڄ
bb	*bh*	*th*	*ṭr*	*ṭh*	*p*	*ph*	*jj*
جھ	ڃ	چ	ڇ	ڌ	ڏ	ڊ	ڍ
jh	*ny*	*ch*	*chh*	*dh*	*ḍḍ*	*ḍr*	*ḍh*
ڙ	ژ	ڪ	ڱ	گ	ڳ	گھ	ڻ
r	*z*	*k*	*ng*	*g*	*gg*	*gh*	*ṇ*

The letter ک (read *k* in Arabic) is read *x*.

QATAR [قطر *qatar*]

The official language is Arabic.

SAUDI ARABIA

[المملكة العربية السعودية
al-mamlakat al-'arabiyat al-su'ūdiyat]

All newspapers are published in Arabic.

SOUTH YEMEN

[جمهورية اليمن الديمقراطية الشعبية *jumhūri-yat al-yaman al-dimoqrātit al-sha'biyat*]

The formal name in Arabic script means People's Democratic Republic of Yemen. The official language is Arabic.

A postage stamp of South Yemen.

SYRIA [سوريا *sūriya*]

Syria is the cradle of Aramaic script. The three Syriac scripts are shown on page 43. The official Syrian language is now Arabic.

TURKEY [TÜRKİYE CUMHURİYETİ]

The official language is Turkish (Turkish/Altaic). Turkish used to be written in Arabic script, but now Latin script is used for all publications. The Latin script used for Turkish contains the additional letters ç, ğ, ı, ö, ş, and ü, and has no q, w, or x. The letters ı and i are distinct; therefore, the corresponding capital letters become I and İ.

A postage stamp of the Ottoman Empire issued in 1916, using Arabic script.

UNITED ARAB EMIRATES

[الامارات العربية المتحدة
al-amārāt al-'arabiyat al-motaxedat]

The official language is Arabic.

YEMEN [اليمن *al-yaman*]

The formal name on the postage stamps, الجمهورية العربية اليمنية, means Yemen Arab Republic. The official language is Arabic.

A postage stamp of Yemen.

Hebrew Script

Hebrew script has not changed since the square Hebrew alphabet developed from Aramaic script in the 2nd century B.C. Its alphabet consists of only twenty-two consonants, and is read from right to left on a horizontal line, as are Phoenician and Aramaic.

At present, Hebrew script is used not only for the Hebrew language in Israel, but also for Arabic, Yiddish (Germanic/Indo-European), Ladino (Italic/Indo-European), and others.

Alphabet

FORM	FINAL FORM	PHONETIC VALUE	NUMERICAL VALUE
א		*a*, [ʾ]	1
ב בּ		*bh* *b*	2
ג גּ		*gh* *g*	3
ד דּ		*dh* *d*	4
ה		*h*	5
ו		*w*	6
ז		*z*	7
ח		*x*	8
ט		*t*	9
י		*y*	10
כ כּ	ך	*kh* *k*	20
ל		*l*	30
מ	ם	*m*	40
נ	ן	*n*	50
ס		*s*	60
ע		[ʿ], *e*	70
פ פּ	ף	*ph* *p*	80
צ	ץ	*s*	90
ק		*q*	100
ר		*r*	200
שׂ שׁ		*s* *sh*	300
ת תּ		*th* *t*	400

Six letters in the above table have enclosed dots to distinguish them from the aspirate letters with the same basic shape. The letter ש has a dot above it, but in different positions to distinguish the sounds *s* and *sh*, which were once written with the same letter. Five letters have final forms, which are used only when the letter appears at the end of a word.

Vowel signs Vowel sounds are ordinarily not written but are mentally supplied between the consonants when Hebrew script is read. The following vowel signs with diacritical marks are sometimes used to make the task of reading easier.

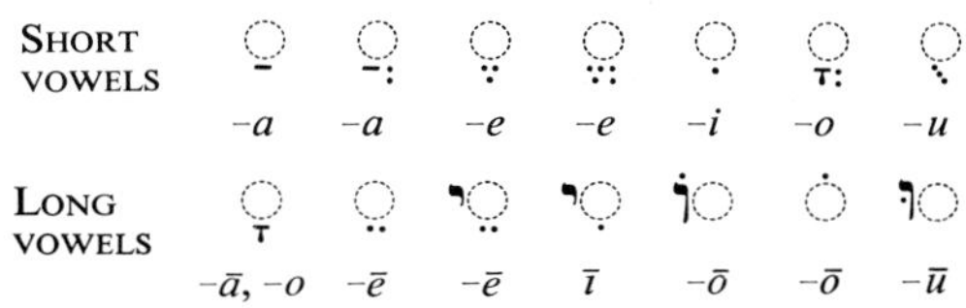

ְ◌(sewa) alone indicates the absence of a vowel. The distinction between short and long vowels is not strict. In addition to the table above, ה is used for *ā*, י for *ē* or *ī*, and ו for *ō* or *ū*. Below is a sample of typesetting of Hebrew script with vowel signs added. Since the page is somewhat unattractive, the dots on consonants and vowels alike are usually omitted in newspapers and other publications.

וְאֵלֶּה הַמִּשְׁפָּטִים אֲשֶׁר תָּשִׂים לִפְנֵיהֶם׃ כִּי תִקְ
נֶה עֶבֶד עִבְרִי שֵׁשׁ שָׁנִים יַעֲבֹד וּבַשְּׁבִעִת יֵצֵא
לַחָפְשִׁי חִנָּם׃ אִם־בְּגַפּוֹ יָבֹא בְּגַפּוֹ יֵצֵא אִם
־בַּעַל אִשָּׁה הוּא וְיָצְאָה אִשְׁתּוֹ עִמּוֹ׃ אִם־
אֲדֹנָיו יִתֶּן־לוֹ אִשָּׁה וְיָלְדָה־לוֹ בָנִים אוֹ בָנוֹת
הָאִשָּׁה וִילָדֶיהָ תִּהְיֶה לַאדֹנֶיהָ וְהוּא יֵצֵא בְגַ

Hebrew script with vowel signs.

Numerals Hebrew letters can also be used for numbers, as shown in the alphabet chart. Nowadays, however, Arabic figures are used.

מעריב

העתון הנפוץ ביותר במדינה • MAARIV

היום 64 עמוד כולל המוסף „קריאת ביניים"

יום ב' 7.8.78 ד' אב תשל"ח

בגין – לוואנס: „אמור לנשיא סאדאת שמוכנים לדון בחיוב בהצעת אל־עריש"

באלכסנדריה תיבחן האפשרות של מיפגש משולש: קארטר־בגין־סאדאת

קציני משטרה מישראל ומצרים ייפגשו היום בסיני

נטייה לחזור להצהרת עקרונות

דיון בין ויצמן לסונדרס:

הצעה להעביר את הגדוד הלבנוני

A Hebrew newspaper published in Israel, printed in Hebrew script with no vowels or diacritical signs. Its title is מעריב *ma'arībh*.

צ"ק קפר"פ באשטעטיקט פאליטיק

פון פארקלענערן די שפאנונג אויף דער וועלט

דער וועג

DER VEG · זו הדרך

3.5.1973 תל־אביב נומער 366

מאסן־אנטייל אין די דעמאנסטראציעס

און מיטינגען פון 1טן מאי

איינדרוקספולע דעמאנסטראציע

פון רק"ח אין תל־אביב

א שותף וואס איז צעגעסן פון קריזיס

25 יאר מדינת־ישראל

A Yiddish newspaper published in the Jewish autonomous region of the USSR. Its title is דער וועג *der veg*, in which *v* is written וו , a doubling of ו *w*. To write vowels in Yiddish, which is a variant of spoken German, א , ו , י , and ע are used.

Arabic Script

Arabic script may be considered Moslem writing, for the area employing it coincides with the area of Moslem influence. The Moslem holy book, the Koran, is usually written and read in Arabic. Arabic is written with twenty-eight letters and is read from right to left on a horizontal line.

Alphabet The chart on the right shows the Arabic alphabet. There is no distinction between capitals and small letters, but there are four forms, independent, initial, medial, and final, determined by where the letter appears in a word. Only the six letters ا , د , ذ , ر , ز , and و have no medial forms because they can only be joined to a preceding letter. This also means that their initial forms are the same as their independent ones, and that following letters are always written in an initial or independent form.

Vowel signs In Arabic, vowel signs are not usually written, but when needed, can be expressed as follows:

	SHORT	EXAMPLE	LONG	EXAMPLE
a SOUND	◌َ -*a*	بَ *ba*	◌َا -*ā*	بَا *bā*
i SOUND	◌ِ -*i*	بِ *bi*	◌ِي -*ī*	بِي *bī*
u SOUND	◌ُ -*u*	بُ *bu*	◌ُو -*ū*	بُو *bū*

Two diphthongs are: ◌َي -*ai* and ◌َو -*au*.

Other signs ◌ْ shows the absence of a vowel: بْ *b*. ◌ّ shows a double consonant: كَسَّرَ *kassara*. ◌ٔ indicates a glottal stop on ا, ي, and و .

Ligatures The many ligatures used in Arabic script make it a difficult language to learn to read. In printing, لا (*l* + *a*) and ة (*t* + *h*) are used frequently.

INDEP. FORM	INITIAL FORM	MEDIAL FORM	FINAL FORM	PHONETIC VALUE	NUMER. VALUE
ا			ـا	*a*	1
ب	بـ	ـبـ	ـب	*b*	2
ت	تـ	ـتـ	ـت	*t*	400
ث	ثـ	ـثـ	ـث	*t*	500
ج	جـ	ـجـ	ـج	*j*	3
ح	حـ	ـحـ	ـح	*x*	8
خ	خـ	ـخـ	ـخ	*kh*	600
د			ـد	*d*	4
ذ			ـذ	*dh*	700
ر			ـر	*r*	200
ز			ـز	*z*	7
س	سـ	ـسـ	ـس	*s*	60
ش	شـ	ـشـ	ـش	*sh*	300
ص	صـ	ـصـ	ـص	*s*	90
ض	ضـ	ـضـ	ـض	*d*	800
ط	طـ	ـطـ	ـط	*t*	9
ظ	ظـ	ـظـ	ـظ	*z*	900
ع	عـ	ـعـ	ـع	[ʿ]	70
غ	غـ	ـغـ	ـغ	*gh*	1,000
ف	فـ	ـفـ	ـف	*f*	80
ق	قـ	ـقـ	ـق	*q*	100
ك	كـ	ـكـ	ـك	*k*	20
ل	لـ	ـلـ	ـل	*l*	30
م	مـ	ـمـ	ـم	*m*	40
ن	نـ	ـنـ	ـن	*n*	50
ه	هـ	ـهـ	ـه	*h*	5
و			ـو	*w,u*	6
ى	يـ	ـيـ	ـى ـي	*y,i*	10

Numerals Arabic figures are written from right to left, but the figure written to the left shows the higher value: ٢٣ *23*.

١	٢	٣	٤	٥	٦	٧	٨	٩	٠
1	2	3	4	5	6	7	8	9	0

بسم الله الرحمن الرحيم

الندوة

٦ قروش

٨ صفحات

رئيس التحرير
حامد مطاوع

AL - NADWA Daily Newspaper MECCA, April 8, 1974 — جريدة يومية تصدر بمكة المكرمة

جلالة الفيصل يتمنى التوفيق لمؤتمر المنظمات الإسلامية

المؤتمر يواصل جلساته ويستمع الى كلمات عدد من الوفود المشتركة

العدو يواصل استخدام طائراته بالجولان

الاشتباكات تشمل جميع قطاعات الجبهة

الملك حسين والسادات: "نحن على اتفاق تام"

ديان يقترح استقالة حكومة مائير

تدهور العلاقات المصرية السوفيتية

New! IC73F

TOSHIBA
In Touch with Tomorrow

A newspaper published in Saudi Arabia printed in Arabic. Its title is الندوة *al-nadwat.*

DATANG SEGERA
PELUANG ISTIMEWA
BAYARAN MURAH
Anda dapat layanan bayaran mudah & murah. TV, Radio-gram dan alat-alat lampu letrik. Service siang & malam.
NEW EXCEL CO,
205, JALAN TUANKU ABDUL RAHMAN, KUALA LUMPUR. TAL: 83678.

اوتوسن ملايو

UTUSAN MELAYU MOST INFLUENTIAL MALAY NATIONAL NEWSPAPER

MASTIKA
BULANAN PENDIDIKAN DAN PENGETAHUAN

KDN 7612 — رابو 10 افريل 1974

جوانتنكواس فوسة MCA
اكن برسيدڠ 17 افريل

ماس دفن
فارتي دبينچڠ

'كاسانوبا مليسيا' دفنجارا لاڬي

A newspaper published in Malaysia written in Malay and printed in Arabic script. Its title is اوتوسن ملايو *utusan malayu.*

Urdu Script

Urdu script is really the beautiful Nastaliq style of Arabic script. However, since the Urdu newspapers published in Pakistan and India do not use movable type but are instead photo-offset printings of pages handwritten in the Nastaliq style, Urdu script seems to be an altogether different kind of script.

Alphabet The Urdu alphabet consists of thirty-six letters as shown in the table. These letters contain the twenty-eight original Arabic letters, four additional letters for Persian (پ, چ, ژ, and گ), and four additional letters for Urdu (ٹ, ڈ, ڑ, and ے). ◌ؕ is also written ◌ٖٖ.

Vowel signs There are three short vowels, ◌َ -*a*, ◌ِ -*i*, and ◌ُ -*u*, but in practice these are seldom written or printed.
As long vowels ا, و, ی, and ے are used. Long *a* is shown by ا: کا *kā*. As an initial it is written آ. Long *i* is shown by ی: میل *mīl*. As an initial it is written ایـ. Long *e* or *ai* is shown by ے: سے *sē*, ہے *hai*. Long *u* and *o* are shown by و: اون *ūn*, لو *lō*.

Aspirate letters In Urdu there are aspirate consonants as in other Indian languages, but Urdu script has no special letters for them. It uses ligatures combining ھ, which is another form of ہ *h*, with other letters: کھ *kh* (ख in Devanagari script), پھ *ph* (फ), چھ *chh* (छ), and so on.

Other signs ◌ٓ (madd) is used over ا to show long *a*: آ *ā*.
◌ّ (tashdid) shows a double consonant: امّاں *amman*. (After a long vowel ن loses its dot.)
◌ْ (jazm) shows that there is no vowel between two consonants: گرْم *garm*.

INDEP. FORM	INITIAL FORM	MEDIAL FORM	FINAL FORM	PHONETIC VALUE
ا			ـا	*a*
ب	بـ	ـبـ	ـب	*b*
پ	پـ	ـپـ	ـپ	*p*
ت	تـ	ـتـ	ـت	*t*
ٹ	ٹـ	ـٹـ	ـٹ	*t*
ث	ثـ	ـثـ	ـث	*s*
ج	جـ	ـجـ	ـج	*j*
چ	چـ	ـچـ	ـچ	*ch*
ح	حـ	ـحـ	ـح	*h*
خ	خـ	ـخـ	ـخ	*x*
د			ـد	*d*
ڈ			ـڈ	*d*
ذ			ـذ	*z*
ر			ـر	*r*
ڑ			ـڑ	*r*
ز			ـز	*z*
ژ			ـژ	*z*
س	سـ	ـسـ	ـس	*s*
ش	شـ	ـشـ	ـش	*sh*
ص	صـ	ـصـ	ـص	*s*
ض	ضـ	ـضـ	ـض	*z*
ط	طـ	ـطـ	ـط	*t*
ظ	ظـ	ـظـ	ـظ	*z*
ع	عـ	ـعـ	ـع	[']
غ	غـ	ـغـ	ـغ	*gh*
ف	فـ	ـفـ	ـف	*f*
ق	قـ	ـقـ	ـق	*q*
ک	کـ	ـکـ	ـک	*k*
گ	گـ	ـگـ	ـگ	*g*
ل	لـ	ـلـ	ـل	*l*
م	مـ	ـمـ	ـم	*m*
ن	نـ	ـنـ	ـن	*n*
و			ـو	*u,w*
ہ	ہـ	ـہـ	ـہ	*h*
ی	یـ	ـیـ	ـی	*y*
ے			ـے	*e*

پاکستان اور برطانیہ کے لیڈروں نے بین الاقوامی صورتحال پر ۳ گھنٹے تک مذاکرات کئے

مشرق

An Urdu newspaper published in Pakistan. Its title is مشرق *mashriq*.

ء (hamza) in Urdu is generally the equivalent of a hyphen to separate vowels: پاؤں *pā-on*.

Reading and punctuation Urdu script runs from right to left on a horizontal line, with a space between each word. The mark (—) is placed at the end of each sentence.

Numerals

۱	۲	۳	۴	۵	۶	۷	۸	۹	۰
1	2	3	4	5	6	7	8	9	0

Maldivian Script

Maldivian script was invented in the 17th century under the influence of Arabic script. However, the forms of the letters in Maldivian script differ greatly from those in Arabic; oddly enough, they resemble the Arabic and Telugu numerals that were used in countries near the Maldives.

Alphabet

FORM	PHONETIC VALUE	FORM	PHONETIC VALUE
ހ	*h*	ތ	*th*
ށ	*sh*	ލ	*l*
ނ	*n*	ގ	*g*
ރ	*r*	ޏ	*ny*
ބ	*b*	ސ	*s*
ޅ	*l*	ޑ	*d*
ކ	*k*	ޒ	*z*
އ	*a*, [’]	ޓ	*t*
ވ	*w, v*	ޔ	*y*
މ	*m*	ޕ	*p*
ފ	*f, ph*	ޖ	*j*
ދ	*d*	ޗ	*ch*

The forms of the first nine letters of the Maldivian alphabet, ހ, ށ, ނ, ރ, ބ, ޅ, ކ, އ, ވ, are similar to those of Arabic numerals in the Nastaliq style: ١, ٢, ٣, ٤, ٥, ٦, ٧, ٨, ٩.

Vowel signs

SHORT VOWELS	◌ަ *-a*	◌ި *-i*	◌ު *-u*	◌ެ *-e*	◌ޮ *-o*
LONG VOWELS	◌ާ *-ā*	◌ީ *-ī*	◌ޫ *-ū*	◌ޭ *-ē*	◌ޯ *-ō*

For the letter ކ *k*:

ކަ *ka* ކާ *kā* ކި *ki* ކީ *kī* ކު *ku* ކޫ *kū*

ކެ *ke* ކޭ *kē* ކޮ *ko* ކޯ *kō*

The signs for *-a*, *-i*, and *-u* are similar to Arabic vowel signs, but the long vowels are unique in that they double the form of the short vowel signs, except for *-ō*.
Single short or long vowels are shown by these signs on އ (alif):

އަ *a*, އި *i*, އޭ *ē*, އޯ *ō*.

A Maldivian letter is never written without a vowel (or vanishing-vowel) sign, though each letter is considered to have an inherent *a*-sound.

Vanishing-vowel sign The sign ◌ް indicates the absence of a vowel as it does in Arabic: ކް *k*, ނަން *nan*. On އ (alif) it denotes a glottal stop: އެކެއް *eke’*.

A postage stamp from the Maldive Islands. Maldivian script is used here only for the monetary unit: ލާރި *lāri*.

Reading and punctuation Maldivian script runs from right to left on a horizontal line, with a space between each word. Maldivian sentences usually contain some Arabic script, which is used to write Arabian names or words borrowed from Arabic.
The comma is [.] and [..] is a period. However [.] is now used for a period as well.

Numerals

١	٢	٣	٤	٥	٦	٧	٨	٩	٠
1	2	3	4	5	6	7	8	9	0

Arabic figures are also used.

A mimeographed newspaper, published in Male. Notice the Arabic script mixed with the Maldivian script. Its title is މޫންލައިޓް *mūnlait*.

Other Scripts in West Asia

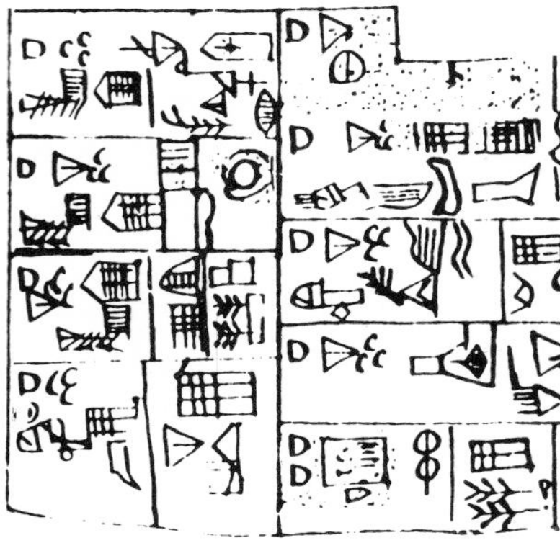

SUMERIAN PICTOGRAMS. The oldest human writing was invented in Mesopotamia about the 32nd century B.C. (Sugi)

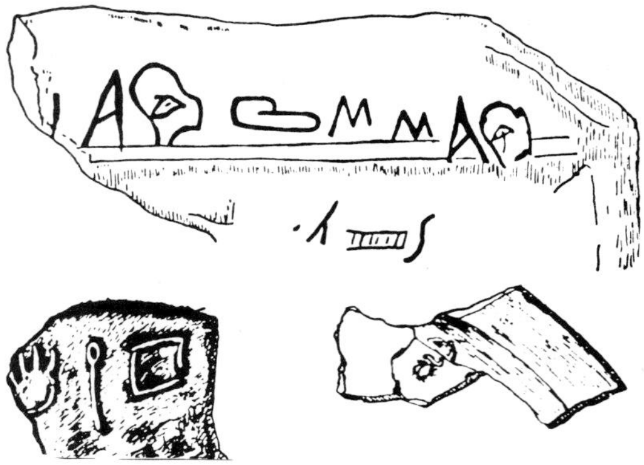

PROTO-PALESTINIAN SCRIPTS. Some of the many characters intermediate between pictograms and phonetic script that have been discovered in Palestine. (Gelb)

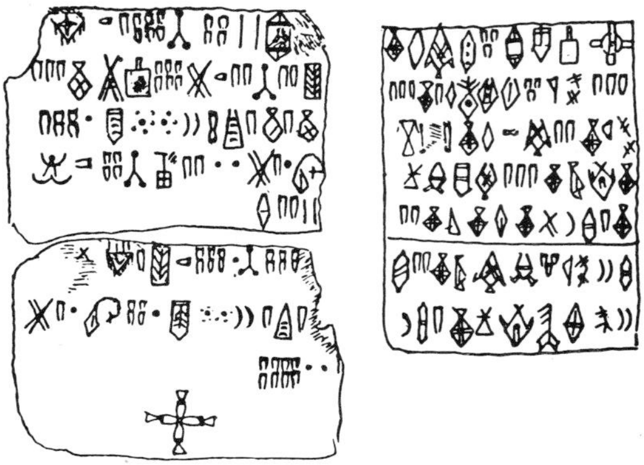

PROTO-ELAMIC SCRIPT. Ancient pictograms from the Elamic district, east of Sumer, from the 30th century B.C. Undeciphered. (Gelb)

HITTITE HIEROGLYPHICS. Hieroglyphics from the ancient Hittite Empire in Asia Minor. Now being deciphered. (Ceram)

INDUS SCRIPT. The writing of the Indus culture in western India about the 25th century B.C. Never deciphered. (Author's drawing)

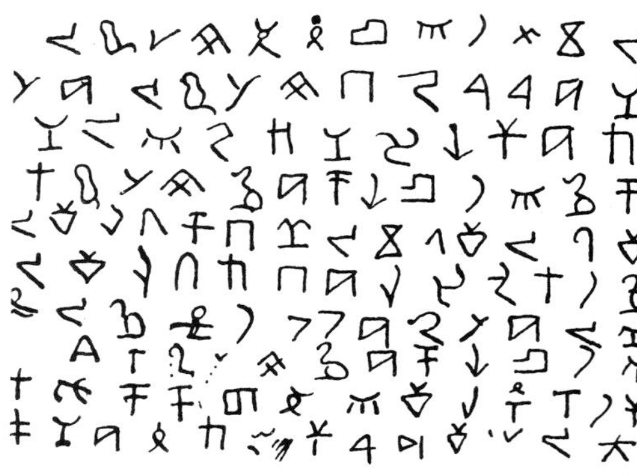

PSEUDO-HIEROGLYPHIC SYLLABARY OF BYBLOS. Used in the 15th–14th century B.C. in Byblos of ancient Phoenicia. Deciphered by E. Dhorme. (Jensen)

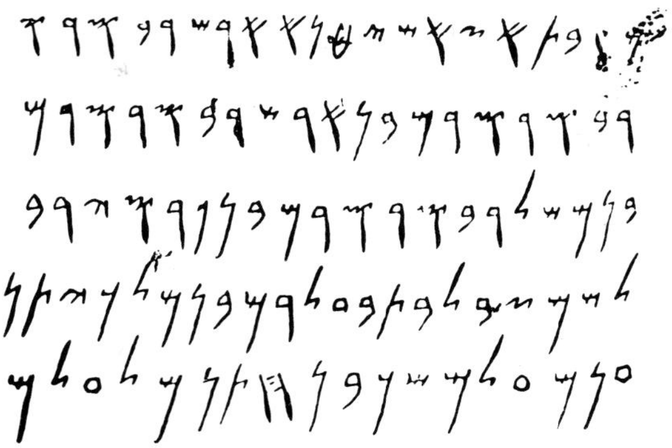

Phoenician script. The writing of ancient Phoenicia consisted of twenty-two letters and was the basis of Western alphabets. (Gelb)

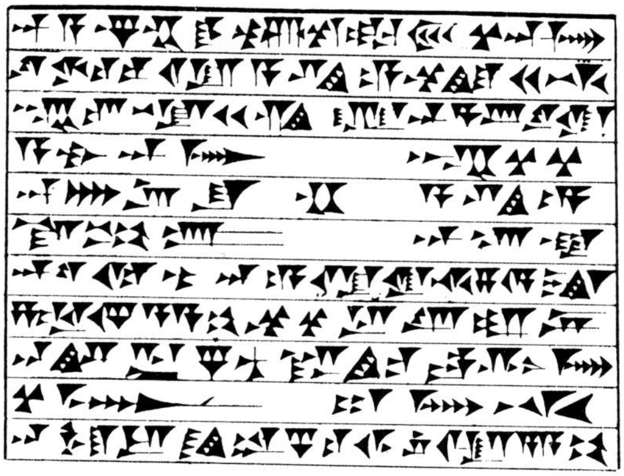

Assyrian cuneiform script. Writing from the ancient Assyrian Empire. It is essentially the same as Babylonian cuneiform script. (Sugi)

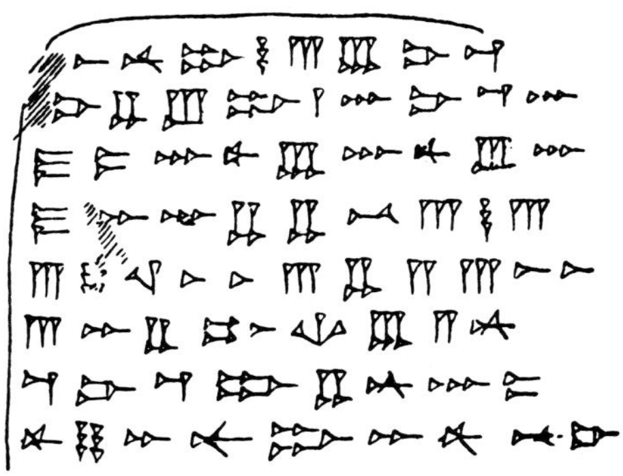

Ugaritic cuneiform script. Cuneiform alphabet discovered at Ras Shamrah in North Syria. Dated around the 15th century B.C. (Ichikawa)

Babylonian cuneiform script. Part of Hammurabi's Code of Laws from the 18th century B.C. It shows the writing of the ancient Babylonian Empire. (Sugi)

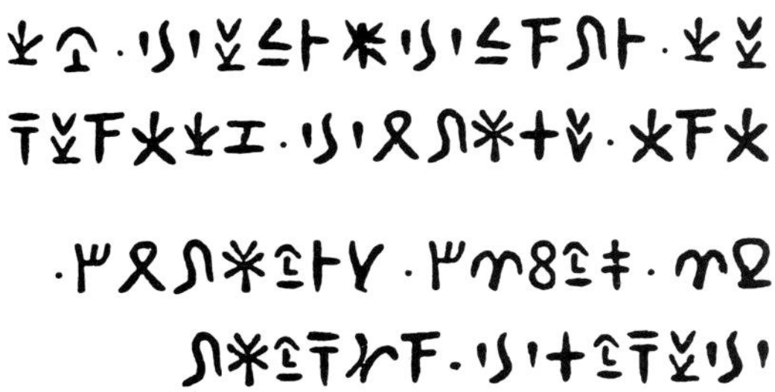

Cypriote syllabary (Classic Cypriote script). Used on the island of Cyprus from the 6th–3rd century B.C. Deciphered. (Fossey)

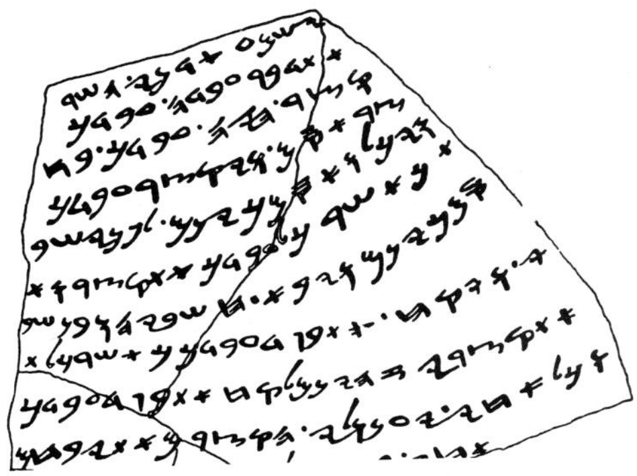

Early Hebrew script. Writing used by pre-exilian Israelites. It is different from square Hebrew. (Diringer)

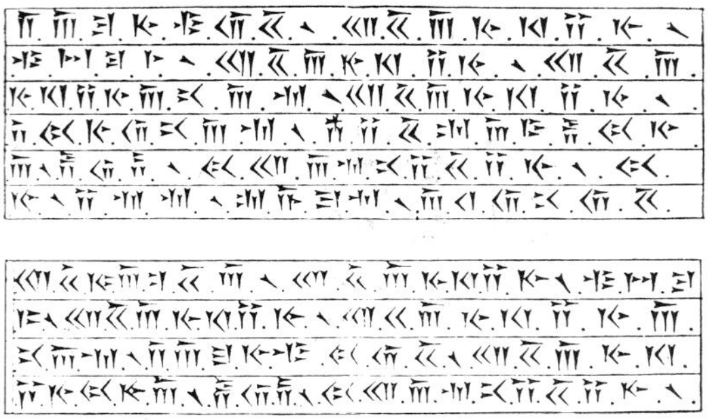

Achaemenid Persian cuneiform script. The writing of the ancient Persian Empire. From the 5th century B.C. (Sugi)

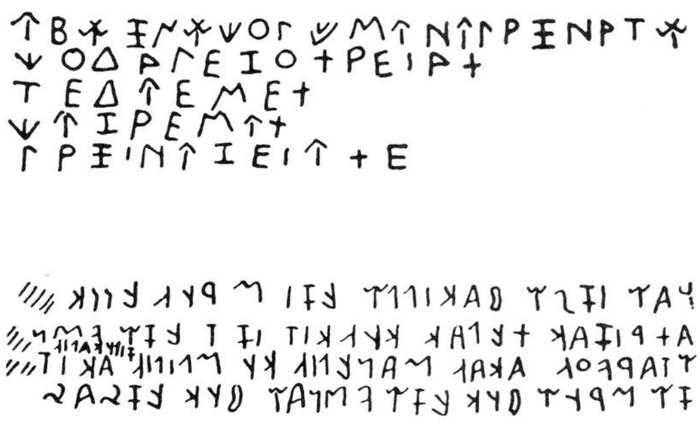

Scripts of Asia Minor. The upper is Lycian script and the lower Lydian script. Both resemble ancient Greek script. (Jensen)

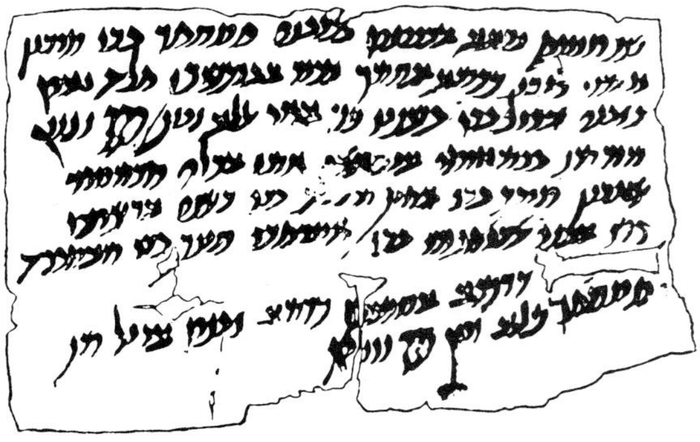

Parthian script. Document from the Arsacid dynasty of the ancient Parthian Empire in Persia. Parthian script was a variety of Aramaic script. (Ito)

Samaritan script. Samaria is an area famous in the Bible. Even now there are Bibles printed in the Samaritan language. (Nida)

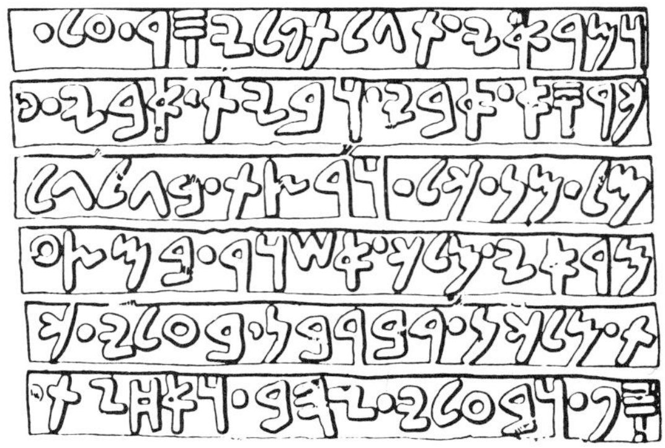

Aramaic script. Aram was a state in ancient Syria. This writing was the basis of Eastern alphabets. (Kato)

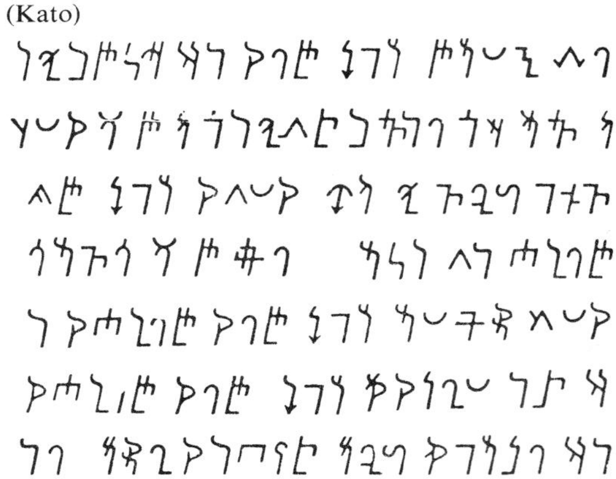

Kharoshthi script. Another writing of ancient India, along with Brahmi script. It extended also to central Asia. (Fossey)

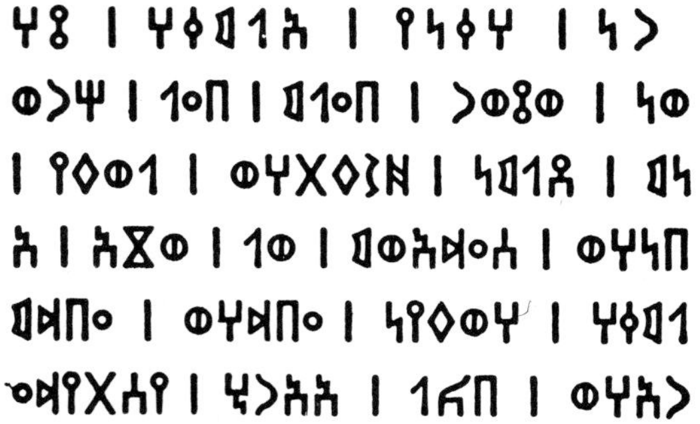

South Arabic script. From the kingdom of the Queen of Sheba in southern Arabia and used 7th century B.C. to 6th century A.D. (Gelb)

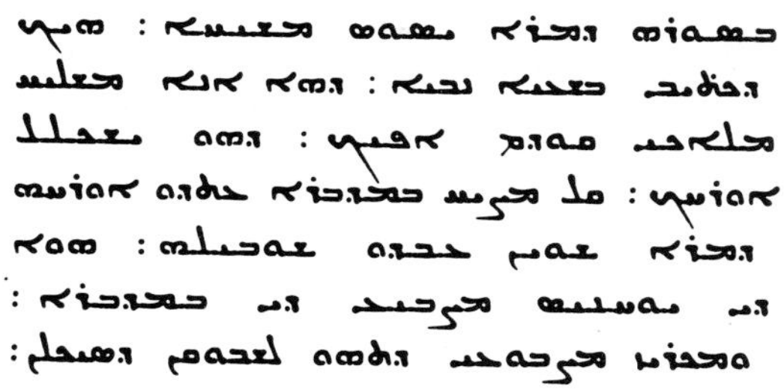

Estrangelo script. One of the three Syriac scripts. It is also found in old documents from central Asia. (Nida)

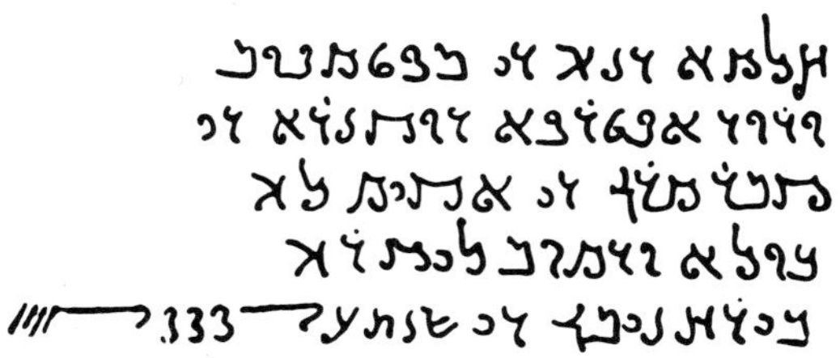

Palmyrene script. Sample from about the 3rd century. Palmyra was an ancient city on an oasis in the Syrian Desert, famous for Queen Zenobia. (Diringer)

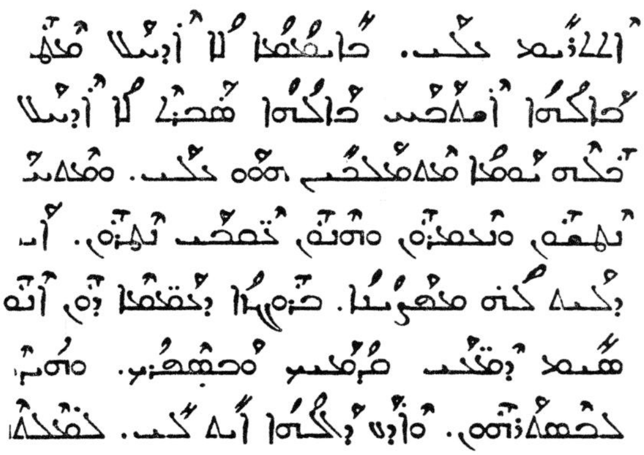

Jacobite script. Used by Syrian Monophysites (Syrian Christians). It is the most ordinal of the Syriac scripts. (Nida)

Nabataean script. Nabatae was in northwestern Arabia. This script later developed into Arabic script. (Jensen)

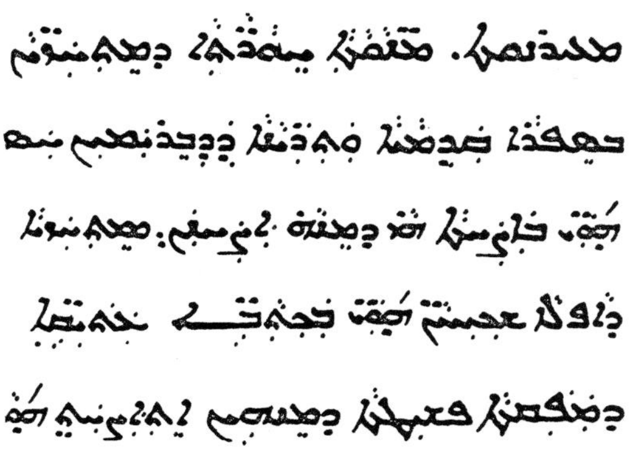

Nestorian script. The writing of Nestorianism, a variety of Christianity. This is also one of the three Syriac scripts. (Nida)

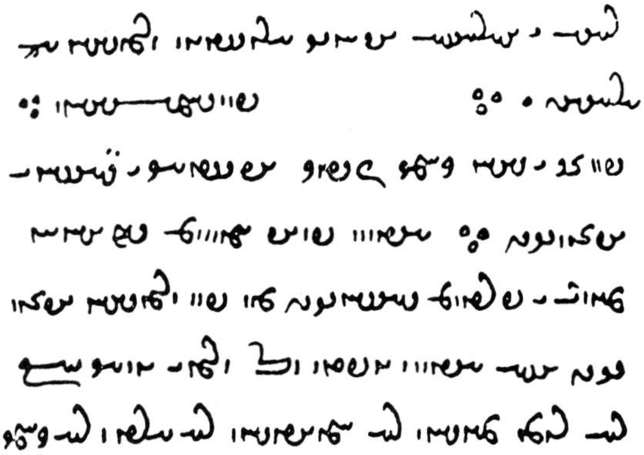

PAHLAVIK SCRIPT (CURSIVE PAHLAVI). The writing of the Sassanian Persian Empire. It is a descendant of Aramaic script. (Ito)

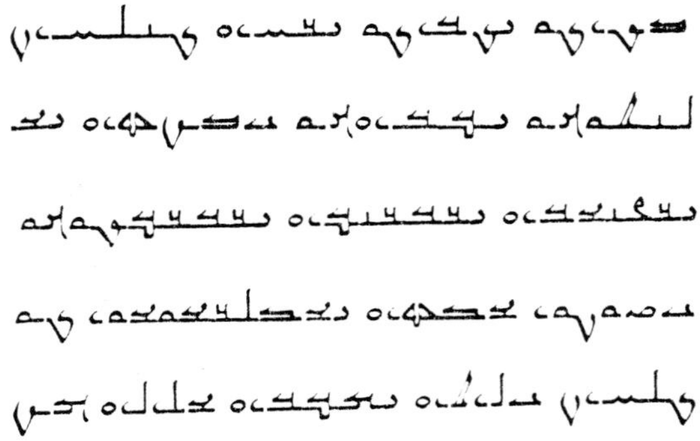

MANDAEAN SCRIPT. Mandaeans have lived in Babylonia and been Christians among Moslems since ancient times. (Fossey)

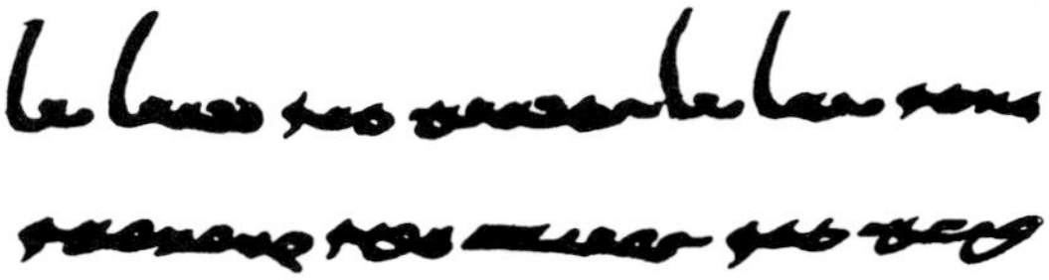

SOGDIAN SCRIPT. Sogdo was in what is now Uzbekistan. The script was widely used in central Asia from the 4th–11th century. (Jensen)

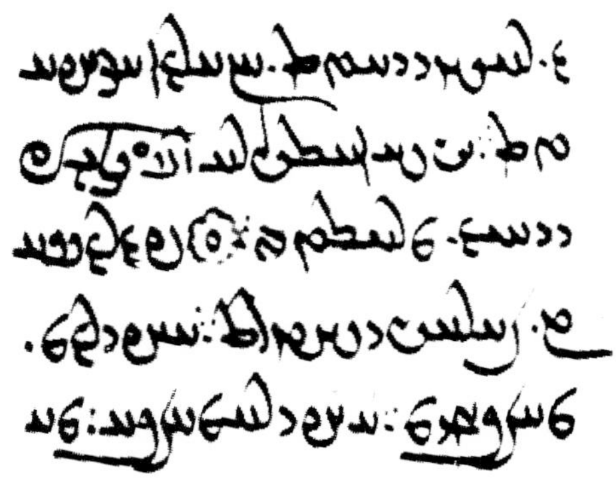

AVESTA (PAZAND) SCRIPT. Writing of Zoroastrianism. From Sassanian Persia. (Diringer)

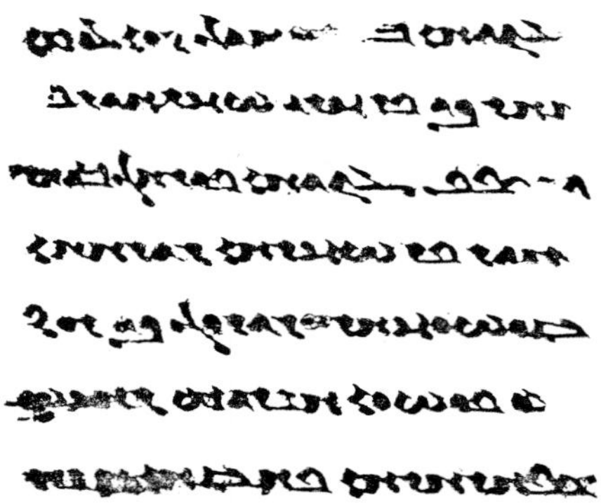

MANICHAEAN SCRIPT. Writing invented by Mani (A.D. 216–277), who was the founder of Manichaeism. (Henning)

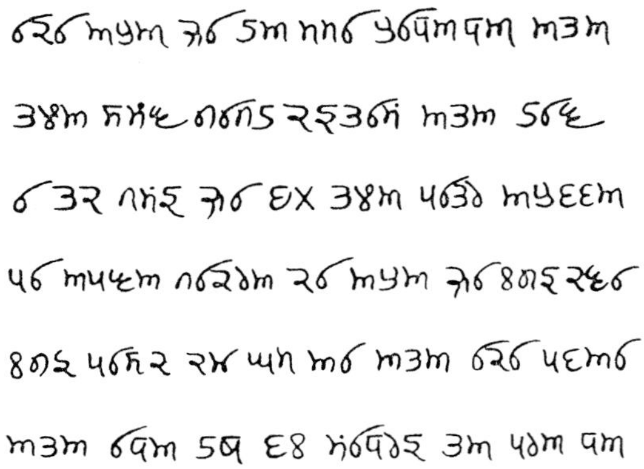

LAHNDA SCRIPT. The original writing for Punjabi and Sindhi in northwestern India. See page 50. (Grierson)

4. SCRIPTS IN AND AROUND INDIA

This chapter includes descriptions of Bangladesh, Bhutan, Nepal, and Sri Lanka because of their close linguistic and historical ties with India, which is itself a treasure box of scripts. See the section on Devanagari script for an explanation of the basic system used for all Indian scripts (page 48).

BANGLADESH [বাংলাদেশ *bāṅglādēś*]

The official language is Bengali (Indian/Indo-European), which is written in Bengali script (page 56). Newspapers are published in Bengali and in English.

A postage stamp of Bangladesh, in which Bengali script is used.

BHUTAN [འབྲུག་ *ṭru*]

The official language is Dzongkha, a dialect of Tibetan, which is written in Tibetan script (see page 88). There is only one newspaper, issued weekly in English.

INDIA [भारत *bhārat*]

India's constitution recognizes fifteen official languages. The picture on this page shows the reverse side of Indian paper money, on which the words "one rupee" are written in these fifteen languages using eleven scripts. From the top, these are Assamese (in Bengali script), Bengali (in Bengali script), Gujarati (in Gujarati script), Kannada (in Kannada or Kanarese script), Kashmiri (in Urdu or Arabic script), Malayalam (in Malayalam script), Marathi (in Devanagari script), Oriya (in Oriya script), Punjabi (in Gurmukhi script), Sanskrit (in Devanagari script), Tamil (in Tamil script), Telugu (in Telugu script), Urdu (in Urdu or Arabic script), Hindi (in Devanagari script; in large letters at the lower left), and English (in Latin script; in large letters at the lower right). Kannada, Malayalam, Tamil, and Telugu belong to the Dravidian languages, and the others (except English) belong to the Indic group of the Indo-European family.

These fifteen languages, with Sindhi in place of Sanskrit, are the major languages used in most of the Indian daily newspapers, of which there are over eight hundred. There are also a few Chinese newspapers published for Chinese living in India. The Republic of India consists of twenty-two states and nine union territories, whose boundaries have been roughly determined by the distribution of the major languages used. Therefore, the languages and scripts in India will be described for each state. English newspapers will not be mentioned since these are published in almost all the states.

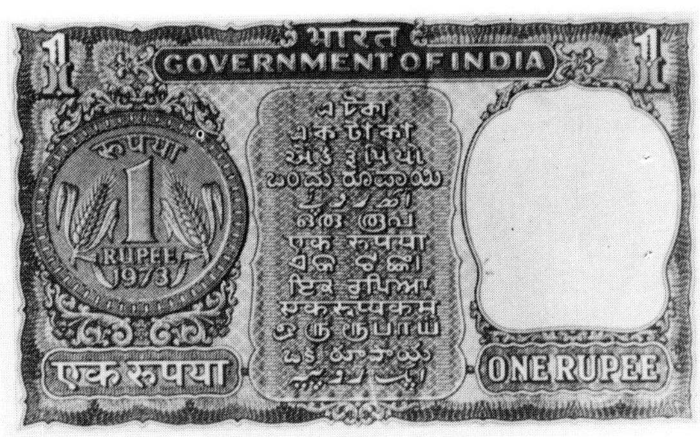

Indian paper money.

Map of India and neighboring countries.

Andhra Pradesh [ఆంధ్రదేశము *āndhra dēsamu*] The main language of this state is Telugu, written in Telugu script (page 60). Urdu and Hindi newspapers are also published.

Assam [আসাম *āsām*] The main language of this state is Assamese, which is written in Bengali script (page 56).

Bihar [बिहार *bihār*] The Bihari language is a dialect of Hindi. Newspapers are published in Hindi and in Urdu. Originally Bihari was written in Kaithi script, which has now become extinct (page 68).

Goa [गोआ *gōa*] In Goa, newspapers are published in Marathi, Portuguese, and Konkani. Konkani (Indic/Indo-European) is on rare occasions printed in Latin script.

Gujarat [ગુજરાત *gujarāt*] Newspapers are published in Gujarati and Sindhi. Gujarati is written in Gujarati script (page 52). Sindhi is printed in Arabic script written in the Naskhi style.

Haryana [हरियाणा *hariyāna*] The main language is Hindi, printed in Devanagari script (page 48).

Himachal Pradesh [हिमाचलप्रदेश *himāchal pradesh*] The main language is Hindi, printed in Devanagari script.

Jammu and Kashmir [جموں کشمیر *jammun kashmīr*] Daily newspapers are published in Kashmiri and in Urdu, both of which are printed in Urdu or Arabic script.

Karnataka [ಕರ್ನಾಟಕ *karnāṭaka*] Formerly, Mysore. The main language is Kannada or Kanarese, which is written in Kannada script (page 62).

Kerala [കേരളം *kēralam*] Newspapers are in Malayalam, which is printed in Malayalam script (page 64).

Madhya Pradesh [मध्य प्रदेश *madhya pradesh*] Most newspapers are published in Hindi; a few are in Urdu.

Maharashtra [महाराष्ट्र *mahārāshtra*] Newspapers are published in Hindi and in Marathi, both of which are printed in Devanagari script.

Meghalaya The main language of this state is Khasi (Mon-Khmer/Austroasiatic), which is printed in Latin script. However, almost all newspapers are published in Bengali.

Orissa [ଉତ୍କଳ *utkala*; ଓଡ଼ିଶା *orīsa*] Newspapers are in Oriya, which is written in Oriya script (page 54).

Punjab [ਪੰਜਾਬ *panjāb*] Newspapers are published in Punjabi, which is written in Gurmukhi script (page 50). There are also Urdu and Hindi newspapers.

Rajasthan [राजस्थान *rājasthān*] The Rajasthani language is a dialect of Hindi. Newspapers are printed in Hindi.

States and Union Territories of Assam In the eastern part of India are many small states and union territories. Some newspapers in these areas are in the Manipuri, Mizo, and Naga languages, all of which belong to the Tibeto-Burman group of Sino-Tibetan languages. These are printed in Bengali script.

Tamil Nadu [தமிழ் நாடு *tamil nāḍu*] Newspapers are in Tamil, which is written in Tamil script (page 58).

Uttar Pradesh [उत्तर प्रदेश *uttar pradesh*] In this state and Delhi, newspapers are published in Hindi and in Urdu.

West Bengal [পশ্চিম বঙ্গ *paschim baṅg*] Newspapers are in Bengali, which is written in Bengali script (page 56).

NEPAL [नेपाल *nepāl*]

The official language is Nepali (Indic/Indo-European), which is written in Devanagari script. Daily newspapers are published in Nepali and in English.

A postage stamp of Nepal.

SRI LANKA (Ceylon) [ශ්‍රී ලංකා *srīlankā*]

The official languages of Sri Lanka are Sinhalese and English. Sinhalese (Indic/Indo-European) is written in Sinhalese script (page 66). Newspapers are published in Sinhalese, in English, and in Tamil.

A postage stamp of Sri Lanka.

Devanagari Script

Devanagari script uses the basic system used for all the Indian scripts described in this chapter. (1) There is neither a distinction between capitals and small letters as in Latin script nor a variation in initial, medial, and final forms as in Arabic script. (2) There are vowels and consonants. (3) Each consonant includes an inherent *a*-vowel. (4) Vowel signs are used; when a consonant's inherent *a*-sound changes to a different vowel, an abridged form of the appropriate vowel letter is attached to the consonant. (5) Conjunct consonants are used; when two or more consonants are combined with no intervening vowel, they are written as one letter. (6) Letters run from left to right on a horizontal line, with a space between each word.

Devanagari script is used to write Sanskrit, Hindi, Marathi, and various other Indian languages. Though its writing system for Sanskrit is very intricate, the following tables suffice for Hindi.

Vowels

अ (अ)	आ	इ	ई	उ	ऊ	
a	*ā*	*i*	*ī*	*u*	*ū*	
ऋ	ए	ऐ	ओ	औ	अं	अः
ri	*ē*	*ai*	*ō*	*au*	*an*	*a'*

Consonants

GUTTURALS	क *ka*	ख *kha*	ग *ga*	घ *gha*	ङ *nga*	
PALATALS	च *cha*	छ *chha*	ज *ja*	झ (झ) *jha*	ञ *nya*	
CEREBRALS	ट *ṭa*	ठ *ṭha*	ड *ḍa*	ढ *ḍha*	ण (ण) *ṇa*	
DENTALS	त *ta*	थ *tha*	द *da*	ध *dha*	न *na*	
LABIALS	प *pa*	फ *pha*	(फ़) *fa*	ब *ba*	भ *bha*	म *ma*
SEMI-VOWELS	य *ya*	र *ra*	ल *la*	व *va, wa*		
SIBILANTS	श *sa, sha*	ष *sha*	स *sa*			
ASPIRATE	ह *ha*					

Vowel signs

◌ *-a* ◌ा *-ā* ि◌ *-i* ◌ी *-ī* ◌ु *-u* ◌ू *-ū*
◌ृ *-ri* ◌े *-ē* ◌ै *-ai* ◌ो *-ō* ◌ौ *-au*
Thus, कि *ki*, के *kē*.

Conjunct consonants Succeeding consonants become subscripts: ङ· *nga* + क *ka* = ङ्क *ṅka*. Preceding consonants become half letters: न्स *nsa*, ष्म *shma*. Such forms are frequently used in printing for convenience: क्‍क → क्क *kka*.
Transformations: क *ka* + ष *sha* = क्ष *ksha*, त ta + त ta = त्त tta.
Preceding *r* becomes ◌र्‍ : र्म *rma*.
Succeeding *r* becomes ◌्र or ◌्र; thus क्र *kra*, ट्र *tra*, प्र *pra*.

Other signs
◌ं (anusvara) shows nasalization: कं *kan*.
◌ः (visarg) shows a weak aspiration: कः *ka'*.
◌् (viram) shows the absence of the inherent *a*: क् *k*. However, the inherent *a*-sound of the last consonant letter of each word is not pronounced, unless there is a viram. If a word ends with an *a* vowel, ◌ा *-ā* is written.

Reading and punctuation Since the top of every Devanagari letter consists of a horizontal stroke, the letters of each word appear to be connected by a single line. The mark 〔 । 〕 is equivalent to a period, and 〔 ॥ 〕 is used at the end of a text.

Numerals

१	२	३	४	५	६	७	८	९	०
1	2	3	4	5	6	7	8	9	0

स्वादिष्ट जलपान शुद्ध व ताजी मिठाइयों का आकर्षण केन्द्र
गुप्ता होटल
नन्दिनी मार्ग, पावर हाउस
भिलाई नगर

देशबन्धु

(नई दुनिया रायपुर सम्मिलित)

DESH BANDHU 2 3 1974

रायपुर शनिवार दिनांक २ मार्च १९७४

लक्ष्मण धारा — हर जगह मिलता है

तीव्र उत्सुकता की घड़ियां : एक के बाद एक सीटों पर कब्जा

उ.प्र. में कांग्रेस को अंततः स्पष्ट बहुमत; बहुगुणा का इस्तीफा : ५ मार्च को शपथ

(ब्रिटिश चुनाव में) (भारतीय पराजित)

उत्तर प्रदेश

दल नेता पद से हटने के तुरंत बाद

चिमन भाई पटेल दल से निष्कासित

शालाओं को व्यवस्थित करने हेतु विधेयक

गुजरात में गोली बारी का एक और दिन : ३ मृत

गुजरात की जनता पर तो

केन्द्र पर खाद्यपूर्ति में

ब्रिटेन चुनाव परिणाम

२१३ वां सत्र बस्ती जो

A Hindi newspaper printed in Devanagari script. Its title is देश बन्धु *dēsh bandhu.*

लोकसत्ता

मुंबई; शुक्रवार, १ मार्च १९७४

सर्वाधिक खपाचे मराठी दैनिक

वर्ष २७ : अंक ४१ किंमत २० पैसे

युनिकेम — औषधि क्षेत्रामध्ये विश्वसनीय नांव

★ ६००० खाली आयकर नाही ★ मद्य, सिगारेट, टी. व्ही., रेफ्रिजरेटर, स्कूटर्स, तलम कापड महागणार ★ प्रॅच्युइटी करमुक्त

केंद्रीय अर्थसंकल्पात १८६ कोटी रु. चे नवे कर

गुजरातेत शांतता प्रस्थापित झाल्याखेरीज

विधिमंडळ विसर्जनासंबंधी निर्णय घेणे शक्य होणार नाही

पंतप्रधान इंदिरा गांधी यांचे निवेदन

लोकसभेत वित्त विधेयक सादर

तरीही वर्षअखेर १२५ कोटि रुपयांची तूट राहणारच

कर चुकविण्याची प्रवृत्ती कमी करण्याचा चव्हाण यांचा प्रयत्न

कामगार घरबांधणी महामंडळ हवे

आ. भाई भोसले यांची सूचना

योजनेसाठी

उत्तर प्रदेशांत काँग्रेस

A Marathi newspaper printed in the same script with the additional letter ळ *la.* Its title is लोकसत्ता *lōkasatta.*

Gurmukhi Script

Gurmukhi script is used to write the Punjabi language. Originally Punjabi was written in Lahnda script (page 44), of which it was said: "It is convenient, with only one fault; it is seldom legible to anyone except the original writer." Misreadings were frequent.

When the Sikh religion developed in the Punjab in the 16th century, the second Sikh Guru (the successor of the leader) improved Lahnda script with reference to the Sanskrit system in order to give exact renderings of the Sikh scriptures. This script has been called Guru-mukhi, which means "script from the mouth of the Guru." Nowadays, it is widely used by others as well as the Sikhs because of its fairly logical arrangement.

Vowels The vowel letters are organized on three bases: ੳ (ura), ਅ (aira), and ੲ (iri).

ਉ	ਊ	ਓ	ਅ	ਆ	ਐ	ਔ
u	*ū*	*ō*	*a*	*ā*	*ai*	*au*
ਇ	ਈ	ਏ				
i	*ī*	*ē*				

Consonants

ਸ	ਹ	ਕ	ਖ	ਗ	ਘ	ਙ
sa	*ha*	*ka*	*kha*	*ga*	*gha*	*nga*
ਚ	ਛ	ਜ	ਝ	ਞ	ਟ	ਠ
cha	*chha*	*ja*	*jha*	*nya*	*ṭa*	*ṭha*
ਡ	ਢ	ਣ	ਤ	ਥ	ਦ	ਧ
ḍa	*ḍha*	*ṇa*	*ta*	*tha*	*da*	*dha*
ਨ	ਪ	ਫ	ਬ	ਭ	ਮ	ਯ
na	*pa*	*pha*	*ba*	*bha*	*ma*	*ya*
ਰ	ਲ	ਵ	ੜ			
ra	*la*	*wa,va*	*ra*			

Additional consonants with dots are:

ਸ਼	ਖ਼	ਗ਼	ਜ਼	ਫ਼
sha	*xa*	*ga*	*za*	*fa*

Vowel signs

◌ –*a* ◌ਾ –*ā* ਿ◌ –*i* ◌ੀ –*ī* ◌ੁ –*u*

◌ੂ –*ū* ◌ੇ –*ē* ◌ੈ –*ai* ◌ੋ –*ō* ◌ੌ –*au*

Thus:

ਕ	ਕਾ	ਕਿ	ਕੀ	ਕੁ	ਕੂ	ਕੇ	ਕੈ	ਕੋ	ਕੌ
ka	*kā*	*ki*	*kī*	*ku*	*kū*	*kē*	*kai*	*kō*	*kau*

Conjunct consonants In Gurmukhi script, there are few conjunct consonants because of the discretionary omission of vowel sounds in juxtaposed consonant letters. For example, ਮਾਰਦਾ , whose spelling should give the pronunciation *māradā*, is actually pronounced *mārda*. This corresponds to the discretionary insertion of vowels when the Punjabi language is written in Arabic script using consonant letters without inherent vowels. There are three subscript forms in use, however:

◌੍ਰ shows succeeding ਰ *ra*: ਪ੍ਰ *pra*.
◌੍ਵ shows succeeding ਵ *wa*: ਸ੍ਵ *swa*.
◌੍ਹ shows succeeding ਹ *ha*: ਨ੍ਹ *nha*.

Tone ਹ does not always indicate the pronunciation of *ha* but sometimes shows a high tone on the preceding vowel: ਜਾਹ *já*. Subscript ਹ (◌੍ਹ) also indicates a high tone: ਪੜ੍ਹ *pár*. Moreover, the five letters ਘ *gha*, ਝ *jha*, ਢ *ḍha*, ਧ *dha*, and ਭ *bha* are used to indicate the high tones. So, ਘਰ , spelled *ghara*, is pronounced *kár*.

Other signs ◌ੰ (tippi) and ◌ਂ (bindi) show the nasalization of vowels: ਬੰ *ban*. ◌ੱ (addak) indicates the doubling of the following consonant: ਸੱਤ *satt*.

Reading and punctuation Gurmukhi script is written from left to right, with a space between each word. The mark 〔 । 〕 shows a period.

Numerals

੧	੨	੩	੪	੫	੬	੭	੮	੯	੦
1	2	3	4	5	6	7	8	9	0

In newspapers Arabic figures are used.

ਅਜੀਤ

ਕਰਨਾਟਕ ਵਿਚ ਇੰਦਰਾ ਕਾਂਗਰਸ ਦੀ ਅਗਵਾਈ ਹੇਠਲੀ ਸਰਕਾਰ ਅਜ ਸਹੁੰ ਚੁਕ ਲਵੇਗੀ

ਇੰਦਰਾ ਗਾਂਧੀ ਵਲੋਂ ਵਜ਼ਾਰਤ ਦੇ ਗਠਨ ਬਾਰੇ ਸਾਥੀਆਂ ਨਾਲ ਮਸ਼ਵਰੇ-ਸੂਚੀ ਤਿਆਰ

ਤ੍ਰਿਪਾਠੀ, ਸਟੀਫਨ, ਕਾਸਮ, ਬਹੁਗੁਣਾ, ਜ਼ੈਲ ਸਿੰਘ, ਨਰਸਿਮ੍ਹਾ, ਫਾਰੂਕ, ਸ਼ਰਮਾ, ਸੁਖਾਡੀਆ, ਗਨੀ ਖਾਂ, ਅੰਤੁਲੇ ਤੇ ਮੋਹਸਿਨਾ ਨੂੰ ਵਜ਼ਾਰਤ ਚ ਲਿਆ ਜਾਣਾ ਯਕੀਨੀ

ਸਿਮ੍ਹਾ ਨੂੰ ਗ੍ਰਹਿ, ਕਾਸਮ ਨੂੰ ਬਦੇਸ਼, ਬਹੁਗੁਣਾ ਨੂੰ ਵਿਤ, ਜ਼ੈਲ ਸਿੰਘ ਨੂੰ ਰਖਿਆ, ਤ੍ਰਿਪਾਠੀ ਨੂੰ ਰੇਲ ਵਜ਼ਾਰਤ ਮਿਲਣੀ ਸੰਭਵ

ਪੰਜਾਬ ਦੀਆਂ ਮੰਗਾਂ ਇੰਦਿਰਾ ਗਾਂਧੀ ਅਗੇ ਰਖਾਂਗਾ

ਸਰਕਾਰ ਨਹੀਂ ਟੁਟਣ ਦਿਆਂਗੇ

ਰੈਡੀ ਨੂੰ ਸੂਚੀ ਕਲ ਪੇਸ਼ ਹੋਵੇਗੀ

ਲੋਕ ਸਭਾ ਚ ਕੌਣ ਕਿਥੇ ਖੜਾ ਹੈ

ਹਿੰਦ ਵਲੋਂ ਰੂਸ ਦਾ ਪੱਖ ਪ੍ਰਵਾਨ

2 ਅਕਾਲੀ ਗੋਲੀ ਨਾਲ ਉਡਾਏ

ਚੀਨੀ ਵਤੀਰਾ ਗ਼ਲਤ ਹੈ-ਪਾਦ

ਇੰਦਰਾ ਦੀ ਜਿਤ : ਨਿਕਮੀ ਸਰਕਾਰ ਵਿਰੁਧ ਲੋਕ ਗੁਸੇ ਦਾ ਪ੍ਰਗਟਾਵਾ

A newspaper in Punjabi written in Gurmukhi script. Its title is ਅਜੀਤ *ajit*, though it is fairly deformed.

Gujarati Script

Gujarati script belongs to the Northern Indian script group, but like Kaithi script (page 68) its letters have no bars on top, in contrast to Devanagari script, which has bars. However, the Gujarati system resembles that of Devanagari.

Vowels

અ	આ	ઇ	ઈ	ઉ	ઊ	ઋ
a	*ā*	*i*	*ī*	*u*	*ū*	*ri*
એ	ઐ	ઓ	ઔ			
ē	*ai*	*ō*	*au*			

Consonants

ક	ખ	ગ	ઘ	ઙ	ચ	છ
ka	*kha*	*ga*	*gha*	*nga*	*cha*	*chha*
જ	ઝ	ઞ	ટ	ઠ	ડ	ઢ
ja	*jha*	*nya*	*ṭa*	*ṭha*	*ḍa*	*ḍha*
ણ	ત	થ	દ	ધ	ન	પ
ṇa	*ta*	*tha*	*da*	*dha*	*na*	*pa*
ફ	બ	ભ	મ	ય	ર	લ
pha	*ba*	*bha*	*ma*	*ya*	*ra*	*la*
વ	શ	ષ	સ	હ	ળ	
wa,va	*sha*	*sha*	*sa*	*ha*	*la*	

Vowel signs

◌ *-a* ◌ા *-ā* િ◌ *-i* ◌ી *-ī*

◌ુ *-u* ◌ૂ *-ū* ◌ૃ *-ri* ◌ે *-ē*

◌ૈ *-ai* ◌ો *-ō* ◌ૌ *-au*

For example, the consonant બ *ba* takes the following forms; note their resemblance to the forms of the independent vowels.

બા	બિ	બી	બુ	બૂ	બૃ
bā	*bi*	*bī*	*bu*	*bū*	*bri*
બે	બૈ	બો	બૌ		
bē	*bai*	*bō*	*bau*		

In addition to the regular forms, there are the following irregular ones:

જા	જી	જુ	ણુ	દૃ	રુ	રૂ
jā	*jī*	*jū*	*ṇu*	*dri*	*ru*	*rū*

Conjunct consonants

Transformations: ક *ka* + ષ *sha* = ક્ષ *ksha*, શ *sha* + ચ *cha* = શ્ચ *shcha*.

Semitransformations: ત *ta* + ન *na* = ત્ન *tna*, દ *da* + ય *ya* = દ્ય *dya*.

Subscriptions: ડ્ન *ḍna*, ખ્ત *khta*.

Using a half letter: ગ *ga* + લ *la* = ગ્લ *gla*.

Double consonants: ટ *ṭa* + ટ *ṭa* = ટ્ટ *ṭṭa*, ત્ત *tta*, ઠ્ઠ *ṭhṭha*, ક્ક *kka*.

◌ર્ shows preceding ર *ra*: ર્ગ *rga*, ર્થ *rtha*.

◌્ર shows succeeding ર *ra*: ત્ર *tra*, ક્ર *kra*.

◌ં shows preceding *n*, *ng*, *ny*, *ṇ*, and *m*: ંગ *ṅga*, ંડ *nda*, ંબ *mba*.

Other signs ◌્ shows the absence of a vowel sound: ક્ *k*. The inherent *a*-vowel of the final letter of a word is not pronounced unless there is a sign: કામ *kām*. When a word ends with *a*, the *-ā* vowel sign is attached: ચા *cha*.

◌ં shows a nasal: ઈં *īn*.

A street scene in Ahmedabad.

Reading and punctuation Gujarati script runs from left to right on a horizontal line, with a space between each word. The mark 〔 । 〕 is a period, but sometimes 〔.〕 is used instead.

Numerals

૧	૨	૩	૪	૫	૬	૭	૮	૯	૦
1	2	3	4	5	6	7	8	9	0

Book your order before budget
Turn on the air of success with
Airtemp Room Airconditioner,
Stockist & service dealer
Freezfast Corporation
Nr. Aradhna Theater,
Baroda-1. Phone. 66051

લોકસત્તા

'ગુજરાત બંધ'માં ફાટી નીકળેલાં વ્યાપક તોફાનો: ચારનાં મોત

ખંભાત—કરમસદ—મહેસાણા અને વિસનગરમાં તોફાનો અને પથ્થરમારો

અમદાવાદ-અંકલેશ્વર-વડોદરા અને વાંસકુઇમાં ગોળીબાર : ૯ જણાને ઇજા

અંકલેશ્વરમાં પોલીસ ગોળીબારમાં બે જણાના મરણ: ભરૂચમાં રોષ

અલ્હાબાદ-કાનપુર રેલવે લાઇન પર સત્યાગ્રહ

આજે દિલ્હી આવતા નવનિર્માણના નેતાઓ

હજારો આદિવાસીઓનો વિદ્યાર્થીઓ પર હુમલો

સીંગતેલ લઇ જતી માલગાડી અટકાવતા ૩ વિદ્યાર્થીઓ

પેરીસ નજીક ભયંકર વિમાની હોનારત: ૩૩૪ મુસાફરોનાં મોત: કોઇજ ન બચ્યું

શિનોરમાં ૫૦૦ મહિલાઓનું સરઘસ

બ્રિટિશ વિમાનનું અપહરણ કરતા ગેરિલાઓ

A newspaper published in Baroda. It is printed in Gujarati script and its title is લોકસત્તા *lōkasatta*.

Oriya Script

Oriya script resembles Northern Indian scripts in structure, but since each Oriya letter has a semicircular line on top, Oriya documents seem like a parade of bald heads. The circular line in Oriya script is considered a deformation of the straight line in Devanagari script. This circular line must have facilitated writing on palm leaves, on which almost all Southern Indian scripts were carved by needles.

Vowels

ଅ	ଆ	ଇ	ଈ	ଉ	ଊ	ଋ	ୠ
a	*ā*	*i*	*ī*	*u*	*ū*	*ru*	*rū*
ଌ	ୡ	ଏ	ଐ	ଓ	ଔ	ଅଂ	ଅଃ
lu	*lū*	*ē*	*ai*	*ō*	*au*	*aṅ*	*a'*

Consonants

କ	ଖ	ଗ	ଘ	ଙ	ଚ	ଛ	ଜ
ka	*kha*	*ga*	*gha*	*nga*	*cha*	*chha*	*ja*
ଝ	ଞ	ଟ	ଠ	ଡ	ଢ	ଣ	ତ
jha	*nya*	*ṭa*	*ṭha*	*ḍa*	*ḍha*	*ṇa*	*ta*
ଥ	ଦ	ଧ	ନ	ପ	ଫ	ବ	ଭ
tha	*da*	*dha*	*na*	*pa*	*pha*	*ba*	*bha*
ମ	ୟ	ଯ	ର	ଲ	ଳ	ୱ	ଶ
ma	*ya*	(*ja*)	*ra*	*la*	*la*	*wa*	*sa*
ଷ	ସ	ହ	କ୍ଷ				
sha	*sa*	*ha*	*khya*				

Vowel signs

◌ *-a* ◌ା *-ā* ◌ି *-i* ◌ୀ *-ī* ◌ୁ *-u*

◌ୂ *-ū* ◌ୃ *-ru* େ◌ *-ē* ୈ◌ *-ai*

ୋ◌ *-ō* ୌ◌ *-au*

For the letter ଗ *ga*:

ଗା	ଗି	ଗୀ	ଗୁ	ଗୂ	ଗୃ
gā	*gi*	*gī*	*gu*	*gū*	*gru*
ଗେ	ଗୈ	ଗୋ	ଗୌ		
gē	*gai*	*gō*	*gau*		

The *-ā* sign is often combined with the right-hand curve of a consonant. The tail of the consonant, if it has one, is then transferred to the left side: ରା → ରା *rā*. Moreover, ଚା *chā* is also written ଚା, the ୵ being added to the vertical line showing the *-ā* to prevent confusion with ଗ *ga*.

The *-i* sign is often sunken into the top curve of the consonant: କି *ki*. The *-i* sign sometimes takes the form ◌ି, as in ଧି → ଧି *dhi*.

The *-ī* sign is also combined with consonants: କୀ → କୀ *kī*.

The *-u* sign ◌ୁ is often written ◌ୁ : ସୁ → ସୁ *su*.

Conjunct consonants These are very intricate and irregular.

Transformations: ନ *na* + ଦ *da* = ନ୍ଦ *nda*, ତ *ta* + ତ *ta* = ତ୍ତ *tta*.

Preceding *nga* becomes two small circles: ଙ *nga* + ଗ *ga* = ଙ୍ଗ *ṅga*, but ଙ୍ଘ *ṅgha*.

Preceding *nya* is unique: ଞ୍ଚ *nycha*, ଞ୍ଜ *nyja*.

◌୍ୟ shows succeeding ଯ *ya*: କ୍ୟ *kya*.

◌୍ର shows succeeding ର *ra*: ଗ୍ର *gra*.

ର୍◌ shows preceding ର *ra*: ର୍କ *rka*.

Subscripts: ଦ୍ଧ *ddha*, ଶ୍ଛ *scha*.

Subscripts without the head: କ୍ଲ *kla*, ଗ୍ନ *gna*.

Subscripts transformed: କ୍ୱ *kwa*, ପ୍ତ *pta*.

Other signs ◌୍ (hasanta) indicates the absence of the *a*-vowel: କ୍ *k*. ◌ଂ (anoswara) shows the sound *ng*: କଂ *kang*.

◌ଃ (bisarga) shows a glottal stop when it is placed on the end of a word. But if it appears in the middle, the consonant preceding it is doubled: ପୁନଃପୁନଃ *punappuna'*. ◌ଁ (chandra bindu) shows a nasal: କଁ *kan*.

Reading and punctuation Oriya script runs from left to right on a horizontal line, with a space between each word. The mark 〔 । 〕 shows a period, but it is written with a space between it and the last word to prevent confusion with ◌ା , the sign of the *-ā* vowel.

Numerals

୧	୨	୩	୪	୫	୬	୭	୮	୯	୦
1	2	3	4	5	6	7	8	9	0

An Oriya newspaper. Its title is ସମାଜ *samāja.*

Bengali Script

At a glance, Bengali resembles Devanagari script, though it is generally more slender and sharp. Bengali script is used to write Assamese, Manipuri, Munda (Austroasiatic), and other East Indian languages as well as Bengali.

Vowels

অ	আ	ই	ঈ	উ	ঊ	ঋ
a	*ā*	*i*	*ī*	*u*	*ū*	*ri*
এ	ঐ	ও	ঔ	অং	অঃ	
ē	*ai*	*ō*	*au*	*aṅ*	*a'*	

Consonants

ক	খ	গ	ঘ	ঙ	চ	ছ	জ
ka	*kha*	*ga*	*gha*	*nga*	*cha*	*chha*	*ja*
ঝ	ঞ	ট	ঠ	ড	ঢ	ণ	ত
jha	*nya*	*ṭa*	*ṭha*	*ḍa*	*ḍha*	*ṇa*	*ta*
থ	দ	ধ	ন	প	ফ	ব	ভ
tha	*da*	*dha*	*na*	*pa*	*pha*	*ba*	*bha*
ম	য়	র	ল	ব	শ	ষ	স
ma	*ya*	*ra*	*la*	*va*	*sa*	*sha*	*sa*
হ							
ha							

Additional consonants: য *za*, ড় *ṛa*, ঢ় *ṛa*

Vowel signs

◌া *–ā* ি◌ *–i* ◌ী *–ī* ◌ু *–u* ◌ূ *–ū*
◌ৃ *–ri* ে◌ *–ē* ৈ◌ *–ai* ে◌া *–ō* ে◌ৗ *–au*

For the letter ক *ka*:

কা	কি	কী	কু	কূ
kā	*ki*	*kī*	*ku*	*kū*
কৃ	কে	কৈ	কো	কৌ
kri	*kē*	*kai*	*kō*	*kau*

Exceptional forms:

গু	রু	শু	হু	রূ	শৃ	হৃ
gu	*ru*	*su*	*hu*	*rū*	*sri*	*hri*

Conjunct consonants Using half letters: স্প *spa*, ন্দ *nda*.
Juxtaposition: ড্গ *dga*, চ্ছ *chchha*.
Subscripts: ম্ব *mba*, গ্ন *gna*.
◌্র shows succeeding *ra*: শ্র *sra*, ক্র *kra*, ত্র *tra*.
◌র্ shows preceding *ra*: র্ক *rka*, র্জ *rja*.
◌্য shows succeeding *ya*: ক্য *kya*, ত্য *tya*.
Other transformations: জ্ঞ *jnya*, ক্ষ *ksha*, হ্ণ *hṇa*, ঙ্গ *ṅga*, ক্ত *kta*.
Double consonants: ক্ক *kka*, চ্চ *chcha*, জ্জ *jja*, ট্ট *ṭṭa*, ড্ড *ḍḍa*, ণ্ণ *ṇṇa*, ত্ত *tta*, ন্ন *nna*, ব্ব *bba*, ম্ম *mma*, ল্ল *lla*.
Though there are many other conjunct consonants, they follow the above rules; for example: ক্ষ্ণ *kshna*, স্ত্র *stra*, ন্দ্র *ndra*, ন্ন্য *nnya*, ম্প্র *mpra*.

Other signs ◌্ (hasanta) indicates the absence of the *a*-vowel: ক্ *k*. An exception is ত *ta*, which does not become ত্ but ৎ *t*. The inherent *a*-vowel of an end letter of a word is not pronounced unless there is a sign. ◌ঁ (chandra bindu) and ◌ং (anusvara) indicate nasals: কঁ *kan*, কং *kang*. ◌ঃ (bisarg) shows a glottal stop: কঃ *ka'*. ৺ denotes the name of God; ৭ is used especially to denote the Hindu god Ganesh.

Reading and punctuation Bengali script runs from left to right on a horizontal line, with a space between each word. The mark (।) shows a period.

Numerals

১	২	৩	৪	৫	৬	৭	৮	৯	০
1	2	3	4	5	6	7	8	9	0

Bengali script also has special signs for fractions. ৴৹ is 1 anna ($\frac{1}{16}$ of a rupee) or $\frac{1}{16}$, ৵৹ is $\frac{1}{8}$, ৶৹ is $\frac{3}{16}$, ৷৹ is $\frac{1}{4}$, ৷৴৹ is $\frac{5}{16}$, ৷৷৹ is $\frac{1}{2}$, ৸৹ is $\frac{3}{4}$, ৸৵৹ is $\frac{7}{8}$, and ১৲ is 1 rupee.

কালির জগতে একটি নতুন নাম
স্টার্লিং ইংক
স্টার্লিং ইংক কোম্পানী
ঢাকা

দৈনিক বাংলা

সর্বপ্রকার ঘড়ি বিক্রয় ও মেরামতের নির্ভরযোগ্য প্রতিষ্ঠান
ন্যাশনাল ট্রেডার্স

লোকের স্বাভাবিক জীবনযাত্রা ব্যাহতকারীরা শ্রমিক শ্রেণীর বন্ধু নয়ঃ বঙ্গবন্ধু

হিংসাত্মক পন্থায় সমস্যার সমাধান হয় না

গতকাল গণভবনে সমবেত বিআরটিসি শ্রমিকদের মাঝে বঙ্গবন্ধু

নৌ-পুলিশের জন্য অবিলম্বে সিদ্ধান্ত নিয়োগের নির্দেশ

আমরা বরকতের ভাই আমরা সালামের ভাই

পুলিশের সাথে সংঘর্ষের পরিণতিতে দুটি ট্রেন ছাড়েনি

কমলাপুরে রেলকর্মীদের আকস্মিক ধর্মঘট

তাঁর অবদান চিরস্মরণীয়ঃ বঙ্গবন্ধু

পরলোকে সৈয়দ মুজতবা আলী

সৈয়দ মুজতবা আলী

কাঁচা মালের অভাবে সাবান শিল্পে সংকট

ছাত্রলীগ কর্মীদের প্রতি বঙ্গবন্ধুর

বঙ্গবন্ধুর আদর্শে উদ্বুদ্ধ হতে হবে

দৌলতপুরে শ্রমিক লীগ নেতা খুন

বিআরটিসি কর্মচারী ইউনিয়নের আহ্বান

ধ্বংসাত্মক কাজের সহযোগীদের শাস্তি দাবী

নরওয়ে বাংলাদেশকে ১৯ কোটি টাকার অনুদান দেবে

সীমান্ত প্রদেশে আফগান অস্ত্রশস্ত্র ?

মস্কোতে ১৭ ব্যক্তি গ্রেফতার

গার্সিয়ায় ইঙ্গ-মার্কিন পাঁয়তারা রুখে দাঁড়ানোর আহ্বান

মুনিরা হত্যারহস্যের তদন্ত শেষঃ চার্জশীট দাখিল

বৃহস্পতিবার বঙ্গবন্ধু জাতীয় সাহিত্য সম্মেলন উদ্বোধন করবেন

লক্ষ ডাড়া বৃদ্ধি না করার আহ্বান

বাংলাদেশের উত্তরাঞ্চলের শিল্পাঞ্চিত শহর সৈয়দপুরে [রংপুর]
কৃষি, শিক্ষা, শিল্প, স্বাস্থ্য ও সাংস্কৃতিক
প্রদর্শনী
স্থান ঃ রেলওয়ে ময়দান
শুভারম্ভ ঃ ২২শে ফেব্রুয়ারী, ১৯৭৪ (মাত্র এক মাসের জন্য)

সর্বশেষ

কায়রো-ওয়াশিংটন পূর্ণাংগ কূটনৈতিক সম্পর্ক আসন্ন

A Bengali newspaper published in Bangladesh. Its title is দৈনিক বাংলা *dainik bāngla.*

Tamil Script

The four scripts of Tamil, Telugu, Kannada, and Malayalam are called Southern Indian scripts of the Dravidian group. Generally they are rounded in form, though their structures are the same as those of the Northern Indian scripts. Tamil script is representative of the Dravidian scripts, but unlike the others, it has neither conjunct consonants nor aspirated letters. A distinct script known as Tamil Granta contains these letters, which are needed to write Sanskrit and Pali (Indic/Indo-European). Ordinary Tamil script, therefore, has a very lucid system.

Vowels

அ	ஆ	இ	ஈ	உ	ஊ	எ
a	*ā*	*i*	*ī*	*u*	*ū*	*e*
ஏ	ஐ	ஒ	ஓ	ஔ		ஃ
ē	*ai*	*o*	*ō*	*au*		*a'*

Consonants

க	ங	ச	ஞ	ட	ண	த	ந
ka,ga	*nga*	*cha,sa*	*nya*	*ṭa,ḍa*	*ṇa*	*ta,da*	*na*

ப	ம	ய	ர	ல	வ	ழ	ள	ற	ன
pa,ba	*ma*	*ya*	*ra*	*la*	*va*	*la*	*la*	*ra*	*na*

Additional consonants for borrowed words:

ஜ	ஷ	ஸ	ஹ	க்ஷ
ja	*sa*	*sa*	*ha*	*ksa*

Vowel signs

◌ா *-ā* ◌ி *-i* ◌ீ *-ī* ◌ு *-u*
◌ூ *-ū* ெ◌ *-e* ே◌ *-ē* ை◌ *-ai*
ெ◌ா *-o* ே◌ா *-ō* ெ◌ள *-au*

For the letter ந *na*: நா *nā*, நி *ni*, நீ *nī*, நு *nu*, நூ *nū*, நெ *ne*, நே *nē*, நை *nai*, நொ *no*, நோ *nō*, நௌ *nau*.

The letter ர *ra* becomes ா when it is not to be confused with the *-ā* sign: ரி *ri*, ரீ *rī*.

The succeeding sign ள *-au* is the same form as the letter ள *la*.

Irregular forms of the *-ā*, *-o*, and *-ō* signs:

ண *ṇa* → ணா *ṇā*, ணொ *ṇo*, ணோ *ṇō*
ற *ra* → றா *rā*, றொ *ro*, றோ *rō*
ன *na* → னா *nā*, னொ *no*, னோ *nō*

Irregular forms of the *-u* and *-ū* signs:

க *ka*, கு *ku*, கூ *kū* ங *nga*, ஙு *ngu*, ஙூ *ngū*
ச *cha*, சு *chu*, சூ *chū* ட *ṭa*, டு *ṭu*, டூ *ṭū*
ப *pa*, பு *pu*, பூ *pū* ம *ma*, மு *mu*, மூ *mū*
ய *ya*, யு *yu*, யூ *yū* ர *ra*, ரு *ru*, ரூ *rū*
வ *va*, வு *vu*, வூ *vū* ழ *la*, ழு *lu*, ழூ *lū*
ள *la*, ளு *lu*, ளூ *lū*

Five additional consonants do not change their forms with *-u* and *-ū*, but ு or ூ is added on the right shoulder: ஜு *ju*, ஜூ *jū*.

Irregular forms of the *-ai* sign: ண *ṇa* → ணை *ṇai*; ல *la* → லை *lai*; ள *la* → ளை *lai*; ன *na* → னை *nai*.

There are no irregular forms for the *-e*, *-ē*, and *-au* signs.

An important sign ◌் is a very important sign in Tamil script, for it shows the absence of the inherent *a*-vowel in consonants: க *ka* → க் *k*. In contrast to other Indian scripts, this sign is often used to denote the absence of the final vowel sound and to make conjunct consonants in ordinary Tamil sentences, where special conjunct-consonant letters are not used: விட்டான் *viṭṭān*. In the other Indian scripts this sign (hasanta) used for showing the absence of the inherent *a*-sound in consonants seldom appears in ordinary sentences.

Reading and punctuation Tamil script runs from left to right on a horizontal line, with a space between each word. Punctuation is now the same as in English.

Numerals

௧	௨	௩	௪	௫	௬	௭	௮	௯	௰	௱	௲
1	2	3	4	5	6	7	8	9	10	100	1,000

Tamil numerals have no sign for zero; thus, ௲௯௱௮௰ *1980*. Now only Arabic figures are used.

பதிவுஎண். எம் 7436

"முரசொலி"
சந்தா விகிதம்

	தபால் மூலம்	விற்பனையாளர் மூலம்
3 மாதங்கள்	25-00	23-00
6 மாதங்கள்	48-00	44-00
1 வருடம்	95-00	88-00

நிர்வாகி

முரசொலி

ஆசிரியர்: மாறன். எம்.ஏ., எம்.பி.,

இன்றையச் செய்தி நாளைய வரலாறு

4 பக்கங்கள் விலை 25 காசு சென்னை 6-1-76 வள்ளுவராண்டு 2006

கைத்தறி உலகினிற்கே ஓர் தனிச்சிறப்பு
சங்கு மார்க் லுங்கிகள் கைக்குட்டைகள்
முகம்மது அபூபக்கர் & கம்பெனி

கலைஞர் கடிதம்

ஒரு தொண்டனின் வேண்டுகோள்!

உடன்பிறப்பே,

★ "கருணாநிதி, முடிவைத் தெரிந்து கொண்டார். கதை அளக்கிறார்"
★ "தர்பாரில் இருந்து இறங்கத் தயாராகிறார்."
★ "கழக ஆட்சியின் காலம் முடிகிறது. கருணாநிதியே அறிவிக்கிறார்."

அன்புள்ள,
மு. க.

இந்த ஆண்டு அமோக விளைச்சலால்
தமிழ்நாட்டில் அடுத்த ஆண்டு
உணவு தட்டுப்பாடு இராது!

அமைச்சர் மாதவன் அறிவிப்பு

சென்னை, ஜன. 6— தமிழகத்தில் இந்த ஆண்டு அமோகமான அளவிற்கு நெல் விளைச்சல் ஏற்பட்டிருப்பதால் அடுத்த ஆண்டு உணவுத் தட்டுப்பாடு இருக்காது. என்று உணவு அமைச்சர் மாதவன் கூறினார்.

பொதுப் பிரச்னையில் ஒத்துழைப்போம்
நாடாளுமன்ற எதிர்க்கட்சிகள்
ஓரணியில் இயங்குவது இயலாது!

மார்க்சிஸ்டு கட்சி கருத்து!

பீகார் சுரங்கவிபத்தில் சிக்கியவர்கள்:
12 தொழிலாளர்கள்
தமிழகத்தைச் சேர்ந்தவர்கள்!

A Tamil newspaper. Its title is முரசொலி *muracholi.*

Telugu Script

Telugu script is one of the four Dravidian scripts; it resembles Kannada script except for its slimmer shapes and the hat-forms above the letters.

Vowels

అ	ఆ	ఇ	ఈ	ఉ	ఊ	ఋ
a	*ā*	*i*	*ī*	*u*	*ū*	*ru*
ఎ	ఏ	ఐ	ఒ	ఓ	ఔ	
e	*ē*	*ai*	*o*	*ō*	*au*	

Consonants

క	ఖ	గ	ఘ	ఙ	చ	ఛ
ka	*kha*	*ga*	*gha*	*nga*	*cha*	*chha*
జ	ఝ	ఞ	ట	ఠ	డ	ఢ
ja	*jha*	*nya*	*ṭa*	*ṭha*	*ḍa*	*ḍha*
ణ	త	థ	ద	ధ	న	ప
ṇa	*ta*	*tha*	*da*	*dha*	*na*	*pa*
ఫ	బ	భ	మ	య	ర	ల
pha	*ba*	*bha*	*ma*	*ya*	*ra*	*la*
ళ	వ	శ	ష	స	హ	
ḷa	*va*	*sa*	*sha*	*sa*	*ha*	

Vowel signs

◌ా *-ā* ◌ి *-i* ◌ీ *-ī* ◌ు *-u* ◌ూ *-ū*
◌ృ *-ru* ◌ె *-e* ◌ే *-ē* ◌ై *-ai*
◌ొ *-o* ◌ో *-ō* ◌ౌ *-au*

When the vowel sign for *-ā, -i, -ī, -e, -ē, -ai, -o, -ō,* or *-au* is to be added to the upper part of a consonant, the hat ✓ on the consonant is dropped. For example, for the letter క *ka*: కా *kā*, కి *ki*, కీ *kī*, కు *ku*, కూ *kū*, కృ *kru*, కె *ke*, కే *kē*, కై *kai*, కొ *ko*, కో *kō*, కౌ *kau*.
When the *-ā* sign ◌ా is added, ఘ *gha*, ఝ *jha*, మ *ma*, and య *ya* do not lose their hats: మా *mā*, యా *yā*.
In ప *pa*, ఫ *pha*, ష *sha*, and శ *sa*, the *-ā* sign ◌ా is written across the upper curve: పా *pā*.
For ఖ *kha*, చ *cha*, ఛ *chha*, న *na*, బ *ba*, భ *bha*, మ *ma*, ల *la*, వ *va*, and శ *sa*, the *-i* and *-ī* signs sink into the heads of the base consonants: ఖి *khi*, మి *mi*, ని *ni*, and నీ *nī*.
For ఠ *ṭha*, థ *tha*, ద *da*, ధ *dha*, and ర *ra*, the *-i* or *-ī* signs are transformed: ది *di*, రి *ri*, and దీ *dī*.
A special case is the letter య *ya*: యి *yi*, యీ *yī*.
If the *-u* or *-ū* sign is added to ప *pa*, వ *va* (distinguished by a space between ు and ✓), or ఫ *pha*, ు or ూ is written large enough to enclose the letter, to avoid confusion with ఘ *gha* or మ *ma*: పు *pu*, పూ *pū*.

Conjunct consonants In Telugu script, conjunct consonants are denoted by subscripts; preceding consonants are written ordinally, and succeeding consonants are subscribed without their hats: ష్ఠ *shṭha*, డ్డ *dda*, and ష్ఠా *shṭhā*.
The following eight letters change their forms when subscribed.

క	త	న	మ	య	ర	ల	వ
◌్క	◌్త	◌్న	◌్మ	◌్య	◌్ర or ◌్ర	◌్ల	◌్వ
ka	*ta*	*na*	*ma*	*ya*	*ra*	*la*	*va*

Thus: క్క *kka*, వ్వు *vvu*, స్త్ర *stra*.
A preceding *ra* is also written ◌ౘ : ఘౘ *rgha* (ర్ఘ is also *rgha*).

Other signs ◌్ indicates the absence of the inherent *a*-vowel: క *ka* → క్ *k*.
◌ః (visarga) denotes an aspiration.
◌ం (sunna) shows nasalization and is pronounced *ng, ṇ, n,* or *m*, according to the following consonant: కం *kan*.

Numerals

౧	౨	౩	౪	౫	౬	౭	౮	౯	౦
1	2	3	4	5	6	7	8	9	0

In addition, ı is $\frac{1}{4}$, ɥ is $\frac{1}{2}$, and ɰ is $\frac{3}{4}$.
Arabic figures are now generally used.

ఆంధ్రభూమి

ఎడిటర్ : గోరా శాస్త్రి

సంపుటి: 16 సంచిక 98 * సికింద్రాబాద్ 8-1-1976 గురువారం * 8 పేజీలు 25 పైసలు

బాలల అకాడెమీ ఏర్పాటుకు రాష్ట్ర మంత్రివర్గ నిర్ణయం

పంచాయతీ ఎన్నికలు త్వరలో జరపవచ్చునట్లు ముఖ్యమంత్రి వెల్లడి

ఫిబ్రవరి 28న రాష్ట్ర బడ్జెట్ సమర్పణ

వాతావరణం

నెదర్లాండ్స్ నుండి 59 కోట్ల సహాయం

ముఖ్యమంత్రి ప్రభుత్వంలకు ఓబుల్ రెడ్డి విందు

శ్రీనగర్‌లో స్వల్ప భూకంపం

అన్నపూర్ణ స్టూడియోకు 14న రాష్ట్రపతి ప్రారంభోత్సవం

మధ్యప్రదేశ్ మంత్రి వర్గం విస్తరణ

గుజరాత్, తమిళనాడు రాష్ట్ర ప్రభుత్వాల పక్షపాత విధానాలపై తీవ్ర ఖండన

దేశంలో విద్యుచ్ఛక్తి పరిస్థితి సంతృప్తికరం

ప్రమాదాలు, ఆరోగ్యభీమాకు మార్చి నుండి కొత్త పథకం

ఉత్తర సరిహద్దులలో సైనికుల అప్రమత్తత

ఆందోళన పడవలసిన పనిలేదని లోక్‌సభలో బన్సీలాల్ ప్రకటన

సి ఆర్ పి ఎఫ్ లో కానిస్టేబుల్స్‌కు షెడ్యూలు కులాల రిక్రూట్‌మెంట్

సోగ్గాడు

పిచ్చిమారాజు

A Telugu newspaper. Its title is ఆంధ్రభూమి *āndhra bhūmi*.

Kannada Script

Kannada or Kanarese script bears a striking resemblance to Telugu script in its structure and form. The form of the hat is an important difference, being ✓ in Telugu and ‿ in Kannada. The vowel *u* is ఉ in Telugu but ಉ in Kannada. Moreover, the vowel sign of *-ī* is ◌ీ in Telugu but ◌ೀ in Kannada, and the consonant *ka* is written క in Telugu and ಕ in Kannada.

Vowels

ಅ	ಆ	ಇ	ಈ	ಉ	ಊ	ಋ
a	*ā*	*i*	*ī*	*u*	*ū*	*ru*
ಎ	ಏ	ಐ	ಒ	ಓ	ಔ	
e	*ē*	*ai*	*o*	*ō*	*au*	

Consonants

ಕ	ಖ	ಗ	ಘ	ಙ	ಚ	ಛ	ಜ	ಝ
ka	*kha*	*ga*	*gha*	*nga*	*cha*	*chha*	*ja*	*jha*
ಞ	ಟ	ಠ	ಡ	ಢ	ಣ	ತ	ಥ	ದ
nya	*ṭa*	*ṭha*	*ḍa*	*ḍha*	*ṇa*	*ta*	*tha*	*da*
ಧ	ನ	ಪ	ಫ	ಬ	ಭ	ಮ	ಯ	ರ
dha	*na*	*pa*	*pha*	*ba*	*bha*	*ma*	*ya*	*ra*
ಲ	ವ	ಶ	ಷ	ಸ	ಹ	ಳ		
la	*va*	*sa*	*sha*	*sa*	*ha*	*la*		

Vowel signs

◌ಾ *-ā* ◌ಿ *-i* ◌ೀ *-ī* ◌ು *-u*
◌ೂ *-ū* ◌ೃ *-ru* ◌ೆ *-e* ◌ೇ *-ē*
◌ೈ *ai* ◌ೊ *-o* ◌ೋ *-ō* ◌ೌ *-au*

Here, when the sign *-ā, -i, -ī, -e, -ē, -ai, -o, -ō,* or *-au* is added the hat ‿ is dropped; thus, for the letter ಕ *ka*:
ಕಾ *kā,* ಕಿ *ki,* ಕೀ *kī,* ಕು *ku,* ಕೂ *kū,* ಕೃ *kru,* ಕೆ *ke,* ಕೇ *kē,* ಕೈ *kai,* ಕೊ *ko,* ಕೋ *kō,* ಕೌ *kau*

Irregular: ಘಾ *ghā,* ಙಾ *ngā,* ಞಾ *nyā,* and ಣಾ *ṇā*; ಞೆ *nye* and ಞೇ *nyē*, but ಘೆ *ghe.*
Special forms for *-i* are ಗಿ *gi,* ಝಿ *jhi,* ಠಿ *ṭhi,* ಡಿ *ḍi,* ಢಿ *ḍhi,* ಥಿ *thi,* ದಿ *di,* ಧಿ *dhi,* and ರಿ *ri*: ಗೀ *gī.*
Also ಛಿ *chhi,* ಟಿ *ṭi,* ನಿ *ni,* ಬಿ *bi,* ಭಿ *bhi,* ಲಿ *li,* ವಿ *vi,* ಳಿ *li*: ಛೀ *chhī.*
ಮ *ma* → ಮಾ *mā,* ಮಿ *mi,* ಮೀ *mī,* and ಮೋ *mō.*
Unique: ಯ *ya* → ಯಾ *yā,* ಯಿ *yi,* ಯೀ *yī,* ಯು *yu,* and ಯೊ *yo.*
Finally, ಪು *pu,* ಫು *phu,* ವು *vu*; also ಪೂ *pū,* and ವೊ *vo.* If *vu* were written regularly as ಮ , it would be confused with *ma*; thus, ವ *va,* ಮ *ma,* ಮು *mu,* ಮೂ *mū,* ವೆ *ve,* ಮೆ *me,* and ಮೊ *mo,* while ವು *vu,* ವೂ *vū,* and ವೊ *vo.*

Conjunct consonants Conjunct consonants are mainly denoted by subscripts. Preceding consonants are written on the ordinal line and the succeeding consonants are subscribed and lose their hats or undergo some type of transformation: ವ್ವ *vva,* ಷ್ಠ *shṭha.*
Several consonants change their forms when subscribed:

ತ	ನ	ಮ	ಯ	ರ	ಲ
◌್ತ	◌್ನ	◌್ಮ	◌್ಯ	◌್ರ	◌್ಲ
ta	*na*	*ma*	*ya*	*ra*	*la*

Thus: ಕ್ರ *kra,* ಜ್ಯ *jya.*
A preceding ರ *ra* is written ◌ರ್ (arka); thus, ವರ್ಗ is not read *vagar*, but *varga.*
For three conjunct consonants: ಸ್ತ್ರ *stra.*

Other signs ◌್ indicates the absence of the inherent *a*-vowel: ಕ *ka* → ಕ್ *k,* ಖ *kha* → ಖ್ *kh.*
◌ಂ (anusvara, or bindu) is commonly used instead of a nasal letter. It can be pronounced *ng, ny, ṇ, n,* or *m*: ಸಂ *san.*
◌ಃ (visarga) denotes an aspiration; it is pronounced as a glottal stop or a double consonant: ದುಃಖ *dukkha.*

Numerals

೧	೨	೩	೪	೫	೬	೭	೮	೯	೦
1	2	3	4	5	6	7	8	9	0

Arabic figures are now generally used.

ಸಂಯುಕ್ತ ಕರ್ನಾಟಕ

CITY

SAMYUKTA KARNATAK KANNADA DAILY. PUBLISHED SIMULTANEOUSLY FROM HUBLI-BANGALORE

Regd No. KRNG 32 — 2-3-1974 — HUBLI

ಸುದ್ದಿ ಸಂಕ್ಷೇಪ

ರಾಗಿ ಲೇವಿ ಸಂಗ್ರಹ ಕೈಬಿಡಲು ನಕಾರ

ಉ. ಪ್ರ. ದಲ್ಲಿ ಕಾಂಗ್ರೆಸ ಮತ್ತೆ ಅಧಿಕಾರ ಗದ್ದುಗೆಗೆ

ನಗರದ ಆಸ್ತಿ ಮಿತಿ ವಿಧೇಯಕಕ್ಕೆ ಒತ್ತಾಯ

ಗೇಣಿ ಜಮೀನು ಸರಕಾರದ ವಶ

ಭೂಸುಧಾರಣೆ ಕಾಯ್ದೆ ಜಾರಿಗೆ

ವಿಧಾನಸಭೆ ಸದಸ್ಯತ್ವಕ್ಕೆ ಚಿಮಣಭಾಯಿ ಪಟೇಲರ ರಾಜೀನಾಮೆ

ಕಾಂಗ್ರೆಸಿನಿಂದ ಚಿಮಣಭಾಯಿ ಪಟೇಲರ ಉಚ್ಚಾಟನೆ

ಜವಳಿ ಕೈಗಾರಿಕೆಗಳಿಗಾಗಿ ಕಾರ್ಪೋರೇಶನ್ ರಚನೆ ಪ್ರಶ್ನೆ

ಸರಕಾರ ಪರಿಶೀಲನೆ ನಡೆಸಿದೆ

ಗುಜರಾತ ಶಾಸಕರಿಂದ ರಾಜೀನಾಮೆ ಸಲ್ಲಿಕೆ

ಚಿಮಣಿ ಎಣ್ಣೆ ಪೆಟ್ರೋಲ ಬೆಲೆ ಮತ್ತೆ ಹೆಚ್ಚಿತು

ಸೋಮವಾರ ಓಡಿಸಾದಲ್ಲಿ ಕಾಂಗ್ರೆಸ ಸಚಿವ ಸಂಪುಟ?

ಬಿಳಿ ಕೂದಲಿನವರಾಗುವದೇಕೆ ?

ಸಾಹಿತ್ಯ ಸಮ್ಮೇಳನಗಳು ಕೇವಲ ಜಾತ್ರೆ ಆಗಬಾರದು

ಗುಜರಾತ ಚಳವಳಿ ಹಿಂದೆ ದೇಶದಲ್ಲಿ ಅವ್ಯವಸ್ಥೆ ಉಂಟುಮಾಡುವ ಹೊಂಚು ಇದೆ

—ಇಂದಿರಾಗಾಂಧಿ

A Kannada newspaper. Its title is ಸಂಯುಕ್ತ ಕರ್ನಾಟಕ *samyukta karnāṭaka.*

Malayalam Script

Malayalam script resembles Tamil script. But where Tamil script has a practical arrangement, Malayalam script seems to have all the complexities of the other Indian scripts.

Vowels

അ	ആ	ഇ	ഈ	ഉ	ഊ	ഋ
a	*ā*	*i*	*ī*	*u*	*ū*	*ru*
എ	ഏ	ഐ	ഒ	ഓ	ഔ	
e	*ē*	*ai*	*o*	*ō*	*au*	

Consonants

ക	ഖ	ഗ	ഘ	ങ	ച	ഛ	
ka	*kha*	*ga*	*gha*	*nga*	*cha*	*chha*	
ജ	ഝ	ഞ	ട	ഠ	ഡ	ഢ	
ja	*jha*	*nya*	*ṭa*	*ṭha*	*ḍa*	*ḍha*	
ണ	ത	ഥ	ദ	ധ	ന	പ	
ṇa	*ta*	*tha*	*da*	*dha*	*na*	*pa*	
ഫ	ബ	ഭ	മ	യ	ര	ല	വ
pha	*ba*	*bha*	*ma*	*ya*	*ra*	*la*	*va*
ശ	ഷ	സ	ഹ	ള	ഴ	റ	
sa	*sha*	*sa*	*ha*	*la*	*ra*	*ra*	

Vowel signs

◌ാ -*ā* ◌ി -*i* ◌ീ -*ī* ◌ു -*u* ◌ൂ -*ū*
◌ൃ -*ru* െ◌ -*e* േ◌ -*ē* ൈ◌ -*ai*
െ◌ാ -*o* േ◌ാ -*ō* െ◌ൗ -*au*

For the letter ട *ṭa*: ടാ *ṭā*, ടി *ṭi*, ടീ *ṭī*, ടു *ṭu*, ടൂ *ṭū*, ടൃ *ṭru*, ടെ *ṭe*, ടേ *ṭē*, ടൈ *ṭai*, ടൊ *ṭo*, ടോ *ṭō*, ടൗ *ṭau*.

However, the signs -*u* and -*ū* are very irregular. For example, ണ *ṇa* and ന *na* enfold the sign ◦ : ണു *ṇu*, ണൂ *ṇū*. The following gives other irregularities involving these signs: ക *ka*, കു *ku*, കൂ *kū*; ഗ *ga*, ഗു *gu*, ഗൂ *gū*; ഛ *chha*, ഛു *chhu*, ഛൂ *chhū*; ജ *ja*, ജു *ju*, ജൂ *jū*; ത *ta*, തു *tu*, തൂ *tū*; ഭ *bha*, ഭു *bhu*, ഭൂ *bhū*; ര *ra*, രു *ru*, രൂ *rū*; ശ *sa*, ശു *su*, ശൂ *sū*; ഹ *ha*, ഹു *hu*, ഹൂ *hū*.

Conjunct consonants Malayalam conjunct consonants are the most intricate among the various Indian scripts.

Double consonants: ക്ക *kka*, ഗ്ഗ *gga*, ച്ച *chcha*, ജ്ജ *jja*, ഞ്ഞ *nynya*, ട്ട *ṭṭa*, ത്ത *tta*, ദ്ദ *dda*, ന്ന *nna*, പ്പ *ppa*, ബ്ബ *bba*, മ്മ *mma*, യ്യ *yya*, ല്ല *lla*, വ്വ *vva*, ശ്ശ *ssa*, ള്ള *lla*.

Succeeding consonants with changed forms:

യ *ya* → ◌്യ : ക്യ *kya*, ക്യു *kyu*
ര *ra* → ◌്ര : ക്ര *kra*, ത്ര *ttra*
ല *la* → ◌്ല : ക്ല *kla*, പ്ലി *pli*

Preceding ര *ra* is shown as ◌ൎ : ൎക *rka*, ൎദു *rdu*, ൎജ്ജൂ *rjjū*.

Subscripts: ച്ഛ *chchha*, സ്ന *sna*, ഷ്മ *shma*, ബ്ദ *bda*, യ്ക്ക *ykka*.

Combined letters:

ക	*ka*	+	വ	*va*	=	ക്വ	*kva*
ക	*ka*	+	ഷ	*sha*	=	ക്ഷ	*ksha*
ന	*na*	+	ദ	*da*	=	ന്ദ	*nda*
ത	*ta*	+	ന	*na*	=	ത്ന	*tna*
ഗ	*ga*	+	ഭ	*bha*	=	ഗ്ഭ	*gbha*

Peculiar combinations: ഹ്മ (*ha* + *ma*) is not *hma* but *mha*; ഹ്ന (*ha* + *na*) is not *hna* but *nha*.

Other signs ◌് indicates the absence of the inherent *a*-vowel: ഴ് *r*, യ് *y*, മ് *m*. However, some consonants take ◌ൽ : ൿ *k*, ൺ *ṇ*, ർ *r*, ൻ *n*. ള *la* transforms into ൾ *l*.

◌ം shows nasalization: ലം *lam*.

◌ഃ shows a glottal stop: അഃ *a'*.

Numerals

൧	൨	൩	൪	൫	൬	൭	൮	൯	൦
1	2	3	4	5	6	7	8	9	0

A postage stamp of the Cochin State issued in 1933. In the uppermost part is written *ko-chchi añchal* (Cochin postage). Written to the left of the head is the figure for six, and in the lowest part *āru pai* (six pies), each in Malayalam script.

ചന്ദ്രിക

CHANDRIKA DAILY

Regd. No. KL/CT/10

പ്രധാനമന്ത്രി "കോൺഗ്രസ്സിൻെറ ചരിത്രം" കണ്ടു

"തിരഞ്ഞെടുപ്പ് യഥാസമയം നടത്തണം"

ലോക്സഭാ തിരഞ്ഞെടുപ്പ് ഒരു വർഷത്തേക്ക് നീട്ടും?

വി. കെ. ഗോവിന്ദൻ നായരുടെ കൃതികൾക്ക് ഓടക്കുഴൽ സമ്മാനം

പഞ്ചായത്ത് ഭരണ സമിതികളുടെ കാലാവധി വീണ്ടും നീട്ടി

ഡി. കെ. ബറൂവ വീണ്ടും കോൺഗ്രസ്സ് പ്രസിഡണ്ട്

അടിയന്തിരാവസ്ഥ ഇപ്പോൾ പിൻവലിക്കില്ല

എറണാകുളം കോർപ്പ: റസ്റ്റ്ഹൗസുൽഘാടനം ചെയ്തു

കോർപ്പറേഷൻ ബസ്സ്റ്റാൻറ് ഉൽഘാടനം ചെയ്തു

പാണക്കാട് തങ്ങൾ സ്മാരക ഗ്രന്ഥം

മനോഹരമായ ത്രിവർണ്ണ മുഖചിത്രം

മാർക്സിസ്റ്റുകളോട് കരാർലംഘനം നടത്തിയിട്ടില്ല

— മന്ത്രി കെ. എം. മാണി

ഫലസ്തീൻ രാഷ്ട്രം സ്ഥാപിക്കാനനുവദിക്കില്ല

— ഇസ്രായിൽ

ഇന്ത്യക്ക് ജയം

ഇ. എസ്. ഐ. പദ്ധതി

നവംബറിൽ $7\frac{1}{4}$ ലക്ഷം ക. നൽകി

A Malayalam newspaper. Its title is ചന്ദ്രിക *chandrika*.

Sinhalese Script

The Sinhalese language belongs to the Indic group of Indo-European languages, which are located principally in northern India, but Sinhalese script resembles the Dravidian script of southern India. For example, the sound *kha* is shown by ഖ in Malayalam, ಖ in Kannada, and ඛ in Sinhalese.

Vowels

අ	ආ	ඇ	ඈ	ඉ	ඊ	උ	ඌ
a	*ā*	*e*	*ē*	*i*	*ī*	*u*	*ū*
ඍ	එ	ඒ	ඓ	ඔ	ඕ	ඖ	
ri	*e*	*ē*	*ai*	*o*	*ō*	*au*	

Consonants

ක	ඛ	ග	ඝ	ඞ	ච	ඡ	ජ	ඣ
ka	*kha*	*ga*	*gha*	*nga*	*cha*	*chha*	*ja*	*jha*
ඤ	ට	ඨ	ඩ	ඪ	ණ	ත	ථ	ද
nya	*ṭa*	*ṭha*	*ḍa*	*ḍha*	*ṇa*	*ta*	*tha*	*da*
ධ	න	ප	ඵ	බ	භ	ම	ය	ර
dha	*na*	*pa*	*pha*	*ba*	*bha*	*ma*	*ya*	*ra*
ල	ව	ශ	ෂ	ස	හ	ළ		
la	*va*	*sa*	*sha*	*sa*	*ha*	*la*		

A new consonant letter, ෆ *fa*, has been added for words adopted from English.

Vowel signs
◌ා *-a* ◌ැ *-e* ◌ෑ *-ē* ◌ි *-i* ◌ී *-ī*
◌ු *-u* ◌ූ *-ū* ◌ෘ *-ri* ෙ◌ *-e* ෙ◌් *-ē*
ෛ◌ *-ai* ෙ◌ා *-o* ෙ◌ෝ *-ō* ෙ◌ෟ *-au*
For the letter න *na*: නා *nā*, නැ *ne*, නෑ *nē*, නි *ni*, නී *nī*, නු *nu*, නූ *nū*, නෘ *nri*, නෙ *ne*, නේ *nē*, නෛ *nai*, නො *no*, නෝ *nō*, නෞ *nau*.
ැ *-e* or ෑ *-ē* with ර *ra* combines as රැ *re* or රෑ *rē*.
The ි *-i* or ී *-ī* sign changes its form according to the shape of the base consonant: කි *ki*, ගි *gi*, චි *chi*, ජි *ji*, and ඨි *ṭhi*.

The *-u* and *-ū* signs take shapes different from ු and ූ in the following five letters: ක *ka*, කු *ku*, කූ *kū*; ග *ga*, ගු *gu*, ගූ *gū*; ත *ta*, තු *tu*, තූ *tū*; භ *bha*, භු *bhu*, භූ *bhū*; ශ *sa*, ශු *su*, ශූ *sū*.
On ර *ra*, the *-u* and *-ū* signs are shown as රු *ru* and රූ *rū*.
The *-ē* sign ෙ◌් becomes ෙ◌ෙ when the upper part of the basic letter forms ◌ : චේ *chē*.

Conjunct consonants The conjunct consonants in Sinhalese script are very complicated, especially when used for writing classical Pali. There are no subscripts, but ligatures are frequently used.
◌ shows preceding ර *ra*: ර්‍ක *rka*, ර්‍ග *rga*.
◌්‍ර shows succeeding ර *ra*: ක්‍ර *kra*, ග්‍ර *gra*.
◌ shows preceding *na*: ඟ *nga*, ඳි *ndi*.
◌්‍ය shows succeeding ය *ya*: ක්‍ය *kya*.
Ligatures: න්‍ථ *ntha*, ත්‍ථ *ttha*, ච්ඡ *chchha*.
Transformations: ඹ *mba*, බ්බ *bba*.
Ligature of three consonants: ර්‍ක්‍ර *rkra*.

Other signs ◌් or ◌් without ෙ indicates the absence of the inherent *a*-vowel: ක් *k*, ඣ් *jh*.
◌ං (anusvara) shows a nasal sound. In modern Sinhalese ං is used for the consonant letter *n*. Thus: ශ්‍රීලංකා *srīlankā*.

Reading and punctuation Sinhalese script runs from left to right on a horizontal line. Formerly, Sinhalese was written with no space between words, and ෴ (kundaliya) was the only punctuation used. This sign was placed at the full stop of the sentence, and sometimes showed a repeating word or an abbreviated sentence. Nowadays, the spacing and punctuation marks used are the same as in English.

Numerals

𑇡	𑇢	𑇣	𑇤	𑇥	𑇦	𑇧	𑇨	𑇩	𑇪	𑇳
1	2	3	4	5	6	7	8	9	10	100

Arabic figures are now commonly used.

ජනදින

2 වෙළුම 278 වෙනි පත්‍රය 1974 අප්‍රේල් මස 17 වෙනි බදාදා මිල ශත 20 යි

ලංගම සේවක සටන නවත්වයි

ශ්‍රී ලංකා මහ බැංකු වාර්තාව පෙන්වා දෙයි

වී අලෙවි මංඩලය ක්‍රමවත් නෑ

ගිස තෙල් ගාන නැකත අද

සිවිල් නීති කැඩූ අයට දඩ ගෙව්වේ මන්ත්‍රී

නිපැයුමට සරිලන ක්‍රියාකාරිත්වයක්

වැඩිවන වී නිෂ්පාදනයට සරිලන සේ වී අලෙවි මණ්ඩලයේ ක්‍රියාකාරිත්වය සම්පූර්ණයෙන් ක්‍රමවත් කළයුතු බව ශ්‍රී ලංකා මහ බැංකුව මගින් මුදල් ඇමතිවරයා වෙත ඉදිරිපත් කොට ඇති 1973 වාර්ෂික වාර්තාව පෙන්වා දෙයි.

සිංහල විරෝධී වැඩවලින් කිසිම පිළිසරණක් නෑ

බෝවෙන රෝග මර්ධන

සෞඛ්‍ය සේවයට විශේෂ පහසුකම්

උක් වගාවට ණය සහන

සමාලෝචනයක්

හාල් මිටි දෙකක් අල්ලා ගනී

මහජන මතය

පාසල් ගොඩනැගිලි වලට රුපියල් කෝටි දෙකහමාරක්

කෘෂි ද්‍රව්‍ය නිපැයුමට සමුපකාර යොදවයි

කුමාරස්වාමිට උප සභාපති පදවියක්

A Sinhalese newspaper. Its title is ජනදින *janadina*.

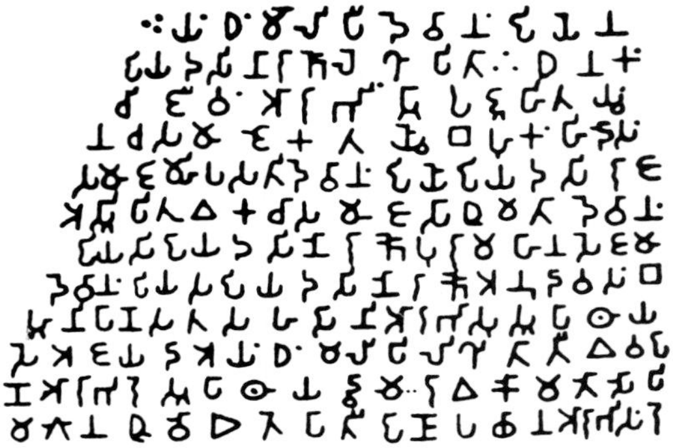

BRAHMI SCRIPT (ASOKA SCRIPT). The writing of the Mauryan dynasty in ancient India. It was the basis for many of the Indian scripts. (Jensen)

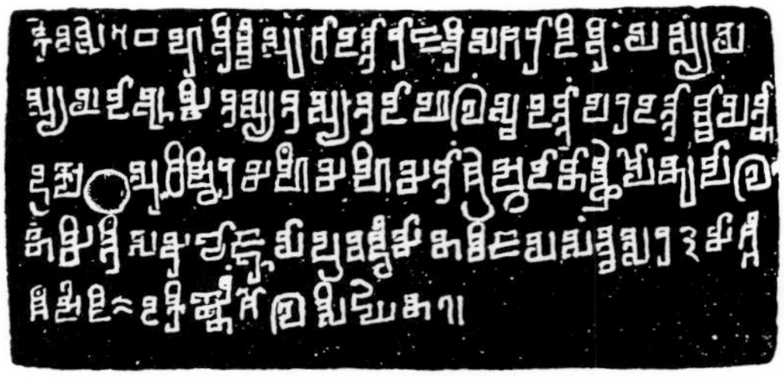

BOX-HEADED SCRIPT. One of the medieval Indian scripts. From the 6th century in or around Madhya Pradesh and Hyderabad in central India. (Diringer)

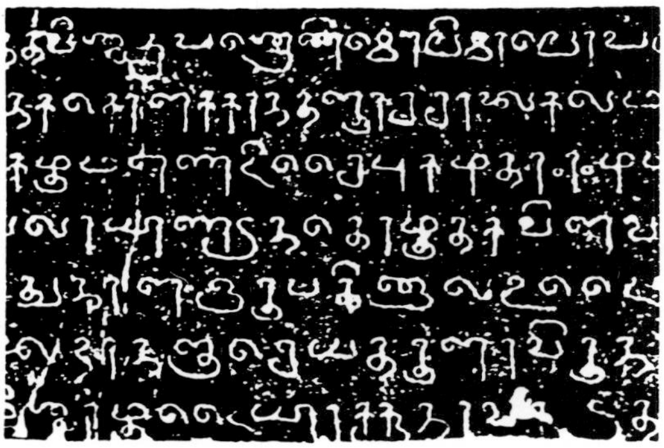

CHOLA SCRIPT. The writing of the Chola dynasty in medieval southern India. One of the Grantha scripts. (Yamamoto)

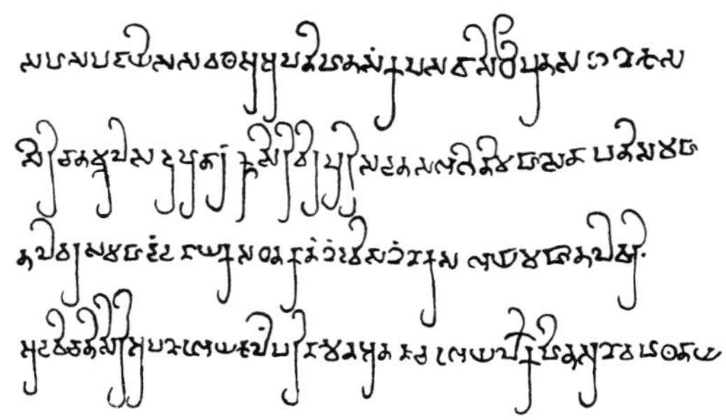

SATAVAHANA SCRIPT. One of the ancient South Indian scripts, very ornamental with elongated vertical strokes. From the 2nd century. (Sivaramamurti)

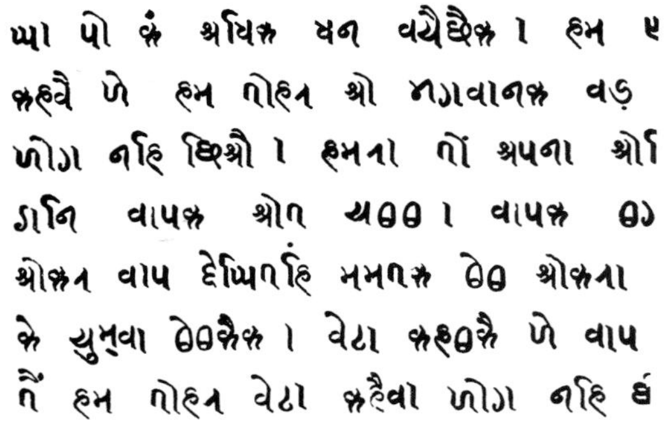

KAITHI SCRIPT. The original writing for the Bihari language in central India. It resembles Gujarati script. (Grierson)

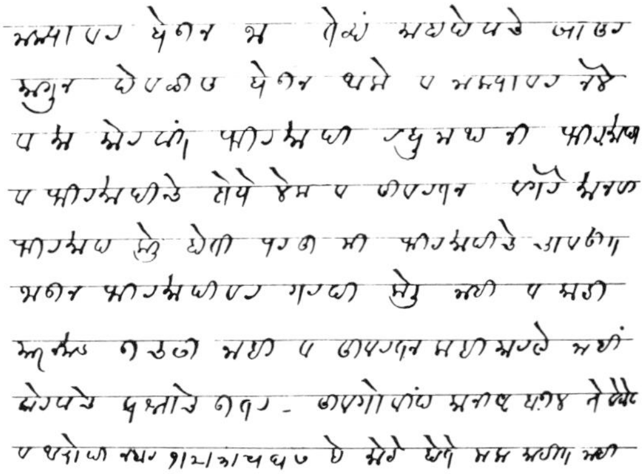

MODI SCRIPT. The original writing for the Marathi language in central India. The letters are bound by one line above. (Grierson)

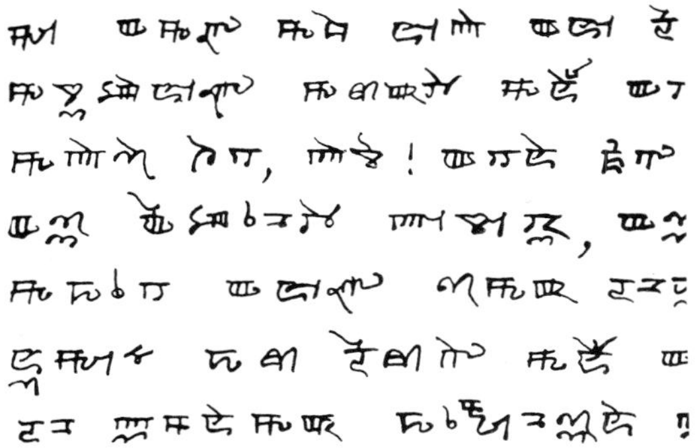

MANIPURI SCRIPT. The original writing for the Manipuri language in the state of Manipur in eastern India. (Grierson)

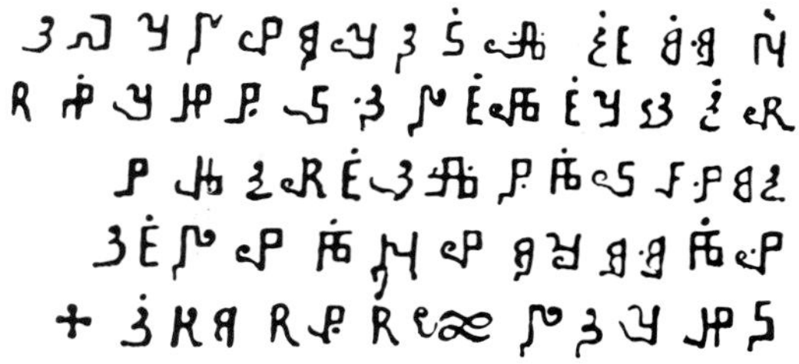

BALTI SCRIPT. The writing of Baltistan in Kashmir in northwestern India. This was a hybrid of Arabic and Indian scripts. (Grierson)

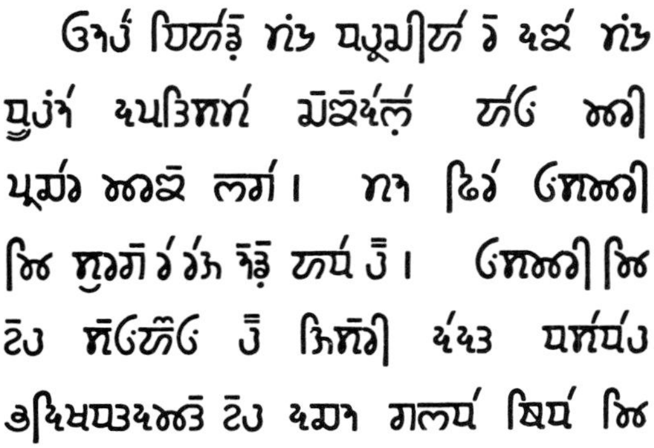

TANKRI SCRIPT. An improved type of Lahnda script. It is used in Himachal Pradesh of northwestern India. (Nida)

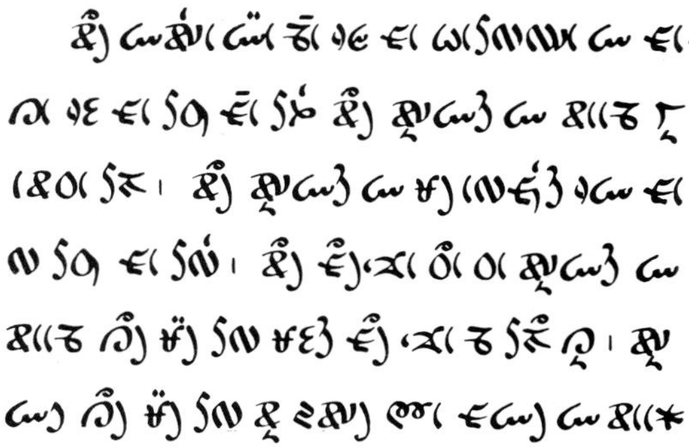

LEPCHA SCRIPT. The writing for the Lepcha language in Sikkim, which lies between India and China. (Nida)

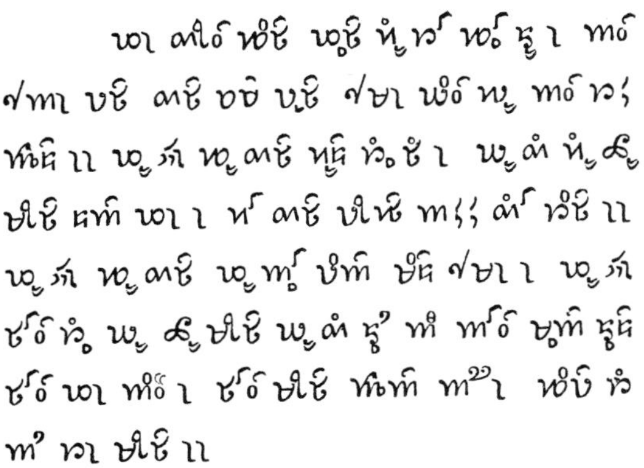

AHOM SCRIPT. Ahom is a Thai tribe in Assam. This script is akin to Shan script. (Author's collection)

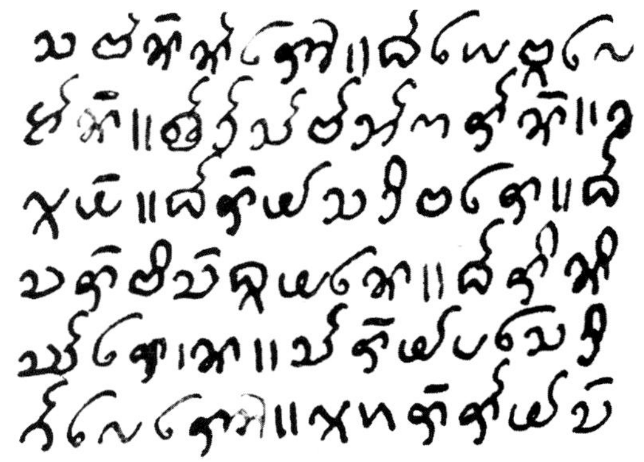

CHAKMA SCRIPT. The Chakma tribe lives in the Chittagong hills in eastern Bangladesh. (Diringer)

5. SCRIPTS OF SOUTHEAST ASIA

Southeast Asia can be considered as belonging to the Indian writing-zone. Most scripts in Southeast Asia are called Further Indian scripts, which is a very fitting name, for Indian scripts in developed or degenerate forms spread over India and the peninsulas and islands of Southeast Asia as far east as the Philippines.

These Southeast Asian scripts are similar to Indian scripts in that the consonant letters contain an inherent vowel-sound and use signs to change the inherent vowel to other vowel sounds.

Chinese characters reached Vietnam and became the Chu Nôm of medieval times, and in the 16th century Arabic script spread to Indonesia and Malaya with Islam. These nations, however, have now adopted Latin script to write their languages.

BURMA [မြန်မာ *myanmā*; ဗမာ *bamā*]

The official language of Burma is Burmese (Tibeto-Burman/Sino-Tibetan). Burmese is used in central Burma, but in the peripheral areas Mon (Mon-Khmer/Austroasiatic), Shan (Thai/Sino-Tibetan), Karen (Thai/Sino-Tibetan), and Kachin (Tibeto-Burman/Sino-Tibetan) are also spoken. These are written in separate scripts, each of which resembles Burmese script, except for Kachin, which is written in Latin script. But they are not used in any daily newspapers. Daily newspapers are published only in Burmese with Burmese script, except for a few English publications. Burmese script is explained on page 72.

The formal name on postage stamps, ပြည်ထောင်စုဆိုရှယ်လစ်သမ္မတမြန်မာနိုင်ငံတော်, means Socialist Republic of the Union of Burma.

CAMBODIA [កម្ពុជា *kampuchie*; ខ្មែរ *khmaer*]

The official language of Cambodia is Khmer or Cambodian (Mon-Khmer/Austroasiatic). It has a peculiar script, explained on page 74. Newspapers are published in Khmer.

INDONESIA

Indonesian (Indonesian/Malayo-Polynesian), the official language of Indonesia, was originally the same as Malay. It is written in Latin script, though it was formerly also written in Arabic script. In Latin script for Indonesian, q and x are not used, and é and ĕ are sometimes used diacritically. Indonesian and Malay spellings in Latin script have been made uniform by the Melindo agreement.

One interesting aspect of Indonesian spelling is that double words indicating the intensive or plural are written by putting a "2" after the single word. Thus "anak 2" or "anak²" is read *ana'-ana'*. In Arabic script, too, it is spelled انق٢ (٢ is "2" in Arabic).

All Indonesian newspapers are printed in Latin script in spite of the fact that separate scripts are used in Sumatra, Java, Bali, and Sulawesi (see pages 80–81); some of these are taught in schools or have been used to ornament sultans' palaces. Some vernacular newspapers, for example, those in Javanese (Indonesian/Malayo-Polynesian), are published in Latin script. English and Chinese newspapers are also published.

LAOS [ລາວ *law*]

The official language of Laos is Lao (Thai/Sino-Tibetan). It has a peculiar script, which is explained on page 78.

Daily newspapers are published in Lao. The formal name on a recent postage stamp, ສາທາລະນະລັດ ປະຊາທິປະໄຕ ປະຊາຊົນລາວ means Peoples' Democratic Republic of Laos.

MALAYSIA [ملايسيا *malaysia*]

Malay (Indonesian/Malayo-Polynesian), the official language of Malaysia, is written in Arabic and in Latin scripts. In Arabic script, its alphabet consists of the basic twenty-eight letters, with five additional ones: چ *ch*, ڠ *ng*, ڤ *p*, ݢ *g*, and ڽ *ny*.

Newspapers are published in Malay printed in either Arabic or Latin script. A sample of a newspaper in Arabic script is shown on page 35. Other daily newspapers are published in English, Chinese, Tamil, and Punjabi.

PHILIPPINES [PILIPINAS]

In the Philippines, before Magellan, several scripts were used for each of the vernacular languages: Tagalog, Visayan, Ilokano, and Pangasinan, all of which belong to the Indonesian group of Malayo-Polynesian languages. Now these scripts are extinct, and all languages are written in Latin script. The picture below shows a Philippine postage stamp issued in 1943. This is a rare sample of the use of ancient Tagalog script, which is written ᜃᜎᜌᜀ ᜈ ᜉᜒᜎᜒᜉᜒᜈ, *ka-la-ya-a na pi-li-pi-na*, under the Latin title.

A Philippine postage stamp.

Newspapers are published using Latin script in English, in Spanish, in Filipino (reformed Tagalog), in Visayan, in Ilokano (partly), and in Pangasinan (partly). There are also newspapers partially in Chinese.

SINGAPORE [SINGAPURA; 新加坡 *sin-chiapo*; சிங்கப்பூர் *singappūr*]

The official languages of Singapore are Malay, English, Chinese, and Tamil. These are used in newspapers and on currency and documents. Malay is printed in Latin script.

THAILAND [ประเทศ ไทย *prathēt thai*]

The state language of Thailand is Thai (Thai/Sino-Tibetan). As in Burma, many different languages are used by minority races in the mountainous regions. Lao, Shan, and Miao (Miao/Sino-Tibetan) are the principal minority languages, and each has its own script. In Northern Thailand, Chieng Mai script (see page 80) is used in school books; but all the daily newspapers are printed in Thai script, except for a few in English and in Chinese. Thai script is explained on page 76.

VIETNAM [VIỆT-NAM; 越南 *vietnam*]

Vietnamese or Annamese (Vietnamese/Sino-Tibetan), the official language of Vietnam, was formerly written in Chu Nôm characters (see page 80); since the 18th century, Latin script has been used.

The Latin script used in Vietnam is called Quôc ngu. It contains the additional letters ă, â, đ, ê, ô, ơ, and ư, and omits f, j, w, and z; thus its alphabet consists of twenty-nine letters. But Vietnamese has six tones, and vowel letters take (besides the above ◌̆, ◌̂, and ◌') five additional signs (◌̀, ◌̉, ◌̃, ◌́, and ◌̣) to show each tone. Since these two kinds of signs can be attached to letters at the same time, movable type for the letter "a" must be prepared in eighteen forms: a à ả ã á ạ ă ằ ẳ ẵ ắ ặ â ầ ẩ ẫ ấ ậ. This is why Vietnamese typesetting seems to be composed of many dots. Newspapers are published in Vietnamese with Quôc ngu Latin script.

The formal name on a recent postage stamp, Việt Nam Dân Chủ Cộng Hòa, means The Democratic Republic of Vietnam.

Burmese Script

Burmese script closely resembles the Southern Indian scripts in form. However, the Burmese language has a system of seven vowels and three tones, making its vowel system more complicated than those of the Southern Indian scripts.

Vowels

အ	အာ	အား	ဣ(အိ)	ဤ(အီ)	ဥ(အု)
a	*ā*	*ā*	*i*	*ī*	*u*
ဦ(အူ)	အေ့	ဧ(အေ)	အဲ	ဪ(အော်)	
ū	*e*	*ē*	*ē*	*ō*	
ဩ(အော)	အို	အံ			
ō	*ō*	*an*			

Consonants All consonants contain the inherent *a*-vowel as in the Indian scripts.

က	ခ	ဂ	ဃ	င	စ	ဆ	ဇ
ka	*kha*	*ga*	*ga*	*nga*	*sa*	*sa*	*za*
ဈ	ည	ဋ	ဌ	ဍ	ဎ	ဏ	တ
za	*nya*	*ta*	*tha*	*da*	*da*	*na*	*ta*
ထ	ဒ	ဓ	န	ပ	ဖ	ဗ	ဘ
tha	*da*	*da*	*na*	*pa*	*pha*	*ba*	*ba*
မ	ယ	ရ	လ	ဝ	သ	ဟ	ဠ
ma	*ya*	*ya(ra)*	*la*	*wa*	*sa*	*ha*	*la*

A comparison with Indian scripts will show that စ was originally *cha*, ဆ was *chha*, and ရ was *ra*. The *r* sound used in adopted foreign words is shown by ရ.

Vowel signs

◌ -*a* ◌ာ -*ā* ◌ား -*ā* ◌ိ -*i* ◌ီ -*ī*
◌ု (◌ု) -*u* ◌ူ (◌ူ) -*ū* ေ◌့ -*e* ေ◌ -*ē*
◌ဲ -*ē* ေ◌ာ် -*ō* ေ◌ာ -*ō* ◌ို -*ō*

ာ is the -*ā* sign for letters consisting of two circles, but it becomes ါ for letters of one circle to avoid confusion: ပ *pa* and ဟ *ha*, but ပါ *pā*, ပေါ် *pō*.

◌ု is the -*u* sign, but ဈ *jha* becomes ဈု *jhu*, and ည *nya* becomes ညု *nyu*.

Tones Burmese has three tones, which are mostly shown by the signs used for the vowels. Short vowels and letters with the sign ◌့ (or ◌့) belong to the 1st tone (short): က *ka*, ကိ *ki*, ကု *ku*, ကေ့ *ke*, ကဲ့ *ke*, ကော့ *ko*, ကို့ *ko*. Almost all the long vowels belong to the 2nd tone (long low): ကာ *kā*, ကီ *kī*, ကူ *kū*, ကေ *kē*, ကယ် *kē*, ကော် *kō*, ကို *kō*.
Long vowels with ◌ဲ or ေ◌ာ (or ဩ), and vowels with ◌း belong to the 3rd tone (long high): ကား *kā*, ကီး *kī*, ကူး *kū*, ကေး *kē*, ကဲ *kē*, ကော *kō*, ကိုး *kō*.

Conjunct consonants Generally, subscripts are used as in the Indian scripts: မ္မ *mma*, ဋ္ဌ *ttha*. ယ *ya*, ရ *ya* (*ra*), ဝ *wa*, and ဟ *ha* change their forms to ◌ျ, ◌ြ, ◌ွ, and ◌ှ, respectively, in combination with other consonant letters: မ *ma*, မျ *mya*, မြ *mya*, မွ *mwa*, မှ *hma*, မျွ *mywa*, မျှ *hmya*, မြှ *hmya*, မွှ *hmwa*, မြို *myo*.

Other signs ◌ံ indicates a final nasal: ဟံ *han*. ◌် indicates the absence of the inherent *a*-vowel: က *ka* → က် *k*.
င် *ṅ* is sometimes written small on other letters, like a sign: င်္ဂ *ṅga*.
ဉ, called small ည *nya*, serves for ည, though its shape is same as ဥ *u*.

Reading and punctuation Burmese spelling is traditional and, like English spelling, does not always follow the pronunciation of words. Burmese script runs horizontally from left to right with no space between words. The mark 〔။〕 is placed at the end of a sentence.

Numerals

၁	၂	၃	၄	၅	၆	၇	၈	၉	၀
1	2	3	4	5	6	7	8	9	0

ဦးကြီးတို့
စပါးစုပေါင်း
ဆက်တိုက်ရောင်း

ကျောက်တန်း ဖေဖော်ဝါရီ ၂၄

ပထမအကြိမ် ပြည်သူ့လွှတ်တော်နှင့် ပြည်သူ့ကောင်စီအဆင့်ဆင့်ဖွဲ့စည်းရေးရက်ပြုကြိုဆိုသောအားဖြင့်ကျောက်တန်းမြို့နယ်ကျုံကန်ကျေးရွာမှ တောင်သူဦးကြီးများသည် စပါးတင်း ၆၀၀၀ ကျော်ကို လှည်းအစီး ၂၄၀ဖြင့် ကျုံကန် စပါးဒိုင်တွင် ဖေဖော်ဝါရီ ၂၃ရက် နံနက်ပိုင်းက စုပေါင်းရောင်းချကြသည်။

အလားတူ စုပေါင်း စပါးရောင်းချပွဲကို ကျောက်တန်းမြို့နယ်အတွင်း ဖေဖော်ဝါရီ ၂၈ရက်ထိ ဆက်တိုက် ပြုလုပ်သွားမည်ဟု သိရသည်။

…o…

ပြင်သစ်
ကိုယ်စားလှယ်အဖွဲ့
ဆိုက်ရောက်လာ

ရန်ကုန် ဖေဖော်ဝါရီ ၂၄

ပြင်သစ်အမျိုးသားလွှတ်တော် ယဉ်ကျေးမှုနှင့် လူမှုရေးရာ ကော်မီရှင်၏ ဒုတိယဥက္ကဋ္ဌ မစ္စတာကာရီရိုး ဦးဆောင်သော ပြင်သစ်ပါလီမန်ကိုယ်စားလှယ်အဖွဲ့သည် ယနေ့ညနေ ၆နာရီခွဲက ရန်ကုန် မင်္ဂလာဒုံလေဆိပ်သို့ ရောက်ရှိကြရာ နိုင်ငံခြားရေး ဝန်ကြီးဌာန နိုင်ငံရေး ဦးစီး ညွှန်ကြားရေးမှူးချုပ် ဦးသောင်းထိုက်နှင့် တာဝန်ရှိ ပုဂ္ဂိုလ်များ၊ မြန်မာ နိုင်ငံ ဆိုင်ရာ ပြင်သစ် သံအမတ်ကြီးနှင့် သံရုံးအရာရှိများက ကြိုဆိုကြသည်။

ဟံသာဝတီ

အမှတ် ၁၅၆၁၊ ၁၃၃၅–ခု တပေါင်းလဆန်း ၅ ရက် တနင်္လာနေ့ ၂၅–၂–၇၄

ဝင်ငွေခွန် ဥပဒေသစ်ပြဋ္ဌာန်း (သတင်း)

ပညာစစ်တန်းသင်

မအူပင် ဖေဖော်ဝါရီ ၂၄

ရောဝတီတိုင်း အခြေခံ ပညာရေးစစ်တန်းကော်ယူရေး နည်းပြသင်တန်းကို ယမန်နေ့နံနက်ပိုင်းက မအူပင် အထက တွင် ဖွင့်လှစ်သည်။

ယင်း နည်းပြ သင်တန်း ကို ပညာရေးသုတေသနမှပုဂ္ဂိုလ်များ လာရောက်ပို့ချရာတိုင်းအတွင်းမြို့နယ် ပညာရေးစစ်တန်း ကော်ယူရေးအဖွဲ့ဝင်များ တက်ရောက်၏။

ဦးကြီးအချို့ ကုန်သည်ထံမှ စပါးပြန် ဝယ်ရ
အစိုးရထံသတ်မှတ်စပါးတင်းရေရောင်းနိုင်ရန်

မန္တလေး ဖေဖော်ဝါရီ ၂၄

မန္တလေးတိုင်းအတွင်း စပါးထွက်သော မြို့နယ်ကျေးရွာများသို့ အထွက်နှုန်းပေါ် သတ်မှတ်ထားသည့် စပါးများ ဝယ်ယူရရှိရေးအတွက် ပါတီ ဗဟိုကော်မီတီဝင်များနှင့်တိုင်းပြည်သူ့ကောင်စီဝင်များ ကွင်းဆင်း စည်းရုံးဝယ်ယူလျက်ရှိရာ ယခင်ကထက်ပိုမိုရောင်းချလာကြသည်ဟုသိရသည်။

ကွင်းဆင်းရှင်း

ယခုအခါ ကွင်းဆင်းစည်းရုံးဝယ်ယူရေး အဖွဲ့ဝင် များ သည် လယ်စိုက်သူတဦးချင်း၏ အထွက်နှုန်းအပေါ် အစိုးရအား ရောင်းချရမည့် စပါးအရေအတွက်များကို မတ်လ ၃၁ ရက် နောက်ဆုံးထားပြီး ရောင်းချကြရန် နှင့် သတ်မှတ်စပါး ရောင်းချခြင်းမပြုသူများအား ကုန်သွယ်ရေး ၁ အမိန့်ကြော်ငြာစာ အမှတ်၄၈အရ အရေးယူသွားမည် ဖြစ်ကြောင်း ကျေးရွာအထိဆင်း၍ ပညာပေးဟောပြောလျက်ရှိသည်။

၁၀ ပြန်ဝယ်

ယင်း ဟောပြောစည်းရုံးချက်အရ အချို့ လယ်ယာ ဦးကြီးတို့သည် အစိုးရထံသို့ သတ်မှတ်သည့်အတိုင်း ပြန်လည် ရောင်းချနိုင်ရေးအတွက် ကုန်သည် များထံ

စာမျက်နှာ၆ ကော်လံ ၃ ★

မန္တလေးမြို့ကားလမ်းဘေး ရွှေကြာ ကျေးရွာတွင် အရေးပေါ်ဖွင့်လှစ်ထားသော ပုသိမ်ကြီးမြို့နယ် စပါးဒိုင်ခွဲသို့ ဖေဖော်ဝါရီ ၂၄ရက် နံနက်က ကျေးရွာအုပ်စု ၃အုပ်စုမှ ဦးကြီးတို့ လာရောက်ရောင်းချနေကြစဉ်။ (သတင်း၆)

ဖေဖော်ဝါရီ ၂၄ ရက် နံနက် ၁၁နာရီက မန္တလေးမြို့ ရွှေဘုန်းရှိန် အမက တိုချဲ့ အဆောက်အဦအတွက် ကျပ်ငွေ ၅၀၀၀ ကို ရှမ်းပွဲရပ်နေ ဦးအောင်သန်း ဒေါ်မြင့်မြင့်ရီတို့က ကျောင်းအုပ်ကြီးလက်သို့ ပေးလှူစဉ်။ (သတင်း၆)

ဘယဆေးကုန်ကြမ်း
ပြည်တွင်းထွက်တိုး

ရန်ကုန် ဖေဖော်ဝါရီ ၂၄

မြန်မာနိုင်ငံ ဆေးဝါးလုပ်ငန်း စက်ရုံသည် ပြည်တွင်းထွက် ဘယဆေး ကုန်ကြမ်းများကို တိုးတက်ဝယ်ယူအသုံးပြုလျက်ရှိရာယခုနှစ်၌ ကျပ် သိန်း ၉၀ ကျော်ဖိုး အထိ ဝယ်ယူ သုံးစွဲသွားမည်ဟုသိရ၏။

စက်ရုံအတွက်လိုအပ်သည့် ကုန်ကြမ်း တန်ဖိုးမှာ သိန်း ၃၅၀ ကျော်ရှိရာ နှစ်အနည်းငယ်အတွင်း ပြည်တွင်း၌သာ အများဆုံး ရရှိဝယ်ယူ နိုင်ရေးအတွက် ဆိုင်ရာတို့က ပူးပေါင်း ဆောင်ရွက်လျက်ရှိသည်ဟုသိရ၏။ (ဝ၃ဝ)

….o….

ကောင်စီ စည်းဝေး လမ်းညွှန်
တဖွဲ့ပြီး တဖွဲ့ အပြီး ရွေးချယ်

ရန်ကုန် ဖေဖော်ဝါရီ ၂၄

ပြည်သူ့ကောင်စီအဆင့်ဆင့်၏ ပထမ အကြိမ် အစည်းအဝေးတွင် ယာယီသဘာပတိတဦးကို ရွေးချယ်တင်မြှောက်၍ ပြည်သူ့ကောင်စီဝင် များက ကတိသစ္စာပြုကြပြီးနောက် သက်ဆိုင်ရာအဖွဲ့အစည်းများကို တခုပြီးတခုရွေးချယ်တင်မြှောက်ဖွဲ့စည်းသွားရန်လိုကြောင်းဖြင့် ပထမအကြိမ် ပြည်သူ့ကောင်စီ အဆင့်ဆင့်တွင်းအဖွဲ့အစည်းများရွေးချယ်တင်မြှောက်ပွဲကျင်းပရေးညွှန်ကြားချက်တွင် ဖော်ပြပါရှိသည်။

ဖွဲ့စည်း

ဖေဖော်ဝါရီ ၂၄ရက်က မန္တလေး၄၄အထက ၌ မူလ တန်းဆရာဖြစ်သင်တန်း တက်လိုသူများ စစ်ဆေးစဉ်။

တော်လှန်ရေးကောင်စီကပြဋ္ဌာန်းထားသောပြည်သူ့ကောင်စီ ဥပဒေနှင့် အညီ ပထမအကြိမ် ပြည်သူ့ကောင်စီ အစည်းအဝေးများက ပြည်သူ့ကောင်စီ

ချောင်ကျေးရွာတွင် စပါးဝယ်ယူရေး ဆွေးနွေးပွဲ ကျင်းပသည်။ တောင်သူ လယ်သမား များက

ကြို တင်ဝယ်စပါး
လကုန် အပြီးသွင်းမည်

တွံတေး ဖေဖော်ဝါရီ ၂၄

တွံတေးမြို့နယ် သမဝါယမ

A Burmese newspaper. Its title is ဟံသာဝတီ *hansāwatī*.

Khmer (Cambodian) Script

The Mon and Khmer languages belong to the Mon-Khmer group of Austroasiatic languages. When the Indian writing system for Indo-European languages reached Southeast Asia, its functions had to be changed to adapt to these languages. Khmer script is as a result in a position between Indian and Thai scripts, the latter being used to write a Sino-Tibetan language.

Vowels

អ	អា	ឥ	ឦ	ឧ	ឩ	ឫ	ឬ
a	*ā*	*i*	*ī*	*u*	*ū*	*ri*	*rī*
ឭ	ឮ	ឯ	ឰ	ឱ	ឲ	ឳ	
li	*lī*	*e*	*ai*	*o*	*ao*	*au*	

Independent vowels are pronounced with a light *q*-sound preceding them. This sound is sometimes considered a consonant, especially when used in subscripts: ក្អក *kqak.*

Consonants

ក	ខ	គ	ឃ	ង	ច	ឆ	ជ
ka	*kha*	*ko*	*kho*	*ngo*	*cha*	*chha*	*cho*
ឈ	ញ	ដ	ឋ	ឌ	ឍ	ណ	ត
chho	*nyo*	*da*	*tha*	*do*	*tho*	*na*	*ta*
ថ	ទ	ធ	ន	ប	ផ	ព	ភ
tha	*to*	*tho*	*no*	*ba*	*pha*	*po*	*pho*
ម	យ	រ	ល	វ	ស	ហ	ឡ
mo	*yo*	*ro*	*lo*	*wo*	*sa*	*ha*	*la*

Some consonants have an inherent *a*-vowel (these are called the 1st series), while others have an inherent *o*-vowel (2nd series).

Vowel signs Attaching a sign to change the inherent vowel produces a different pronunciation in the first and second series. For example, ◌ិ with ខ *kha*, which belongs to the 1st series, is pronounced *khe*, while ◌ិ with ឃ *kho*, which belongs to the 2nd series, is pronounced *khi*. The attached signs and their pronunciations are shown in the table below.

Conjunct consonants A succeeding consonant is written as a peculiar subscript below the preceding consonant. In most cases, the subscript is a smaller version of the original without the hat ◌៉ (ក្ត *kta*), but some letters are written both to the right and under the first consonant: ◌្ខ *-kh-*, ◌្ឆ *-chh-*, ◌្ឋ *-th-*, ◌្ប *-b-*, ◌្យ *-y-*, ◌្ស *-s-*. Some consonants also change their forms when used as subscripts: ◌្ង *-ng-*, ◌្ច *-ch-*, ◌្ញ *-ny-*, ◌្ដ *-d-*, ◌្ថ *-th-*, ◌្ត *-t-*, ◌្ធ *-th-*, ◌្ន *-n-*, ◌្ម *-m-*, ◌្រ *-r-*, ◌្ល *-l-*, ◌្វ *-w-*.

Other signs ◌់ on a final consonant shortens the vowel in its syllable: បន់ *ban.* (The inherent vowel of the last letter of a syllable is dropped when there is no sign.)

◌៉ converts a 2nd-series consonant to a 1st-series one (ម *mo* → ម៉ *ma*) or converts ប *ba* to ប៉ *pa*, យ *yo* to យ៉ *ya*.

◌៊ converts a 1st-series consonant to a 2nd-series one: ប *ba* → ប៊ *bo*.

◌ំ shows the nasal: ខំ *kham*, ជុំ *chum*, ទុំ *tum*.

◌ះ shows a final *h*: និះ *nih*.

◌័ is the same as ◌ា◌់.

◌+ shows a high intonation.

◌៍ on an etymological spelling shows that the letter is not to be pronounced.

VOWEL SIGNS	◌	◌ា	◌ិ	◌ី	◌ឹ	◌ឺ	◌ុ	◌ូ	◌ួ	◌ើ	◌ឿ	◌ៀ	◌េ	◌ែ	◌ៃ	◌ោ	◌ៅ
1ST SERIES	*-a*	*-ā*	*-e*	*-ei*	*-e*	*-ei*	*-o*	*-ou*	*-ue*	*-ae*	*-ie*	*-ie*	*-ei*	*-ae*	*-ai*	*-ao*	*-au*
2ND SERIES	*-o*	*-ie*	*-i*	*-ī*	*-i*	*-ī*	*-u*	*-ū*	*-ue*	*-ē*	*-ie*	*-ie*	*-i*	*-ē*	*-ī*	*-ō*	*-iu*

A Khmer newspaper published in what was then the Kingdom of Cambodia. It is printed in the slanted, standing, and Cambodian styles. Its title is សុជីវធម៌ *sochiwotho.*

Styles of type There are standing and slanted styles in Khmer script as well as the so-called Cambodian style, which resembles classic Khmer script and is used frequently in titles. Examples which differ from the ordinary slanted style are:

ក = ក *ka*	ង = ង *ngo*
ជ = ជ *cho*	ណ = ណ *na*
ត = ត *to*	ន = ន *no*
ា = ា *–a* or *–ie*	

Reading and punctuation Khmer script runs horizontally from left to right, with no space between words. A space is left where a comma would usually be used in English. ។ is put at the end of the sentence like the period in English. ៗ is a repeating sign.

Numerals

១	២	៣	៤	៥	៦	៧	៨	៩	០
1	2	3	4	5	6	7	8	9	0

Thai Script

Thai script has no independent vowel letters like those in Khmer script; all the independent letters are consonants. There are more consonant symbols than in Khmer script, and the inherent vowel in each consonant letter is *o*.

Consonants

ก	ข	ฃ	ค	ฅ	ฆ	ง	
ko	*kho*	*kho*	*kho*	*kho*	*kho*	*ngo*	
จ	ฉ	ช	ซ	ฌ	ญ		
cho	*chho*	*chho*	*so*	*chho*	*yo*		
ฎ	ฏ	ฐ	ฑ	ฒ	ณ		
do	*to*	*tho*	*tho*	*tho*	*no*		
ด	ต	ถ	ท	ธ	น		
do	*to*	*tho*	*tho*	*tho*	*no*		
บ	ป	ผ	ฝ	พ	ฟ	ภ	ม
bo	*po*	*pho*	*fo*	*pho*	*fo*	*pho*	*mo*
ย	ร	ล	ว	ศ	ษ	ส	
yo	*ro*	*lo*	*wo*	*so*	*so*	*so*	
ห	ฬ	อ	ฮ				
ho	*lo*	*'o*	*ho*				

Vowel signs

◌ *-o* ◌ะ *-a* ◌ั *-a* ◌า *-ā* ◌ิ *-i*

◌ี *-ī* ◌ึ *-u* ◌ื *-ū* ◌ุ *-u* ◌ู *-ū*

เ◌ะ *-e* เ◌ *-ē* เ◌็ *-e* แ◌ะ *-e* แ◌ *-ē*

โ◌ะ *-o* โ◌ *-ō* เ◌าะ *-o* ◌ำ *-am*

ใ◌ *-ai* ไ◌ *-ai* เ◌า *-au*

For the letter ก *ko*: กะ *ka*, กั *ka*, กา *kā*, กิ *ki*, กี *kī*, กึ *ku*, กื *kū*, กุ *ku*, กู *kū*, เกะ *ke*, เก *kē*, เก็ *ke*, แกะ *ke*, แก *kē*, โกะ *ko*, โก *kō*, เกาะ *ko*, ใก *kai*, ไก *kai*, เกา *kau*.

Vowels Independent vowels are written with vowel signs on the letter อ: อะ *a*, อิ *i*, อุ *u*, เอะ *e*, and โอะ *o*. Exceptions are the independent vowel letters ฤ *ru* or *ri* (the long vowel is ฤๅ *rī*) and ฦ *lu*, which are only used to write words borrowed from Pali.

To express double vowels, the consonant letters อ, ย, and ว are used, which makes the vowel system of Thai fairly complex: เ◌ีย *-iā*, เ◌ียะ *-ia*, ◌ัว *-uā*, and so on.

Conjunct consonants Thai script has no conjunct consonants; two consonants pronounced with no intervening vowel are merely juxtaposed: กลม *klom*, ตรง *trong*. In fact, Thai script is sometimes said to have not syllabic symbols containing the *o* vowel (which when written is sometimes not pronounced) but phonemic symbols consisting only of consonants (for the *o* vowel is sometimes not written at all).

A Thai postage stamp.

Syllables and tones Thai is in principle a monosyllabic language: one word is represented by one syllable consisting of a head consonant (sometimes combined), a vowel with a tone, and a final consonant.

The head consonant letter belongs inherently to one of three classes; high, middle, or low. Four signs for tones are also used: ◌่ 1st, ◌้ 2nd, ◌๊ 3rd, and ◌๋ 4th. These four signs, plus the absence of a sign, are used to indicate the tone of each syllable, though there is not always a correspondence of one sign for one tone. The tone sign is placed on the right shoulder of the letter. When there is a vowel sign on the letter, the tone sign is placed above: ฟั้ *fa* (2nd tone).

The final sound of a syllable is either an open tone (nasal and vowel) or a closed tone (consonants *k*, *t*, and *p*). All final consonants become one of eight sounds: ก, ข, ค, and

รายละเอียดคดีกรรมกรอ้อมน้อยพ้นผิด หน้า ๒-๓

สยามรัฐ

ปีที่ ๓๐ ฉบับที่ ๑๐๐๐๐ วันพฤหัสบดีที่ ๑๖ สิงหาคม ๒๕๒๒ ราคา ๑.๕๐ บาท

นายจ้างขอจ่าย ๒ ระยะ

ค่าแรงขึ้น ๓ อัตรา ลูกจ้างใหม่ให้ ๓๕

คณะกรรมการค่าจ้าง ลงมติให้ค่าจ้างขั้นต่ำเป็น ๓ อัตรา กรุงเทพฯ และจังหวัดใกล้เคียง ๔๕ บาทภาคกลางและใต้๓๘บาท ภาคเหนือและอีสาน ๓๕ บาท เริ่มใช้ ๑ ตุลาคม แต่ฝ่ายนายจ้างขอตั้งข้อสังเกตขึ้น ให้จ่ายเป็น ๒ ระยะ ๆ แรก ๔๐ บาท และระยะที่สองต้นปีหน้า ๔๕ บาท รวมทั้งให้คนงานใหม่ ๓๕ บาท

นายเดชชาติ วงศ์โกมลเชษฐ รองปลัดกระทรวง มหาดไทย และประธานคณะกรรมการ ค่าจ้าง เฉียงเหนือ ๓๕ บาท หรือคิดเป็นเปอร์เซ็นต์ ที่ เพิ่มขึ้นคือจาก๓๘บาทเป็น ๔๕ บาท ๒๘ เปอร์เซ็นต์ จาก

'คึกฤทธิ์' ว่า เร่งส่งออก ยังไม่เห็น ทางสำเร็จ

ม.ร.ว. คึกฤทธิ์ว่า ปัญหาของบ้านเมืองในขณะนี้ประชาชน ต้องเผชิญกับภาวการณ์ต่าง ๆ หลายชนิด ทั้งเศรษฐกิจตกต่ำ และสภาวะทางการเมือง

ม.ร.ว. คึก ฤทธิ์ ปราโมชได้รับเชิญไปเป็นองค์ปาฐกแก่สมาชิกสมาคมศิษย์เก่านักศึกษาบัญชีมหาวิทยาลัยธรรม ศาสตร์ ที่โรงแรมอินทราเมื่อเที่ยงวานนี้ในหัวข้อเรื่อง "ปัญหาบ้านเมือง" โดยสรุปได้ว่า ในปัจจุบันประชาชนของประเทศทุกกลุ่มต้องเผชิญกับปัญหาทั้งเศรษฐกิจและการเมืองหลายด้าน ทำให้เกิด คว าม เดือด ร้อน แก่ประชาชนทั่ว ประเทศทุกหมู่เหล่า เช่นการขึ้นราคาสินค้า อันเนื่องมาจากการขึ้นราคาน้ำมัน ซึ่งทำให้ต้อง มีการ เรียก ร้องปรับค่าแรงงานขั้นต่ำอย่างหลีกเลี่ยงไม่ได้ ส่วนผลกระทบที่จะตามมา คือ บรรดานายจ้างจะหันไปใช้เครื่อง

□ อ่านต่อหน้า ๑๒

นายพิชิต สรรพอาสา ผู้บัญชาการเรือนจำคลองเปรม ชี้แจงแก่ผู้สื่อข่าวถึงเรื่องหมายปล่อย

พบน้ำมัน ที่ฝางอีก

กรม การ พลัง งานทหารพบบ่อน้ำมันดิบที่ ฝางอีก มีคุณภาพเหมือนกับน้ำมันเซงลี่ของจีน

แหล่ง ข่าวจากกระทรวงกลาโหมเปิด เผยกับ "สยามรัฐ" ว่า กรมการพลังงานทหารได้ค้นพบบ่อน้ำมันดิบแห่งใหม่ที่ตำบล

□ อ่านต่อหน้า ๑๒

เตรียมยึดน้ำมัน กว่า๓หมื่นบาเรล มากลั่นในไทย

เกรียงศักดิ์ งง ถูกซัมมิทยื่นหนังสือบีบ ๒ รัฐมนตรีออกเดินทาง ไปซาอุดีอาระเบีย ต้นเดือนหน้า เตรียมยึดน้ำมันดิบ ๓๕,๐๐๐ บาเรลกลับมากลั่นในไทย

นายประสิทธิ์ ณรงค์เดช รัฐมนตรีว่าการกระ-

A Thai newspaper. Its title is *สยาม รัฐ syam rat.*

ฆ are pronounced *k*; จ, ช, ฌ, ฎ, ฏ, ฐ, ฑ, ฒ, ด, ต, ถ, ท, ธ, ศ, ษ, and ส are *t*; ง is *ng*; ญ, ณ, น, ร, ล, and ฬ are *n*; ม is *m*; บ, ป, พ, ฟ, and ภ are *p*; ย is *y*; and ว is *w*.

Other signs ◌ํ shows the nasal: *กํา kam.* ◌์ means that the letter reflects an etymological spelling and should not be pronounced. *จันทร์* is read as *chan*, and *dr* is not read because this word was derived from the Indian *chandra*, meaning "moon."

ๆ is a repeating sign: *บ่อยๆ boy boy.*

Reading and punctuation Thai script runs horizontally from left to right, with no spaces between words. A space is left where a comma would be used in English. Usually, in a Thai sentence, neither the period nor the comma is used.

ฯ is a small ellipsis showing that following letters have been omitted; *กรุงเทพฯ krung thēp* is the Thai name for Bangkok, whose original name was very long.

ฯลฯ means "etc."

Numerals

๑	๒	๓	๔	๕	๖	๗	๘	๙	๐
1	2	3	4	5	6	7	8	9	0

Lao Script

Lao script used to be divided into two groups: Western Lao or Chieng Mai script in northern Thailand, and Eastern Lao or Luangpraban script in Laos.

In 1960, the Lao government instituted Modern Lao script. It is improved Luangpraban script written more simply and for more exact pronunciation. Silent letters in borrowed words, abbreviated forms, and irregular spellings have been totally abolished. Modern Lao script more closely resembles Thai script. All independent letters are consonants.

Consonants

ກ	ຂ	ຄ	ງ	ຈ	ສ	ຊ
ko	*kho*	*kho*	*ngo*	*cho*	*so*	*so*
ຍ	ດ	ຕ	ຖ	ທ	ນ	ບ
nyo	*do*	*to*	*tho*	*tho*	*no*	*bo*
ປ	ຜ	ຝ	ພ	ຟ	ມ	ຢ
po	*pho*	*fo*	*pho*	*fo*	*mo*	*yo*
ຣ	ລ	ວ	ຫ	ອ	ຮ	
ro	*lo*	*wo*	*ho*	*'o*	*ho*	

ຣ *ro* is a new letter for borrowed words.
Lao is monosyllabic with tones, and letters are classified into high, middle, and low classes. Thus, in the table above there are different-shaped letters with the same pronunciation. The letter ຂ *kho* belongs to the high class, and ຄ *kho* belongs to the low class. The letter ມ *mo* belongs to the low class, and though there is no corresponding high-class letter, high-class *mo* is written ຫມ, in which the ຫ (high-class *ho*) is not pronounced.
ຫມ is also written ໝ as a ligature. In the same way, ໜ is *ho* + *no*, ຫຼ is *ho* + *ro* or *ho* + *lo*, and ຫຍ is *ho* + *nyo*.
◌ຼ is also used with combined consonants; ພຼ *phro*.

Vowel signs

◌	*–o*	◌ະ	*–a*	◌ັ◌	*–a–*	◌າ	*–ā*
◌ິ	*–i*	◌ີ	*–ī*	◌ຶ	*–u*	◌ື	*–ū*
◌ຸ	*–u*	◌ູ	*–ū*	ເ◌ະ	*–e*	ເ◌ັ◌	*–e–*
ເ◌	*–ē*	ແ◌ະ	*–e*	ແ◌ັ◌	*–e–*	ແ◌	*–ē*
ໂ◌ະ	*–o*	◌ົ◌	*–o–*	ໂ◌	*–ō*	ເ◌າະ	*–o*
ເ◌ິ	*–e*	ເ◌ີ	*–ē*	ເ◌ັຽະ	*–ia*	ເ◌ັຽ	*–ia*
◌ຽ◌	*–ia–*	ເ◌ຶອ	*–ua*	ເ◌ືອ	*–uā*		
◌ົວ◌	*–ua–*	◌ົວ	*–uā*	ໄ◌	*–ay*		
ໃ◌	*–ay*	ເ◌ົາ	*–au*	◌ຳ	*–am*		

An independent vowel is written with a sign attached to the base letter ອ : ອະ *a*, ອິ *i*, ອຸ *u*, ແອະ *e*, and ໂອະ *o*.

Tones As in Thai, Lao has four tone signs: ່ 1st, ້ 2nd, ໊ 3rd, and ໋ 4th, of which ໊ and ໋ are seldom used. The tone of a Lao word is determined by the combination of tone signs (່ , ້ , and no sign), the classification of the head consonant, the presence or absence of the final consonant, and the length of the vowel.

A Lao postage stamp.

Reading and punctuation Lao script runs horizontally from left to right, with no space between each word. Punctuation is now the same as in English.
ໆ is a repeating sign.
ຯ is an ellipsis.
ຯລຯ is an ellipsis for an entire sentence.

Numerals

໑	໒	໓	໔	໕	໖	໗	໘	໙	໐
1	2	3	4	5	6	7	8	9	0

Arabic figures are also used.

ສຽງປະຊາຊົນ

ປີທີ 5 ສະບັບທີ 1249 (ລາຄາ 10 ກີບ) ວັນຈັນ 6 / 8 / 1979

A Lao newspaper. Its title is ສຽງປະຊາຊົນ *siang pasāson.*

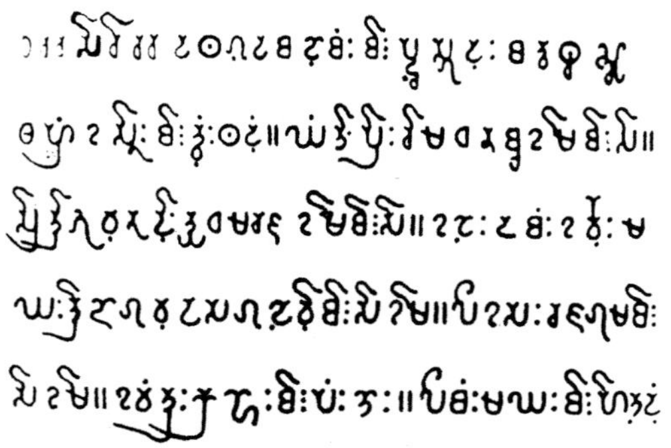

PYU SCRIPT. The Pyu were a cultured tribe in ancient Burma (7th–12th century). This is part of the Myazedi inscription. (U Tha Myat)

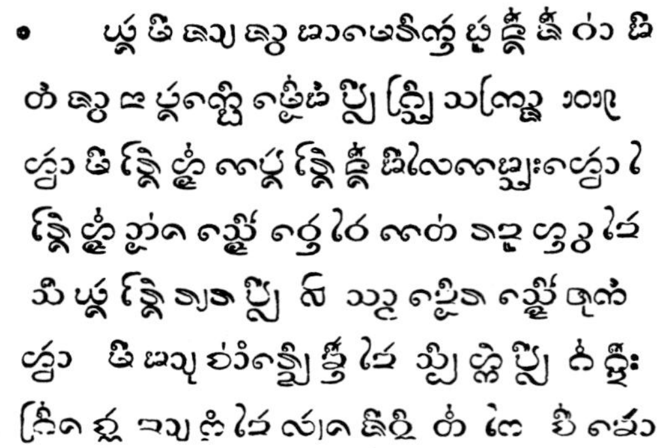

CHIENG MAI SCRIPT. The Lao writing of northern Thailand. It differs from the Thai and Lao scripts, being closer to Khmer script. (School book)

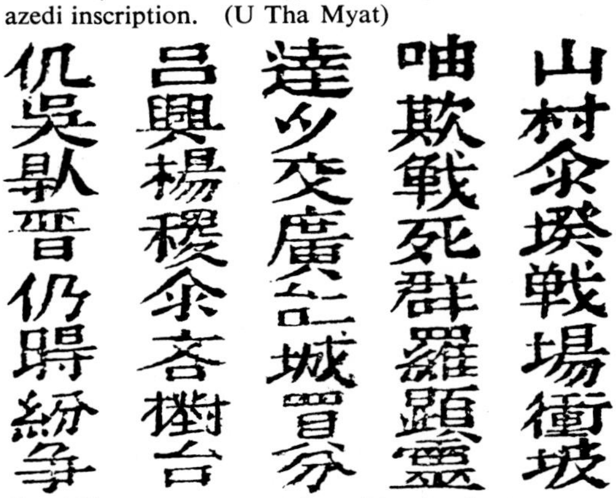

CHU NÔM CHARACTERS. The writing for the Annamese language, used after the 14th century. It was written with a mixture of Chinese characters. (Old book)

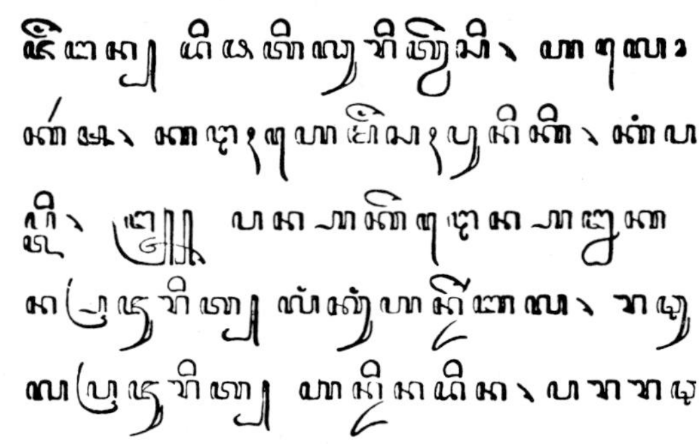

JAVANESE SCRIPT. The writing used in Java after the Majapahit dynasty. It is related to the Indian scripts. (Author's collection)

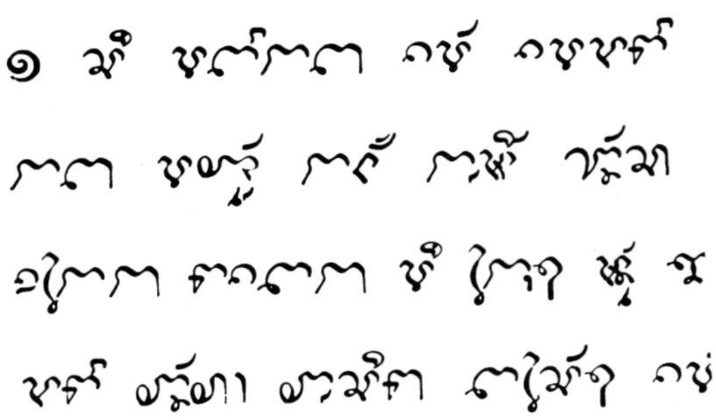

CHAM SCRIPT. Cham is in southern Vietnam and Cambodia. It has the oldest Malayo-Polynesian culture. (Fossey)

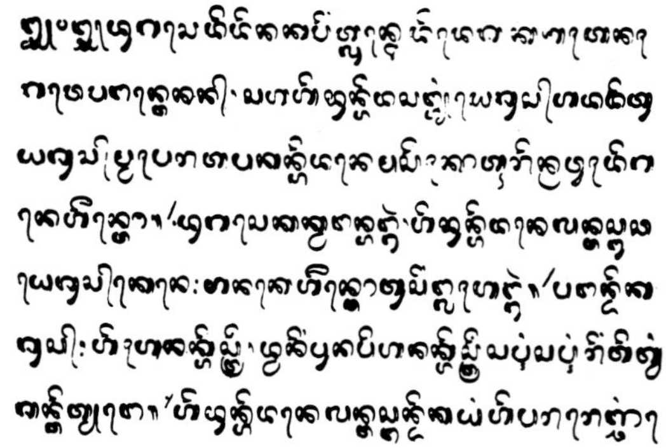

BALINESE SCRIPT. The writing of the island of Bali in Indonesia. It is close to Javanese script. (Nida)

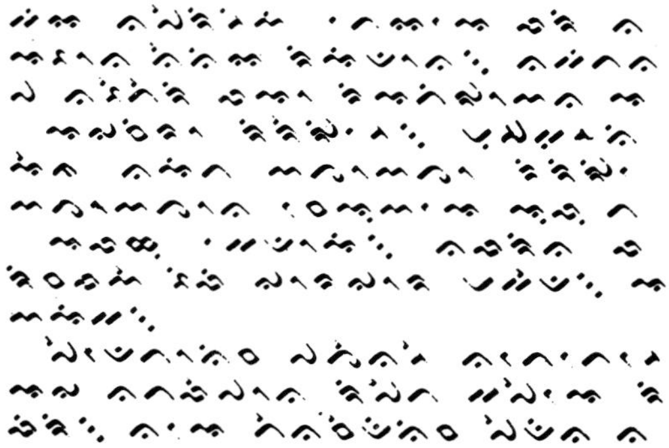

BUGINESE SCRIPT (MAKASSAR SCRIPT). The writing of the island of Sulawesi. It represents the easternmost extension of the Indian scripts. (School book)

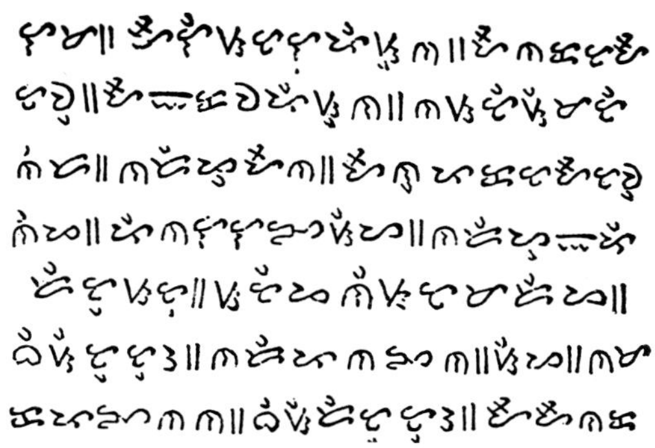

TAGALOG SCRIPT. Representative of the various Philippine scripts before the Spanish invasion. Used in Luzon. (Old book)

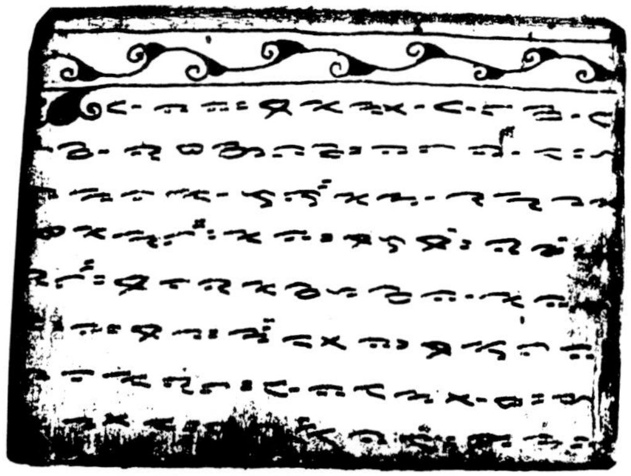

BATAK SCRIPT. The writing of the Batak tribe in the northern part of the island of Sumatra. Seldom used today. (Author's collection)

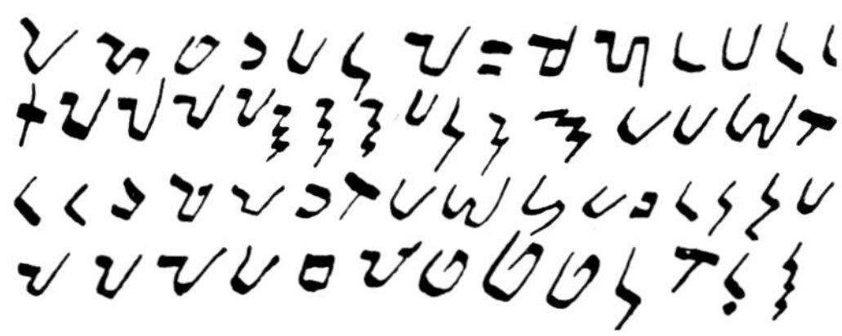

BUHID SCRIPT. This Philippine script has remained on the island of Mindoro, where it has been cut into bamboo. (Gardner)

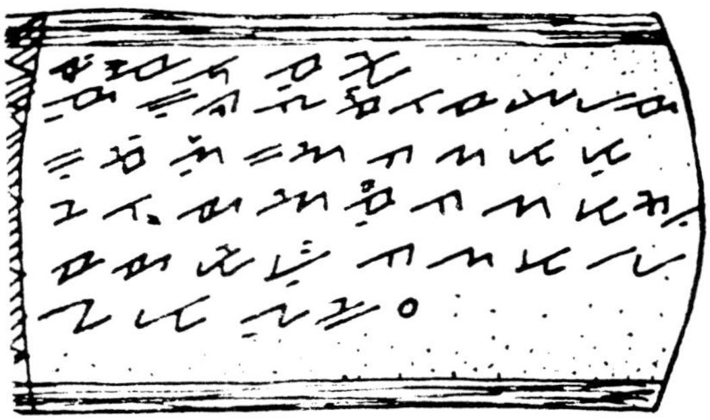

REJANG SCRIPT. One of the vernacular scripts on the island of Sumatra, Indonesia. It has also been cut into bamboo. (Jaspan)

MANGYAN SCRIPT. A native script on Mindoro Island, the Philippines. It is still used. (Postma)

6. SCRIPTS OF EAST ASIA

China is situated in the center of East Asia. The writing system of China is unique because of its enormous number of characters with ideographic functions and irregular pronunciations. All modern scripts in the world are the descendants of Phoenician script or were invented under its influence, except for Chinese characters and those of nearby countries influenced by China.

The Japanese Kana scripts, for instance, are pure syllabaries, while Korean script uses syllabic signs composed of elements. Khitan characters used in medieval times in North China were combinations of syllabic elements. Nuchen characters were a mixture of ideograms and syllabics, while Hsihsia characters were constructed theoretically. Lolo characters remaining in Yunnan are syllabic but ideographic, while Moso characters are primitive ideograms that suggest the origin of Chinese characters.

Nomads in northern Asia scarcely employed such intricate characters; they invented simpler scripts: Uighur, Mongolian, and Manchu. These are descendants of Aramaic script, being composed of pure phonemic signs. Tibetan, Khotanese, Lepcha, and Passepa scripts, however, are related to Indian scripts.

Specimens of the above characters and scripts are shown on pages 96–98.

Generally, the languages of East Asia,

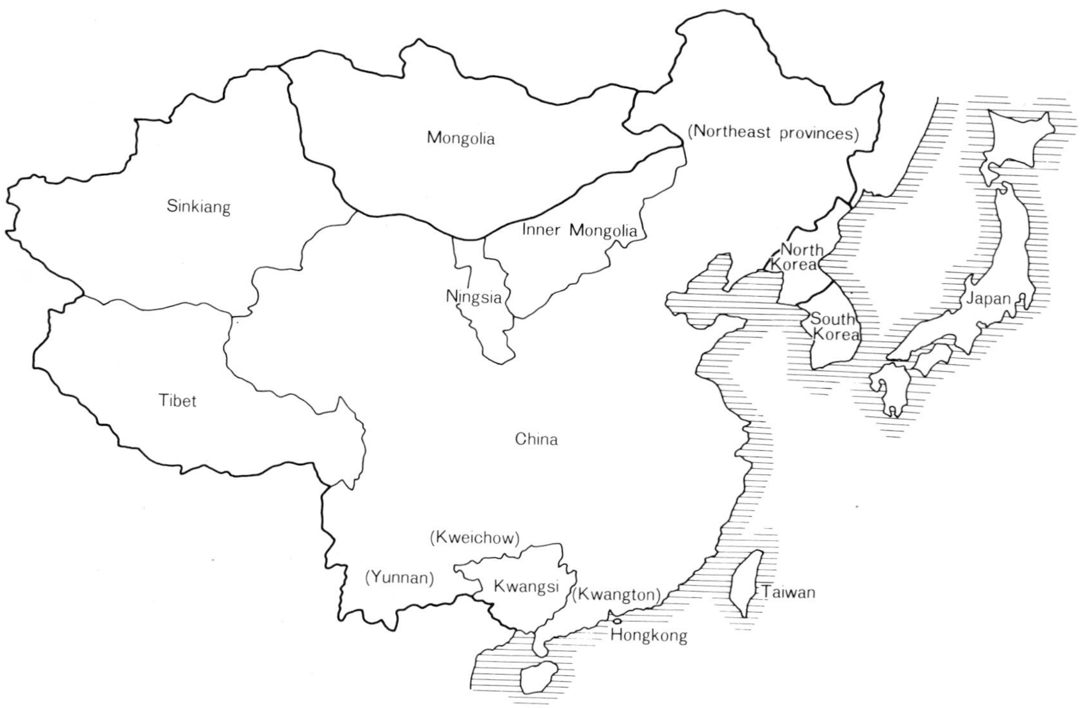

especially Sino-Tibetan languages, are poor in consonants and rich in vowels, with one word consisting of one syllable and many words having the same sound. Therefore, many languages employ tones. When such East Asian languages introduced the Western scripts used for Indo-European or Semitic-Hamitic languages, which are rich in consonants and poor in vowels and contain polysyllabic words, many contrivances were necessary and their writing systems became complex.

The Tibetan script in remote ages, the Thai script of the modern age, and the Quôc ngu alphabet of Vietnam are good examples of this complexity. The complexity involved also explains why any attempt to write the Chinese languages in Latin script is so difficult and why so few systems have been successful.

Since the Altaic languages of northern Asia are polysyllabic and without tones, Western scripts were more easily accepted there. In contrast, the Khitan people, who invented peculiar characters like Chinese ones, seem to have had some difficulty because of their polysyllabic system and the need to express auxiliary words.

CHINA [中华人民共和国 *chuňhua renmin kungxekuo*; ZHONGHUA RENMIN GONGHEGUO]

The state language of China is Chinese (Chinese/Sino-Tibetan), which is written in Chinese characters and in Latin script. Chinese characters are the only pure ideograms in the present world and have a very peculiar system. Nowadays, in Chinese characters, there are three forms, of which Chianthitsi (简体字), the simplified form, is used in modern China. These Chinese characters and other forms are explained on page 86.

Recently Latin script has been used for Chinese and the other languages spoken in China. However, its phonetic values differ from those of the European languages. For example, Peking is spelled "Beijing" in China. (In the older Wade-Giles system, Peking is spelled "Peiching.") The Chinese phonetic values of Latin letters are shown on the lower lines in the table below.

A	B	C	D	E	F	G	H	I	J	K
a	*p*	*ts*	*t*	*e*	*f*	*k*	*x*	*i*	*ch*	*kh*
L	M	N	O	P	Q	R	S	T	U	V
l	*m*	*n*	*o*	*ph*	*chh*	*r*	*s*	*th*	*u*	*v*
W	X	Y	Z							
w	*sh*	*y*	*ts*							

In China there is also a special alphabet called Chu Yin phonetic script, which was developed in 1918 and is used in children's books and in dictionaries to transcribe Chinese and minority languages.

The Chinese Chu Yin phonetic script consists of forty symbols as follows.

CONSONANTS

ㄅ	ㄆ	ㄇ	ㄈ	ㄪ	ㄉ	ㄊ	ㄋ	ㄌ
p	*ph*	*m*	*f*	*v*	*t*	*th*	*n*	*l*
ㄍ	ㄎ	ㄫ	ㄏ	ㄐ	ㄑ	ㄬ	ㄒ	ㄓ
k	*kh*	*ng*	*x*	*ch*	*chh*	*n*	*sh*	*ch*
ㄔ	ㄕ	ㄖ	ㄗ	ㄘ	ㄙ			
ch	*sh*	*r, ri*	*ts*	*ts*	*s*			

VOWELS

ㄚ	ㄛ	ㄜ	ㄝ	ㄧ	ㄨ	ㄩ	ㄦ	ㄞ
a	*o*	*e*	*e*	*i*	*u*	*yu*	*er*	*ai*
ㄟ	ㄠ	ㄡ	ㄢ	ㄣ	ㄤ	ㄥ		
ei	*ao*	*ou*	*an*	*en*	*ang*	*eng, ng*		

The Chinese language has four tones, which are indicated by signs: ◌̄ 1st (upper level), ◌́ 2nd (lower level), ◌̌ 3rd (rising), and ◌̀ 4th (vanishing). These are placed above the vowel letters of the Latin script and beside or above those of the Chu Yin phonetic script. In the Wade-Giles system, tones are indicated by superior numbers after a syllable. Thus, the Chinese character 共 is spelled as "gòng" or ㄍㄨㄥ in China and as "Kung^4" in the Wade-Giles system.

China is a huge multiracial nation that comprises twenty-one provinces and five autonomous regions, in both of which many minority races (the Chinese government counts fifty-four) live and in which vernacular languages are used. In twenty-one provinces, Chinese is generally spoken, Chinese characters are used, and newspapers are published in Chinese with Chinese characters. Manchu (Tungusic/Altaic) and Korean in the Northeast provinces; Lolo (Tibeto-Burman/Sino-Tibetan), Tai (Thai/Sino-Tibetan), and Moso (Tibeto-Burman/Sino-Tibetan) in Yunnan province; Miao (Miao-Yao/Sino-Tibetan) in Kweichow province; and Yao (Miao-Yao/Sino-Tibetan) in Kwangton province are also spoken and are written in special scripts as main minority languages. In autonomous regions, however, distinct languages and scripts are used. The picture below shows a portion of a bill of Chinese currency, on which "Chinese People's Bank, Two Chiao" is printed in four languages and scripts. "China" is written as ᠳᠤᠮᠳᠠᠳᠤ ᠤᠯᠤᠰ in Mongolian, ཀྲུང་གོ་ in Tibetan, جۇڭگو in Uighur, and "Cuŋƅ goƨ" in Chuang; in addition to these, 中国 and "ZHONGGUO" are written in Chinese on the other parts.

Inner Mongolia [ᠥᠪᠦᠷ ᠮᠣᠩᠭᠣᠯ *obor mongol*; 内蒙古 *neimenku*] In the Inner Mongolian autonomous region, Mongolian (Mongolian/Altaic) is generally spoken and newspapers are published in it. Mongolian is written in Mongolian script in Inner Mongolia, while in (Outer) Mongolia Russian script is used. Mongolian script is explained on page 90.

Kwangsi [广西 *kuangshī*] In the Kwangsi-Chuang autonomous region, Chuang (Thai/Sino-Tibetan) is spoken. The Chuang are the largest minority race in China. Though Chuang was once written in a mixture of borrowed Chinese characters (e.g., 可, 隆) and Chuang characters (e.g., 跖, 荟, 名), it is now written in Latin script with the additional letters Ƃ, ƌ, ə, ŋ, ɵ, and ɯ, but without j, q, w, x, and z. The Chuang alphabet also contains five letters for tones: ƨ (2nd tone), з (3rd tone), ч (4th tone), ƽ (5th tone), and ƅ (6th tone). These letters for tones are placed after each syllable, while the absence of any letter for tone indicates the 1st tone; thus, 南宁 *nanning* is spelled "Namƨ niŋƨ."

Ningsia [宁夏 *ningshia*] In the Ningsia Moslem autonomous region, Chinese is spoken as in other Chinese areas, though the inhabitants are pious Moslems and constitute a minority race.

Sinkiang [شىنجاڭ *shinjang*; 新疆 *shinchiang*] In the Sinkiang Uighur autonomous region, Uighur (Turkish/Altaic) and Kazakh (Turkish/Altaic) are spoken; both are written in Arabic script. The Arabic alphabet for Uighur consists of thirty letters, adding ئا *a*, ئە *e*, پ *p*, چ *ch*, ژ *j*, گ *g*, ڭ *ng*, ۋ *v*, ئۇ *u*, ې *e*, and ى *i*, and excluding ث, ح, ذ, ص, ض, ط, ظ, and ع. This Arabic writing system expresses vowels completely. Recently, Latin script has also been used for Uighur and Kazakh.

Tibet [བོད་ཡུལ་ *pho-yul*; 西藏 *shītsang*] In the Tibetan autonomous region, Tibetan is used generally. Tibetan (Tibeto-Burman/Sino-Tibetan) is written in its own script (page 88).

HONGKONG [香港 *xoṅkong*]

Daily newspapers are published in Chinese and in English. The Chinese newspapers are printed in original-form (i.e., unsimplified) Chinese characters printed vertically.

A postage stamp from Hongkong.

JAPAN [日本, ニッポン *nippon*; にほん *nihon*]

Daily newspapers are mostly published in Japanese (Japanese/Altaic) which is written in Japanese Kana script mixed with Chinese characters printed from top to bottom in vertical columns shifting from right to left. The standard group of Chinese characters used for Japanese is the so-called Toyo Kanji (当用漢字), which is explained on page 86; Japanese Kana script is explained on page 94. In Japan a few newspapers are also issued in Korean and in English.

A Japanese postage stamp.

KOREA, NORTH [朝鮮, 조선 *choson*]

Korean (Korean/Altaic) is the official language and is written in Korean script or Hangul, which is explained on page 92. In North Korea, newspapers are printed in Korean script from left to right on horizontal lines; Chinese characters are not mixed. The formal name of North Korea is 조선민주주의인민공화국, which is read as *choson minjujuwi inmingoṅhwaguk* and means Democratic People's Republic of Korea.

KOREA, SOUTH [大韓民國, 대한민국 *tehan minguk*]

The official language is Korean. Newspapers are published in Korean and in English. Korean newspapers are printed from top to bottom in vertical columns which shift from right to left and also contain original-form Chinese characters.

A Korean postage stamp.

MONGOLIA [МОНГОЛ, ᠮᠣᠩᠭᠣᠯ *moṅgol*]

Formerly, Outer Mongolia. The official language is Mongolian, which has been written in Russian script with the additional letters ө and ү since 1941. Newspapers are published in Mongolian with Russian script, but traditional Mongolian script is also in daily use.

A postage stamp from Mongolia. The Mongolian script on the left shows *moṅgol un unen.*

TAIWAN [臺灣 *taiwan*]

Daily newspapers are published in Chinese and in English. The Chinese newspapers are printed in original-form Chinese characters and are written from top to bottom, in columns shifting from right to left. The name on postage stamps issued on Taiwan is 國民華中, which is read from right to left as *chuṅhuaminkuo* and means Republic of China.

A postage stamp from Taiwan.

Chinese Characters

Chinese characters (sometimes called picto-grams or ideograms) are unique because of their special system of construction, their long history, their irregular pronunciations, and the many thousands which are used.

Construction Each Chinese character consists of one or more elements. Those consisting of one element are generally pictographic characters: 月 (moon), 女 (woman), 山 (mountain), 木 (tree). A few are symbolic: 三 (three), 上 (above), 本 (origin; the character represents the base of a tree).

In most characters consisting of two or more elements, one element indicates the phonetic value and the other the general category. Elements are juxtaposed in various ways: right and left, above and below, around and center, and so on:

被 *pi* (suffer) = 衣 or 衤 (cloth) + 皮 *pi*
裏 *ri* (reverse) = 衣 (cloth) + 里 *ri*
袋 *tai* (sack) = 衣 (cloth) + 代 *tai*

Some characters are produced by two or more pictographic elements:

明 (bright) = 日 (sun) + 月 (moon)
森 (forest) = 木 (tree) + 木 (tree) + 木 (tree)
困 (be in trouble) = 木 (tree) growing in a □ (box)

Three forms There are three forms of Chinese characters in general use. Original-form characters on the whole contain more strokes and are more clearly pictorial. They have hardly changed at all since early times. Japanese characters for daily use (called the Toyo Kanji) are of simpler construction. The most simplified forms are those developed on the mainland in recent years to speed up the educational process. Some characters in all three systems are the same. The chart gives examples of characters that differ.

Forms			Sounds			Def.
Orig.	Jap.	Simp.	Chinese	Japanese	Korean	
廣	広	广	*kuang*	*ko* *hiro-i*	*kwang*	wide
與	与	与	*yu*	*yo* *ata-eru*	*yo*	give
習	習	习	*shi*	*shu* *nara-u*	*sup*	learn
鬪	闘	斗	*tou*	*to* *tataka-u*	*thu*	fight
專	専	专	*chuan*	*sen* *moppa-ra*	*chon*	solely
勸	勧	劝	*chhuan*	*kan* *susu-meru*	*kwon*	advise
讀	読	读	*tou*	*doku* *yo-mu*	*tok*	read

Sounds Chinese characters are read with sounds that vary according to the language or dialect which uses them. In Japanese most characters have two or more sounds; "On" sounds are derived from original Chinese; "Kun" sounds express native Japanese words.

Meanings The meanings represented by Chinese characters are generally constant, despite the varying pronunciations given them in different languages. Some have of course changed due to historical influences.

Reading and punctuation Chinese characters are traditionally written from top to bottom in a vertical line that shifts from right to left, but nowadays many texts are written from left to right on a horizontal line. In Taiwan articles in the same newspaper may be written on a horizontal line from right to left or from left to right with no indication. There are no spaces between words. The mark 〔。〕 is a period, and 〔、〕 is a comma, but 〔. 〕 and 〔, 〕 are also used in horizontal sentences.

Numerals

一	二	三	四	五	六	七	八	九	十	百	千
1	2	3	4	5	6	7	8	9	10	100	1,000

Arabic figures are now commonly used when Chinese characters are written horizontally.

人民日報

RENMIN RIBAO

1980年5月
8
星期四
庚申年三月二十四
北京地区天气预报
白天 晴间多云
风向 偏北转南风
风力 二、三级
夜间 晴间多云
风向 偏北
风力 一、二级
温度 最高 23°
最低 9°

我国党政代表团吊唁铁托总统逝世

南斯拉夫党政领导人会见我代表团

新华社贝尔格莱德五月六日电 以中共中央主席、国务院总理华国锋为团长的中国党政代表团六日下午抵达贝尔格莱德后立即前往联邦议会大厦会见南斯拉夫党政领导人，对约·布·铁托总统逝世表示哀悼。

南斯拉夫联邦主席团主席科利舍夫斯基、南共联盟中央主席团执行主席多罗尼斯基、联邦执行委员会主席久拉诺维奇、南共联盟中央主席团委员米洛什·米尼奇、联邦主席团秘书长伊·多尔尼查尔等同志会见了中国党政代表团。

会见时，华国锋同志首先代表中国人民、中国共产党和中国政府为铁托同志不幸逝世向南斯拉夫人民、南共联盟和南斯拉夫政府表示最沉痛哀悼。

华国锋同志向科利舍夫斯基同志递交了中国党政代表团的悼词。

会见时，双方进行了亲切友好的谈话。

会见结束后，华国锋同志在铁托总统的吊唁簿上题词："伟大的马克思主义者、杰出的无产阶级革命家、反法西斯战争的著名英雄、不结盟运动的创始人、南斯拉夫人民敬爱的领袖、中国人民尊敬的朋友铁托同志永垂不朽！"中国党政代表团团员姬鹏飞、张海峰、周秋野也在题词后面签了字。

新华社贝尔格莱德五月六日电 中国党政代表团今晚向铁托总统遗体敬献了花圈。

铁托同志的灵柩安放在联邦议会大厦的中央大厅里。晚七时三十分，华国锋同志和中国党政代表团其他成员缓步进入庄严、肃穆的议会大厦中央大厅。中国党政代表团在灵柩前敬献了花圈。花圈的缎带上写着："约瑟普·布罗兹·铁托同志永垂不朽 中国党政代表团敬献"

中国党政代表团全体同志在铁托同志的灵柩前默哀一分钟。

华国锋同志递交代表团的悼词

对铁托同志逝世表示最沉痛的哀悼

新华社贝尔格莱德五月六日电 中国党政代表团团长华国锋五月六日下午在贝尔格莱德向南斯拉夫联邦主席团主席科利舍夫斯基递交了中国党政代表团对铁托同志逝世的悼词。悼词全文如下：

中国党政代表团对铁托同志逝世的悼词

公里的土地上第一次建立起各族人民友爱团结的社会主义新国家。铁托同志领导南斯拉夫共产主义者联盟，创造性地把马克思主义同本国实际相结合，建立了一套适合本国情况的社会主义自治制度，战胜了国内外各种敌对势力的破坏和颠覆，为维护国家的独立、主

图为朱德、周恩来、毛泽东、刘少奇同志在一起。

加强党的建设是搞好军队工作的关键

全军政治工作会议提出，要充分发挥党委核心领导、党支部战斗堡垒和党员的先锋模范作用，来带动全军各项工作

新华社北京五月七日电 要把现代化革命军队建设搞上去，一定要加强党的建设，充分发挥各级党委核心领导作用、党支部战斗堡垒作用和共产党员的先锋模范作用，来带动军队各方面的工作。这是最近召开的全军政治工作会议的中心议题。

四月二十九日，中共中央主席、中央军委主席华国锋到会讲了话。耿飚、韦国清、张廷发、杨得志、韩先楚、杨勇、王平、肖克、张爱萍、张震、迟浩田、梁必业、傅钟、甘渭汉、黄玉昆、颜金生、朱云谦、史进前、华楠、洪学智、李耀文、高厚良、宋承志、金如柏、李水清、陈鹤桥、黄新廷、莫文骅、谭善和、陈再道、吕正操、周泰和、相炜、段苏权、林浩、唐亮、陈漫远、李聚奎、秦基伟、梅嘉生、黎光等出席会议。

华国锋同志说，这次会议着重研究在军队中坚持和改善党的领导，提高党的战斗力问题，抓住了当前军队政治工作的关键。他说，全党工作着重点转移以后，我们面临着社会主义现代化、包括国防现代化的任务，迫切需要通过强有力的政治工作，保证党的路线和方针政策的执行。他重申，在四化建设的新的历史时期，政治工作仍然是经济工作的生命线，也是军队工作的生命线。

华国锋同志指出，加强政治工作就要开展兴无灭资的教育和斗争。 （下转第四版）

A newspaper published on mainland China, written horizontally and in simplified-form Chinese characters. Its title is 人民日報 *renmin ripao*.

中華民國六十五年五月二日 中央日報 星期日

中央日報

行政院新聞局出版事業登記證局版臺報字第〇〇一八號 地址臺北市忠孝西路一段八三號

中華郵政第一四八號執照登記爲第一類新聞紙類 今日三大張每份二元五角 郵區一〇〇

CENTRAL DAILY NEWS

北平俄「使館」被炸事件 實係青年抗暴壯舉

圖造成匪俄緊張困擾匪新頭目

携帶炸藥青年多在混鬥中犧牲

〔合衆國際社東京一日電〕一家日本報紙今天說，對於在北平的蘇俄「大使館」的攻擊，似乎是一種「自殺行爲」，目的在引起中共和蘇俄間的緊張情勢，藉以使中共的「新領導階層」處於困境。

「朝日新聞」在一則北平電訊中並說，前天炸死蘇俄「大使館」前面兩名中共警衛的爆炸事件，可被視爲對於繼續對已被免職的「副總理」鄧小平進行抨擊一事所作的一項「對抗行動」。

該報說，約有五、六個中國青年嘗試攜帶着炸藥進入「大使館」的大門，但三名守衛「大使館」的中共「解放軍」士兵攔阻他們，於是一場混鬥隨即發生。該報說，在混鬥之中，炸藥爆炸，擊斃了兩名警衛，這些青年大都也被炸死。

該報說，炸藥非常强烈，死者的傷殘肢體散在於「大使館」場地上，窗玻璃破碎，在大約一百八十英尺之外的「大使館」大廳的牆壁也被炸壞。

世盟亞盟聯合大會 昨在韓國揭幕

朴正熙促自由國家加强團結

〔中央社漢城一日專電〕爲期三天的世界反共聯盟與亞洲人民反共聯盟聯合大會，今天上午在汝矣島的國會大廈舉行，共有來自六十六個國家和數個世界反共組織的兩百多位代表與會。

繼新任世盟主席與韓國反共聯盟主席林炳稷以及世盟榮譽主席谷正綱發表揭幕致詞後（谷氏致詞要點刊第二版），美國衆議員黑變也曾在揭幕式中發表演說。中華民國總統嚴家淦的賀詞，由中華民國首席代表……

臺省議會舉行酒會 慶祝成立卅年

互勉爲共同目標努力

A newspaper published in Taiwan written vertically in original-form Chinese characters. Headlines are written horizontally from right to left. Its title, written vertically, is 中央日報 *tsuṅyang ripao*.

Tibetan Script

Tibetan script is descended from the Indian scripts and can be understood by using the principles of the Indian writing system. Since the Tibetan language is monosyllabic, however, the spelling construction in Tibetan script is different from that in Indian scripts, which are used to represent polysyllabic languages.

Alphabet

ཀ	ཁ	ག	ང	ཅ	ཆ	ཇ	ཉ
ka	*kha*	*ga*	*nga*	*cha*	*chha*	*ja*	*nya*
ཏ	ཐ	ད	ན	པ	ཕ	བ	མ
ta	*tha*	*da*	*na*	*pa*	*pha*	*ba*	*ma*
ཙ	ཚ	ཛ	ཝ	ཞ	ཟ	འ	ཡ
tsa	*tsa*	*za*	*wa*	*sha*	*za*	*'a*	*ya*
ར	ལ	ཤ	ས	ཧ		ཨ	
ra	*la*	*sha*	*sa*	*ha*		*a*	

ཨ *a* is the only independent vowel.

There are also five additional letters for borrowed words:

ཊ	ཋ	ཌ	ཎ	ཥ
ṭa	*ṭha*	*ḍa*	*ṇa*	*sha*

The forms of these cerebral letters are the reverse of those of the similarly pronounced dental letters that appear in the table above.

Vowel signs

◌ -*a* ◌ི -*i* ◌ུ -*u* ◌ེ -*e* ◌ོ -*o*

For the letter ཀ *ka*: ཀི *ki*, ཀུ *ku*, ཀེ *ke*, ཀོ *ko*. Independent vowels can be shown by attaching these vowel signs to the letter ཨ *a*: ཨི *i*, ཨུ *u*, ཨེ *e*, ཨོ *o*.

In Tibetan originally there were no long vowels, but when they are necessary for Sanskrit or other languages, འ *ha* is written small at the bottom: ཨཱ *ā*, ཨཱི *ī*, ཀཱ *kā*, གཱེ *gē*, མཱོ *mō*.

Conjunct consonants Three preceding consonants (ར *ra*, ལ *la*, and ས *sa*) are written above succeeding consonants: ལྐ *lka*, སྐ *ska*. A preceding ར *ra* changes its form to ◌: རྐ *rka* (but རྙ *rnya*).

Succeeding consonants (ཡ *ya*, ར *ra*, ལ *la*, ཝ *wa*, and ཧ *ha*) are written beneath preceding consonants: ཀླ *kla*, གྷ *gha*. A succeeding *ya* changes its form to ◌ྱ, ར *ra* to ◌ྲ, and ཝ *wa* to ◌ྭ: རྐྱ *rkya*, ཀྲ *kra*, ཀྲུ *kru*, ཀྭ *kwa*.

Other conjunct consonants: ཀྵ *ksha*, ངྐ *ngka*, ཎྞ *nna*, ནྡ *nda*, དྡྷ *ddha*.

Reading, other signs, and punctuation Tibetan script runs from left to right on a horizontal line, with a special sign (་) (tseg) placed between each syllable. A Tibetan syllable consists of from one to four letters, of which one is basic. Signs of vowels and consonants are attached to the basic letter, and the other letters lose the inherent *a*-sounds: མིག་ *mig*. If a syllable is to end in an *a* sound, འ is added at the end: དག་ *dag*, but དགའ་ *dga*. Tibetan pronunciations frequently do not reflect their spellings due to the silence of all consonants except the base: for example, བརྒྱད་ is pronounced *gye* though it is spelled *ba-rgya-da*. Such spellings reflect the fact that Tibetan spelling has changed very little in the 1,300 years since the 7th century when Tibetan script originated.

A postage stamp from Bhutan.

(།) was a comma, and (༎) was a period. Nowadays, (,) and (.) are used.

༄༅༅ or ༄༅ was an ornament placed at the beginning of a text or sutra. ༈ was placed at the beginning of written charms.

Numerals

༡	༢	༣	༤	༥	༦	༧	༨	༩	༠
1	2	3	4	5	6	7	8	9	0

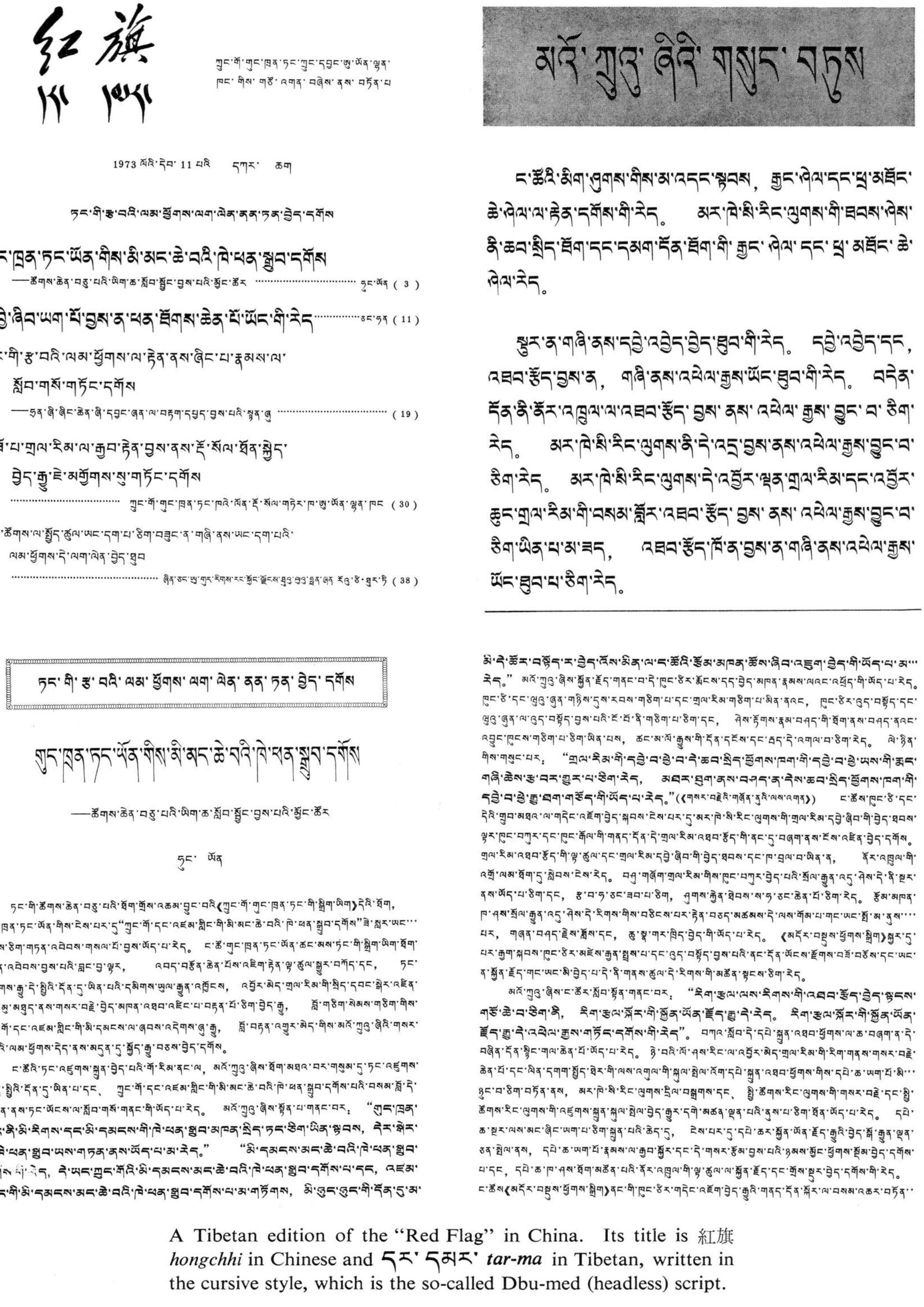

A Tibetan edition of the "Red Flag" in China. Its title is 紅旗 *hongchhi* in Chinese and དར་དམར་ *tar-ma* in Tibetan, written in the cursive style, which is the so-called Dbu-med (headless) script.

Mongolian Script

Mongolian script traces its origin to ancient Aramaic script via Sogdian and Uighur scripts. It has a pure phonemic system and has an impressive appearance because of the vertical line of each word.

Alphabet The table at right gives the usual Mongolian alphabet. There is no distinction between capital and small letters but there are three forms: initial, medial, and final. Sometimes, the same form is used for different letters, according to the position; for example, initial ᠭ is *g* but final ᠶ is *y*; initial ᠪ is *b* but final ᠪ is *o*; ᠨ is *n* but when doubled becomes ᠩ *g*. Mongolian vowels are classified as masculine, feminine, and neuter; masculine and feminine vowels should never appear together in one word. This is called the principle of vowel harmony, and it allows readers to distinguish between vowels whose medial or final forms are the same.

ᠢ *i* is written ᠢ after a vowel: ᠠᠢᠯ *ail.* ᠧ or ᠧ *e* is used in foreign words: ᠯᠧᠨᠢᠨ *lenin.* The final form ᠠ is *a* or *e* after a consonant, while it is *n* after a vowel: ᠨᠠ *na*, ᠤᠨ *un.* ᠠ is written after ᠪ and ᠫ with ᠠ inserted: ᠪᠠ *ba.*

ᠠ is also written separately after the final forms of ᠬ *q*, ᠭ *g*, ᠶ *y*, ᠮ *m*, ᠨ *n*, and ᠷ *r*: ᠬᠠ *qa*, ᠭᠠ *ga*, ᠮᠠ *ma*, ᠨᠠ *na.*

Preceding ᠺ *k* or *g*, ᠪ *b*, and ᠫ *p* enfold ᠣ *o*: ᠺᠣ *ko*, ᠪᠣ *bo*, ᠫᠣ *po.*

The final form ᠣ *o* is used in foreign words: ᠲᠣᠭᠣ *togo.*

The medial form of feminine *o* ᠥ is used in first syllables, that is, as the second letter of a word. In other places the medial form of *o* is written as ᠣ because, by the principle of vowel harmony, there is no confusion with masculine *o*.

In masculine words ᠬ *q* or ᠭ *g* is used, while in feminine words ᠭ is used for *k* or *g*. The medials ᠨ and ᠩ lose their dots when they are before a consonant or at the end of a syllable: ᠨᠠᠭᠵᠢᠭᠠᠷ *nagjigar.*

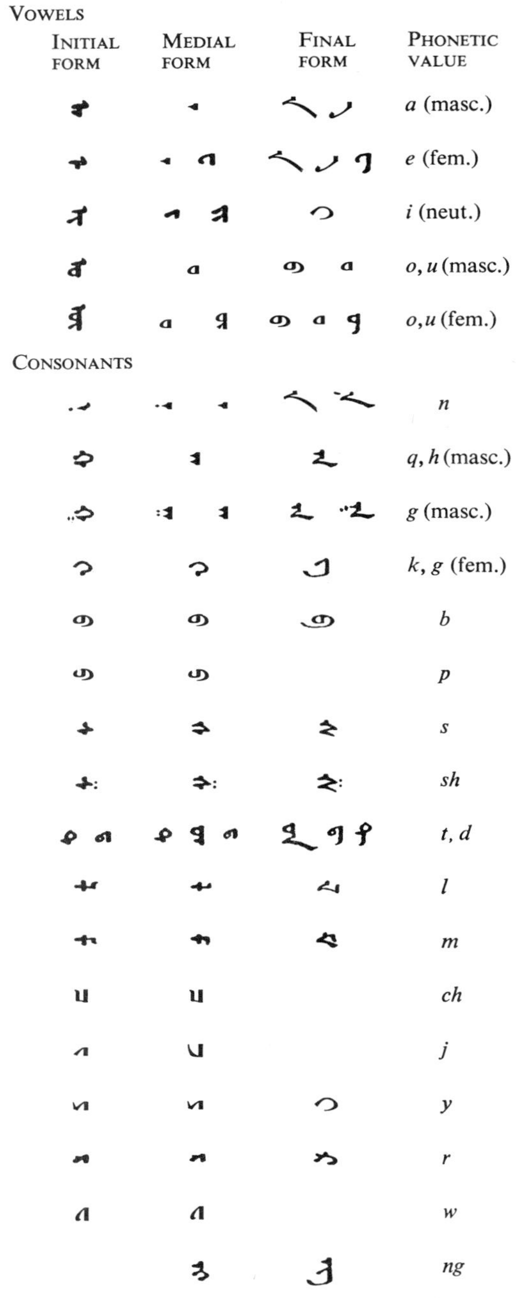

A Mongolian newspaper from Inner Mongolia in China. Its title is ᠥᠪᠥᠷ ᠮᠣᠩᠭᠣᠯ ᠤᠨ ᠡᠳᠦᠷ ᠤᠨ ᠰᠣᠨᠢᠨ *obor mon̆gol un edur un sonin.*

There is no distinction between ᠲ and ᠳ *t* or *d* in pure mongol words, but in foreign words ᠲ is always *t* and ᠳ is *d*. In the medial form ᠳ precedes a vowel, while ᠳ precedes a consonant or appears at the end of a syllable, and is read always *d*.

ᠴ *ch*, ᠵ *j*, and ᠸ *w* seldom appear at the end of a word.

Additional letters The letters ᠹ *f*, ᠺ *k*, ᠼ *ts*, ᠽ ts, and ᠾ *h* are used for foreign words.

Reading and punctuation Mongolian script runs from top to bottom on vertical columns shifting from left to right, with a space between each word. In Mongolian punctuation, ᠀ shows the beginning of a text, 〔᠂〕 is used as a comma, 〔᠃〕 is a period, and 〔᠉〕 is put at the end of a chapter.

Numerals

᠑	᠒	᠓	᠔	᠕	᠖	᠗	᠘	᠙	᠐
1	2	3	4	5	6	7	8	9	0

Korean Script

Korean script or Hangul uses a peculiar system in which one syllabic letter consists of a consonant sign or signs and a vowel sign in its original form. Such a syllabary is unique in the world. Korean script was devised in 1443 by King Sejong, and modern Korean script differs little from it. Korean letters are divided into two categories: element signs (phonemes) and combined scripts (syllabics). One Korean syllabic consists of a consonant element, a vowel element, and sometimes one or more final consonant elements.

Consonant elements The basic signs are:

ㄱ	ㄴ	ㄷ	ㄹ	ㅁ	ㅂ	ㅅ
g,k	*n*	*d,t*	*r,l*	*m*	*b,p*	*s, sh*
ㅇ	ㅈ	ㅊ	ㅋ	ㅌ	ㅍ	ㅎ
〔'〕, *ng*	*j,ch*	*chh*	*kh*	*th*	*ph*	*h*

ㄱ *g*, ㄷ *d*, ㅂ *b*, and ㅈ *j* at the beginning of a word are, respectively, heard as *k*, *t*, *p*, and *ch* by non-Korean speakers.
ㅇ at the top of a syllabic is a base for vowels; thus, 아 is not *nga* but *a*.
Double-element signs:

	ㄲ	ㄸ	ㅃ	ㅆ	ㅉ
(strong)	*'k*	*'t*	*'p*	*'s*	*'ch*

Vowel elements The basic signs are:

ㅏ	ㅑ	ㅓ	ㅕ	ㅗ	ㅛ	ㅜ	ㅠ	ㅡ	ㅣ
a	*ya*	*o*	*yo*	*o*	*yo*	*u*	*yu*	*u*	*i*

Combined vowel signs are:

ㅐ	ㅒ	ㅔ	ㅖ	ㅚ	ㅟ	ㅢ	ㅘ	ㅝ	ㅙ	ㅞ
e	*ye*	*e*	*ye*	*o*	*i*	*wi*	*wa*	*wo*	*we*	*we*

Combination of elements Each letter of Korean script consists of two or more elements. The way of combining two elements (a consonant and a vowel) is determined by the form of each vowel element. This is shown here for the consonant ㄱ *k*:

가	갸	거	겨	고	교	구	규	그
ka	*kya*	*ko*	*kyo*	*ko*	*kyo*	*ku*	*kyu*	*ku*
기	개	걔	게	계	괴	귀	긔	과
ki	*ke*	*kye*	*ke*	*kye*	*ko*	*ki*	*kwi*	*kwa*
궈	괘	궤						
kwo	*kwe*	*kwe*						

Independent vowels are expressed by the sign ㅇ (silent) and a vowel element: 아 *a*, 이 *i*, 우 *u*, 에 *e*, 오 *o*.
Examples of syllabics containing the vowel ㅗ *o* are:

고	노	도	로	모	보	소	오	조	초
ko	*no*	*to*	*ro*	*mo*	*po*	*so*	*o*	*cho*	*chho*
코	토	포	호	꼬	또	뽀	쏘	쪼	
kho	*tho*	*pho*	*ho*	*'ko*	*'to*	*'po*	*'so*	*'cho*	

By adding a final consonant, which consists of one or two elements, to the combined letters, other syllabics can be made.

각	간	갇	갈	감	갑	갓	강	갖
kak	*kan*	*kat*	*kal*	*kam*	*kap*	*kat*	*kang*	*kat*
갗	같	갚	갛	갉	값	갔		
kat	*kat*	*kap*	*ka'*	*kak*	*kap*	*kat*		

The number of possible combinations of two or more elements is enormous, but about 2,300 movable types suffice for Korean printing because some combinations are not actually used.

Reading and punctuation Korean script is written, often in a mixture of Chinese characters, in syllables arranged from top to bottom in vertical columns shifting from right to left, with a space between each word. At present, however, many Korean texts are written from left to right on a horizontal line and without Chinese characters. The mark 〔。〕 is a period and 〔、〕 is a comma in vertical texts, while 〔.〕 and 〔,〕 are used in horizontal texts.

Numerals Korean script has no numerals; Chinese characters or Arabic figures are used instead.

위대한 수령 김일성동지께 무한히 충직한 혁명전사가 되자!

로동청년

조선사회주의로동청년동맹 중앙위원회기관지

제38호 [루계 제6744호] 1974년 2월 23일 (토요일)

전체 청년들은 조국의 통일과 혁명을 위하여 당과 수령을 목숨으로 보위하며 수령의 명령지시 관철에서 근위대, 결사대가 되자!

경애하는 수령 김일성동지께서

재일본조선인총련합회 제10차전체대회앞으로 축하문을 보내시였다

축 하 문

재일본조선인총련합회 제10차전체대회 앞

조선로동당 중앙위원회 총비서

조선민주주의인민공화국 주석

김 일 성

1974년 2월 23일

A newspaper published in **North Korea**. It is written horizontally **without Chinese characters. Its title is** 로동청년 *rodong chhongnyon.*

The Seoul Shinmun 1977年6月3日 (金曜日) 第9985號 [日刊]

서울신문

모범援護對象者 55명 포상

崔總理 致辭 "愛國精神을 體現한 산 龜鑑"

政府發注 공사 늦지않게 補完

崔總理 지시…庶政刷新 무준히

2년제 技能大學 설립

經濟閣議 法案의결 1차로 79년 昌原에

기존大學 일부 人文

文敎部, 對象校 報告 지시

에너지協議機構 설치에 失敗

파리 南北會談 共同聲明 開發國부채輕減등 4項만 合意

朴大統領 예방 케냐國會議長

駐韓美地 防衛계획

A newspaper published in South Korea. It is written vertically and contains Chinese characters. Its title is 서울신문 *soul shinmun.*

Japanese (Kana) Script

Modern Japanese writing is a mixture of Chinese characters and two different Japanese scripts, Katakana and Hiragana. These scripts are the only two pure syllabaries extant today. All of the symbols, except the single vowel letters and *n*, represent a single consonant sound followed by a single vowel sound.

Katakana Katakana is an angular script which is most often used for borrowed words and emphasis. It is arranged in the Gojūon-jun, meaning the "order of fifty sounds."

ア	イ	ウ	エ	オ	カ	キ	ク	ケ	コ
a	*i*	*u*	*e*	*o*	*ka*	*ki*	*ku*	*ke*	*ko*
サ	シ	ス	セ	ソ	タ	チ	ツ	テ	ト
sa	*shi*	*su*	*se*	*so*	*ta*	*chi*	*tsu*	*te*	*to*
ナ	ニ	ヌ	ネ	ノ	ハ	ヒ	フ	ヘ	ホ
na	*ni*	*nu*	*ne*	*no*	*ha*	*hi*	*hu*	*he*	*ho*
マ	ミ	ム	メ	モ	ヤ	イ	ユ	エ	ヨ
ma	*mi*	*mu*	*me*	*mo*	*ya*	*i*	*yu*	*e*	*yo*
ラ	リ	ル	レ	ロ	ワ	ヰ	ウ	ヱ	ヲ
ra	*ri*	*ru*	*re*	*ro*	*wa*	*i*	*u*	*e*	*o*
ガ	ギ	グ	ゲ	ゴ	ザ	ジ	ズ	ゼ	ゾ
ga	*gi*	*gu*	*ge*	*go*	*za*	*ji*	*zu*	*ze*	*zo*
ダ	ヂ	ヅ	デ	ド	バ	ビ	ブ	ベ	ボ
da	*ji*	*zu*	*de*	*do*	*ba*	*bi*	*bu*	*be*	*bo*
パ	ピ	プ	ペ	ポ	ヴ	ン			
pa	*pi*	*pu*	*pe*	*po*	*vu*	*n*			

ヰ *i* and ヱ *e* are usually not used but are replaced by イ *i* and エ *e*.

ン *n* is a nasal sign and is pronounced *ng* (*ṅ*), *m*, or *n* depending on the succeeding consonant: テンマンジングウ *temmanjiṅgū*.

ヽ is a repeating sign: コヽ *koko*.

LONG VOWELS The sign〔｜〕is used in vertical text; it becomes〔—〕in horizontal text. It is only used in borrowed words: ボール *bōru* (ball, bowl), スター *sutā* (star).

Long vowels are usually indicated by actually writing the vowel letters contained in the sound, except *o* which is added as ウ *u*: アア *ā*, シイカ *shīka*, リュウ *ryū*, ネエサン *nēsan*, but トウリ *tōri* (not トオリ).

LETTERS WRITTEN SMALL ヤ *ya*, ユ *yu*, ヨ *yo*, and ワ *wa* are written small to express contracted sounds: キャ *kya*, キュ *kyu*, キョ *kyo*; シャ *sha*, シュ *shu*, ショ *sho*; ニャ *nya*, ニュ *nyu*, ニョ *nyo*; チャ *cha*, チュ *chu*, チョ *cho*; ミャ *mya*, ミュ *myu*, ミョ *myo*; リャ *rya*, リュ *ryu*, リョ *ryo*; ギャ *gya*, ギュ *gyu*, ギョ *gyo*; ジャ *ja*, ジュ *ju*, ジョ *jo*; ビャ *bya*, ビュ *byu*, ビョ *byo*; ピャ *pya*, ピュ *pyu*, ピョ *pyo*; クヮ *kwa*.

ツ *tsu* is sometimes written small to express double consonants: ブツダ *butsuda*, but ブッダ *budda*. Thus: カッパ *kappa*, モッコ *mokko*, キッテ *kitte*, テッサ *tessa*.

ア *a*, イ *i*, ウ *u*, エ *e*, and オ *o* are also written small to express borrowed sounds: ファ *fa*, ディ *di*, ヴィ *vi*, トゥ *tu*, チェ *che*, ツォ *tso*.

Hiragana Hiragana is a cursive script whose sounds correspond to those in Katakana. It is used in usual Japanese text together with Chinese characters. Hiragana script is arranged in the Iroha order, which by itself makes up a famous Buddhist poem.

い	ろ	は	に	ほ	へ	と	ち	り	ぬ
i	*ro*	*ha*	*ni*	*ho*	*he*	*to*	*chi*	*ri*	*nu*
る	を	わ	か	よ	た	れ	そ	つ	ね
ru	*o*	*wa*	*ka*	*yo*	*ta*	*re*	*so*	*tsu*	*ne*
な	ら	む	う	ゐ	の	お	く	や	ま
na	*ra*	*mu*	*u*	*i*	*no*	*o*	*ku*	*ya*	*ma*
け	ふ	こ	え	て	あ	さ	き	ゆ	め
ke	*hu*	*ko*	*e*	*te*	*a*	*sa*	*ki*	*yu*	*me*
み	し	ゑ	ひ	も	せ	す			
mi	*shi*	*e*	*hi*	*mo*	*se*	*su*			

Letters with two dots or a small circle on the shoulder and a nasal sign are also used: が *ga*, ぎ *gi*, ぐ *gu*, げ *ge*, ご *go*; ざ *za*, じ *ji*, ず *zu*, ぜ *ze*, ぞ *zo*; だ *da*, ぢ *ji*, づ *zu*, で *de*, ど *do*; ば *ba*, び *bi*, ぶ *bu*, べ *be*, ぼ *bo*; ぱ *pa*, ぴ *pi*, ぷ *pu*, ぺ *pe*, ぽ *po*; ん *n*.

4/18 (金曜日) 昭和55年 (1980) 日刊 13546号

サンケイ

産業経済新聞

積立ファミリー交通傷害保険

安田火災海上

イラン制裁「ECと行動」鮮明に

米要請に積極対応

防衛力増強で三原則

首相講演 外人記者クラブ

食糧、医薬品も禁輸

米、追加措置を事前通告

京都ニュース

林田体制一期目仕上げへ

企画部門の強化柱

昇任、人事交流を積極推進

サラリー

開業

A Japanese newspaper in which Chinese characters, Hiragana, Katakana, and Latin script are used. Its title is サンケイ *sankei.*

All the preceding remarks for Katakana apply to Hiragana, except those for the long sign 〔｜〕 (or 〔ー〕). The repeating sign for Hiragana is ゝ, and Hiragana, when written vertically, uses repeating signs for two letters:

ころ〱 *korokoro*　　ぼう〲 *bōbō*　　てん〲 *tenden*

Reading and punctuation All Japanese script originally ran from top to bottom on vertical lines which shifted from right to left, but now many texts are written from left to right on a horizontal line. Spaces are not used between words. In punctuation, 〔。〕 is a period and 〔、〕 is a comma. In horizontal texts 〔.〕 and 〔,〕 are also used.

Numerals Japanese script has no numerals. Chinese characters and Arabic figures are commonly used.

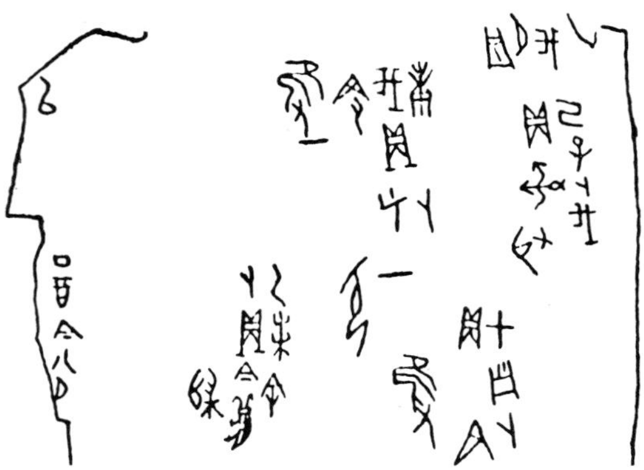

BONE-AND-SHELL SCRIPT. The writing of the ancient Yin Empire in central China (*ca.* 14th century B.C.), it shows original-form Chinese characters. (Kaizuka)

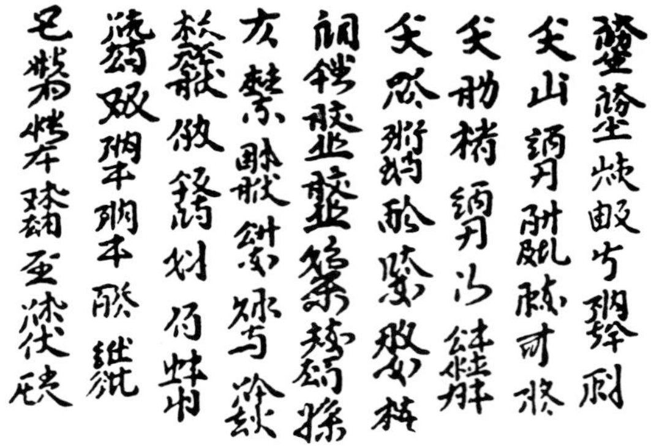

KHITAN CHARACTERS. The writing of the Liao Empire in northern China about the 10th century. Undeciphered. (Tamura)

KÖK TURKI RUNES (ORKHON SCRIPT). The writing of pre-Islamic Turkic peoples in northern China about the 6th century. (Malov)

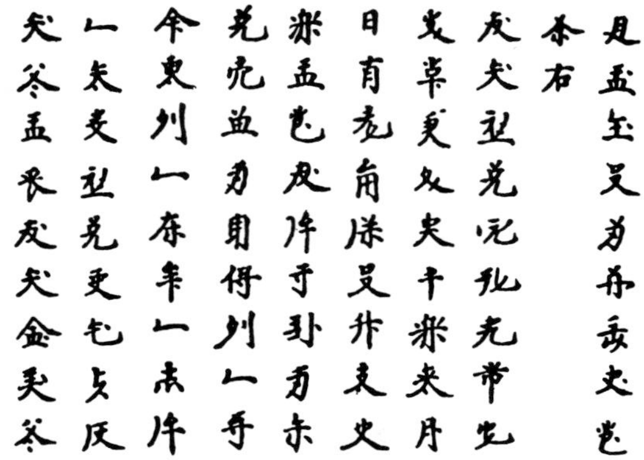

NUCHEN CHARACTERS. The writing of the Chin Empire in northern China about the 12th century. Only partly deciphered. (Old book)

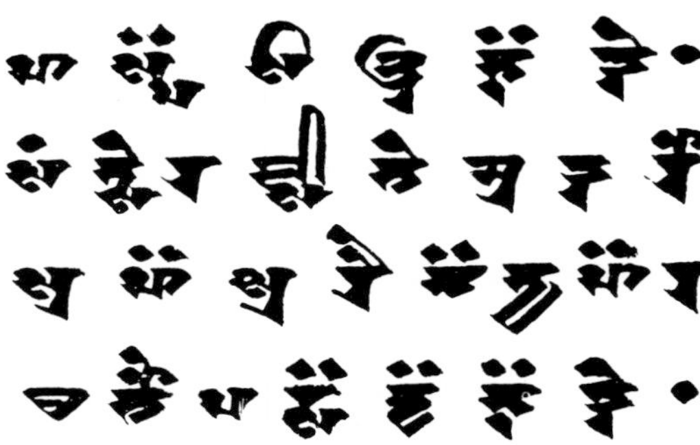

KHOTANESE SCRIPT. The writing of ancient Khotan in central Asia. It is within the genealogy of Gupta scripts. (Ishihama)

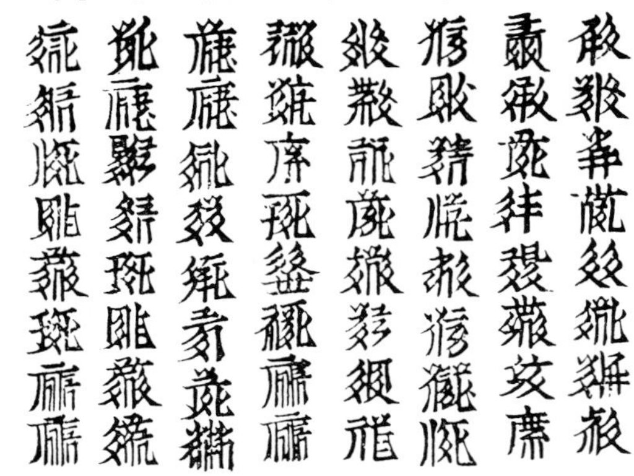

HSIHSIA CHARACTERS. The writing of the Hsihsia kingdom in western China about the 12th century. Deciphered by Dr. Tatsuo Nishida. (Nishida)

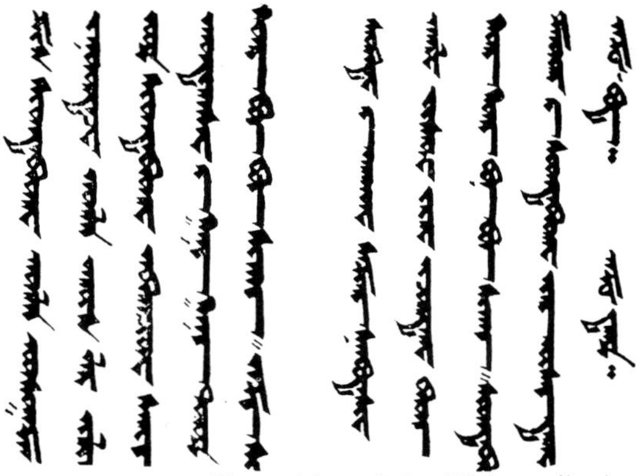

UIGHUR SCRIPT. The writing of the Uighur tribe in central Asia and western China in the medieval ages. Sometimes written horizontally. (Old book)

PASSEPA SCRIPT. Established by Kublai Khan in the 12th century as the official international script of the Great Mongolian Empire. (Ishihama)

MOSO (NASI) IDEOGRAMS. The writing of the Moso or Nasi tribe in Yunnan province in southwestern China. Very primitive, but still in use now. (Nishida)

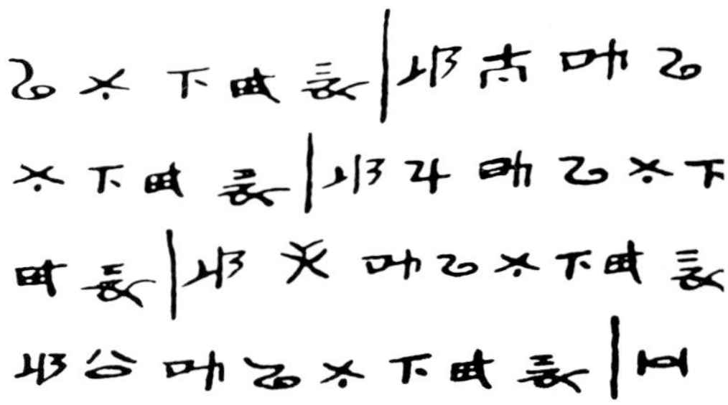

MOSO PHONETIC SCRIPT. Another Moso writing developed from their ideograms. (Rock)

LOLO SCRIPT. The writing of the Lolo tribe in Yunnan province. A kind of syllabary. (Old book)

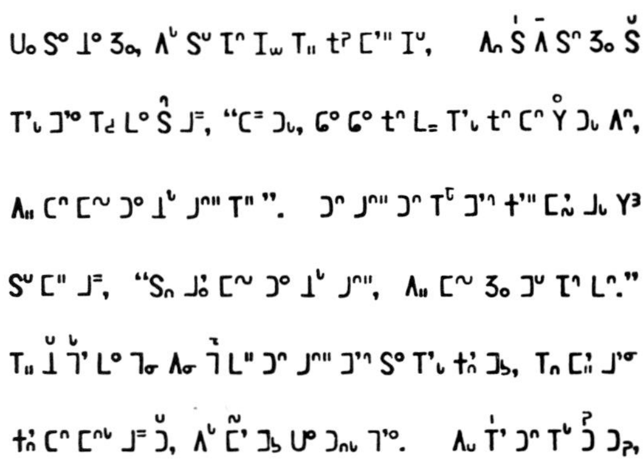

POLLARD PHONETIC SCRIPT. A syllabary invented by Samuel Pollard to write the languages of minority races in Yunnan province in the 19th century. (Nida)

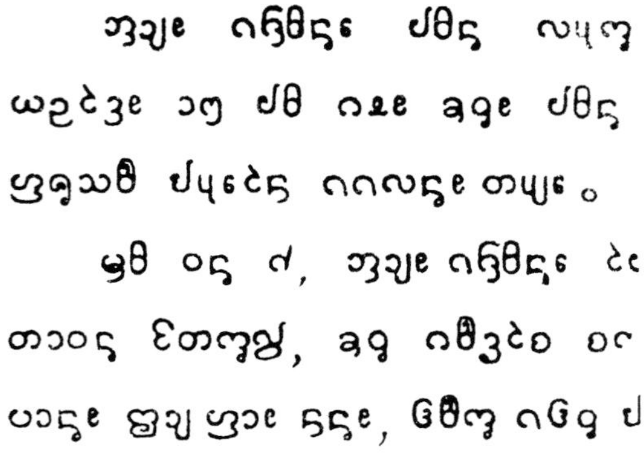

Tai Lu script. Tai Lu is a Thai tribe in southern Yunnan. Its script is similar to Lao script. (Gilyarevsky)

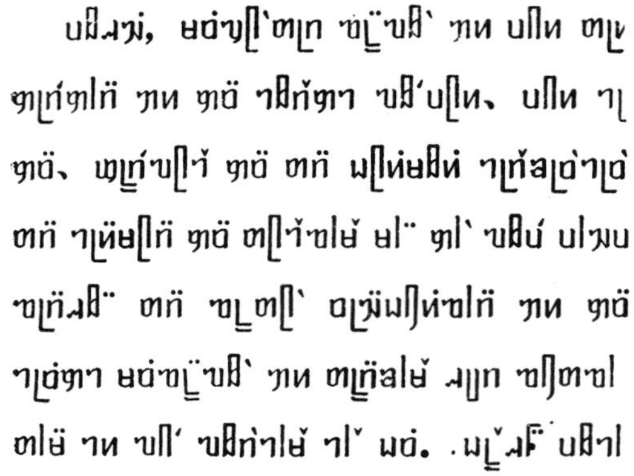

Tai Nua script. Tai Nua is a Thai tribe in southwestern Yunnan. This script was developed recently. (Author's collection)

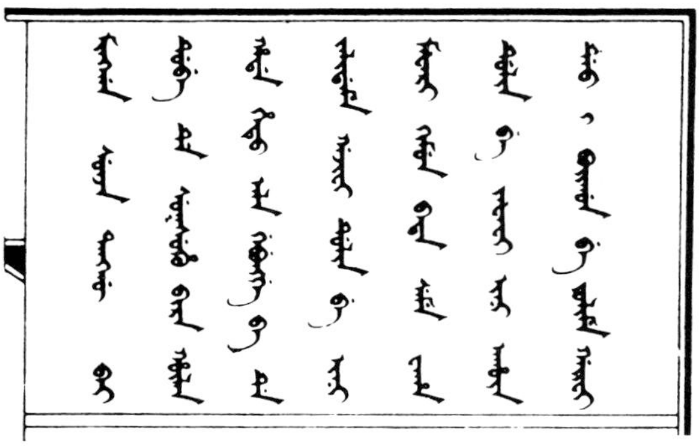

Manchu script. The official writing of the Chinese Ch'ing Empire. It is an improved form of Mongolian script. (Old book)

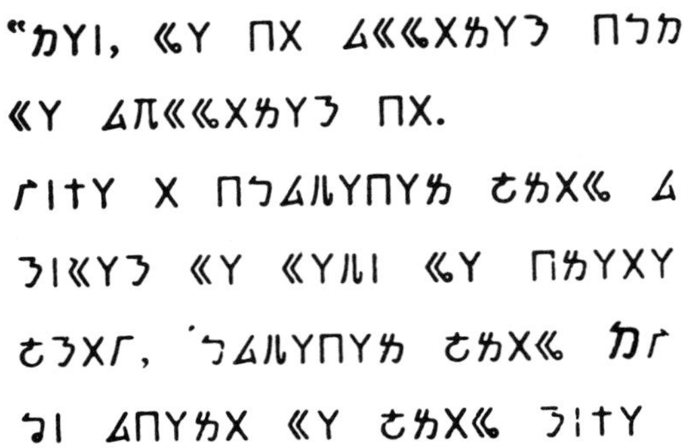

Kuoyu script. Writing adapted for native mountain tribes in Taiwan. It is based on Chu Yin phonetic script. (Nida)

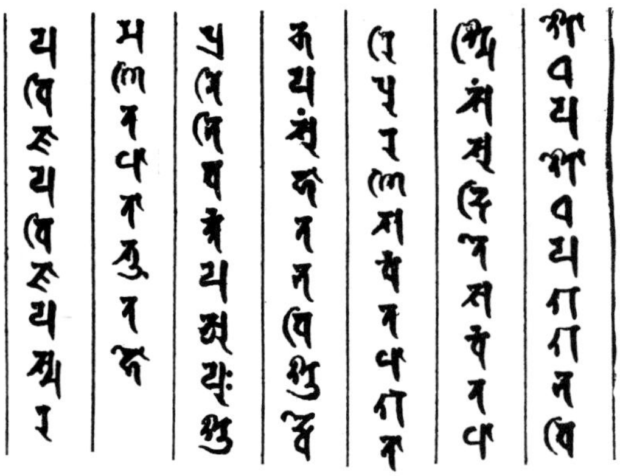

Shittan script. A variant of Indian Nagari script used by Buddhists in the Far East. It is written vertically. (Kawakatsu)

Jindai script. A script for the Japanese Shinto religion. This picture is a red seal for an amulet of a shrine. (Author's collection)

7. SCRIPTS OF AFRICA

Africa's written characters can be divided into three main zones. The first zone extends from south of the Mediterranean Sea to the Sahara, where the ancient Egyptian Empire in the east and the Phoenician colonies in the west prospered in ancient times. In the medieval ages, this area made up the territories of the Saracen Empire, and since then only the Arabic language and script have been used. A descendant of Phoenician scripts remains in the Sahara Desert.

The second zone covers Ethiopia. Southern Arabic script was introduced across the Red Sea before Christ and developed into Amharic (or Ethiopian) script, which is used to write Amharic and other Ethiopian languages.

The third zone is located south of the Sahara, so-called Black Africa, where no written characters were known until relatively modern times when Arabic and Latin scripts were introduced. In the 19th century this zone was divided into colonies governed by various European powers. Many of these former colonies have now become independent. These nations use, as their national languages, the languages of their former suzerains and their vernacular languages. In both cases Latin script is used.

ALGERIA [ALGERIE; الجزائر *al-jazā'ir*]

Newspapers are in Arabic and in French.

ANGOLA

The official language is Portuguese.

BENIN

Formerly Dahomey. Newspapers are in French and in Fon (Sudan Guinean/African).

BOTSWANA

Formerly, Bechuanaland. The official language is English.

BURUNDI

Newspapers are in French and in Swahili (Bantu/African), which was written in Arabic script before the 19th century but which is now written in Latin script without q and x.

CAMEROON [CAMEROUN]

Newspapers are in French and in English.

CENTRAL AFRICAN REPUBLIC

[REPUBLIQUE CENTRAFRICAINE]

Newspapers are published in French and in Sangs (Sudan-Guinean/African), which is written in Latin script.

CHAD [REPUBLIQUE DU TCHAD]

French is used in newspapers.

CONGO

Formerly, Brazzaville Congo. Newspapers are published in French.

EGYPT [مصر *misr*]

One of the oldest scripts, Egyptian hieroglyphics (see page 104), was invented in this country. Nowadays Arabic is used generally. Newspapers are published in Arabic, in English, and in French. The formal name on postage stamps is جمهورية مصر العربية , which means Arab Republic of Egypt (AR Egypt).

EQUATORIAL GUINEA

[GUINEA ECUATORIAL]

The official language is Spanish.

ETHIOPIA (Abyssinia) [ኢትዮጵያ *'ītyōpyā*]

The official languages of Ethiopia are English and Amharic (Southwest Semitic/Semitic-Hamitic). Newspapers are published in English, in French, in Arabic, in Amharic, in Oromo (Cushite/Semitic-Hamitic), and in Tigrinya (Southwest Semitic/Semitic-Hamitic). Amharic, Oromo, and Tigrinya are written in Amharic script, explained on page 102.

A postage stamp of Ethiopia.

GABON [REPUBLIQUE GABONAISE]

Newspapers are in French.

THE GAMBIA

Newspapers are in English.

GHANA

Formerly, Gold Coast. Most newspapers are published in English, but some are in Ewe (Sudan-Guinean/African). Ewe is written in Latin script.

GUINEA [GUINEE]

Newspapers are published in French, but some parts are printed in Mandingo (Sudan-Guinean/African) written in Latin script.

IVORY COAST [COTE D'IVOIRE]

Newspapers are published in French.

KENYA

Newspapers are in English and in Swahili.

LESOTHO

Formerly, Basutoland. The official language is English.

LIBERIA

Newspapers are published in English.

LIBYA [ليبيا *lībiya*]

Newspapers are published in Arabic only. The formal name on postage stamps is الجمهورية العربية الليبية, which means Libyan Arab Republic (LAR).

MALAGASY

Formerly, Madagascar. The official languages are French and Malagasy. Newspapers are published in both these languages. Malagasy (Indonesian/Malayo-Polynesian) is written in Latin script with the additional letters à and n'. It contains no c, j, q, u, w, or x.

MALAWI

Formerly, Nyasaland. The official languages are English and Nyanja (Bantu/African), which is written in Latin script.

MALI

Newspapers are published in French and in Bambara (Sudan-Guinean/African), which is written in Latin script. The Tuareg tribes, Saharan nomads, use Tifinagh script (see page 105), which descended from ancient Libyan script, to write their Tamahaq language (Libya-Berber/Semitic-Hamitic). Tifinagh script is not used in newspapers.

MAURITANIA [موريتانيا *mōrītāniya*]

The official languages are Arabic and French. The formal names on postage stamps are الجمهورية الاسلامية الموريتانية in Arabic, and Republique Islamique du Mauritanie in French.

MOROCCO [مراكش *marrākish*]

Newspapers are published in Arabic and in French. In Arabic, the formal name on postage stamps is المملكة المغربية (Kingdom of Maghrib), but in French it is Royaume du Maroc.

MOZAMBIQUE [MOÇAMBIQUE]

The official language is Portuguese.

NAMIBIA (Southwest Africa, SWA)
[SUIDWES AFRIKA]

The official languages are English and Afrikaans. Afrikaans (German/Indo-European) is written in Latin script with the additional letters ë, ê, and 'n, and without q.

NIGER

Newspapers are published in French.

NIGERIA

Newspapers are published in English, Yoruba (Sudan-Guinean/African), Hausa (Chad/Semitic-Hamitic), and Ibo (Sudan-Guinean/African). All of these are written in Latin script.

RWANDA [REPUBLIQUE RWANDAISE]

Newspapers are in French and in Swahili.

SAHARA

Formerly, Spanish Sahara or Rio de Oro. Arabic and Spanish are used.

SENEGAL

Newspapers are published in French, the official language.

SIERRA LEONE

Newspapers are in English, with parts in Mandingo and Temne (Sudan-Guinean/African).

SOMALIA [صوماليا *sōmāliya*; SOOMAALIYA]

The English, Arabic, Italian, and Somali languages are used. Somali (Cushite/Semitic-Hamitic) is written in Latin script, but a new script, known as Osmanya script (page 105), is being developed.

SOUTH AFRICA
[REPUBLIEK VAN SUID-AFRIKA]

The official languages are English and Afrikaans; newspapers are published in both.

SUDAN [السودان *al-sūdān*]

Newspapers are in English and in Arabic.

SWAZILAND

The official language is English.

TANZANIA

Newspapers are published in English and in Swahili.

TOGO [REPUBLIQUE TOGOLAISE]

Newspapers are published in French and in Ewe.

TUNISIA [تونس *tūnis*]

The formal name is الجمهورية التونسية in Arabic or Republique Tunisienne in French. Newspapers are published in both these languages.

UGANDA

Newspapers are in English and in Swahili.

UPPER VOLTA
[REPUBLIQUE DE HAUTE VOLTA]

Newspapers are published in French, the official language.

ZAIRE

Formerly, Kinshasa Congo. The official language is French, in which newspapers are published. Swahili newspapers are published in the north and west, and Lingala(Bantu/African) newspapers in the east and in Katanga.

ZAMBIA

Formerly, Northern Rhodesia. Newspapers are published in English, in Tonga (Bantu/African), in Nyanja, and in Bemba (Bantu/African).

ZIMBABWE

Formerly, Southern Rhodesia. Newspapers are published in English.

Amharic (Ethiopian) Script

Amharic script consists of the classical Ethiopian alphabet and additional letters adapted for the Amharic language. It is used for not only Amharic but also Oromo, Tigre, Tigrinya, and other languages in Ethiopia and Somalia. Amharic script is descended from Southern Arabic script.

Syllabary Amharic script is syllabic. The basic form contains an inherent *a*-vowel, and by slightly changing the basic forms, other syllabics are made, as shown in the table.

Letters containing *e* are also used as phonemes without a vowel.

By attaching ᐨ to the underside of some letters, syllabics containing *ua* are made: ሏ *lua*, ሷ *sua*. ቨ *va* was devised for borrowed words.

Reading and punctuation Amharic script runs horizontally from left to right, with 〔 ፡ 〕 between each word. 〔 ፣ 〕 is a comma, 〔 ፤ 〕 is a semicolon, and 〔 ። 〕 is a period.

Numerals Numerals are written with 〔 ̅ ̲ 〕.

፩	፪	፫	፬	፭	፮	፯	፰	፱	፲	፻
1	2	3	4	5	6	7	8	9	10	100

PHONETIC VALUE	*a*	*ū*	*ī*	*ā*	*ē*	*e*	*ō*
h	ሀ	ሁ	ሂ	ሃ	ሄ	ህ	ሆ
l	ለ	ሉ	ሊ	ላ	ሌ	ል	ሎ
h	ሐ	ሑ	ሒ	ሓ	ሔ	ሕ	ሖ
m	መ	ሙ	ሚ	ማ	ሜ	ም	ሞ
s	ሠ	ሡ	ሢ	ሣ	ሤ	ሥ	ሦ
r	ረ	ሩ	ሪ	ራ	ሬ	ር	ሮ
s	ሰ	ሱ	ሲ	ሳ	ሴ	ስ	ሶ
sh	ሸ	ሹ	ሺ	ሻ	ሼ	ሽ	ሾ
k	ቀ	ቁ	ቂ	ቃ	ቄ	ቅ	ቆ
b	በ	ቡ	ቢ	ባ	ቤ	ብ	ቦ
t	ተ	ቱ	ቲ	ታ	ቴ	ት	ቶ
ch	ቸ	ቹ	ቺ	ቻ	ቼ	ች	ቾ
x	ኀ	ኁ	ኂ	ኃ	ኄ	ኅ	ኆ
n	ነ	ኑ	ኒ	ና	ኔ	ን	ኖ
ny	ኘ	ኙ	ኚ	ኛ	ኜ	ኝ	ኞ
〔'〕	አ	ኡ	ኢ	ኣ	ኤ	እ	ኦ
k	ከ	ኩ	ኪ	ካ	ኬ	ክ	ኮ
kh	ኸ	ኹ	ኺ	ኻ	ኼ	ኽ	ኾ
w	ወ	ዉ	ዊ	ዋ	ዌ	ው	ዎ

PHONETIC VALUE	*a*	*ū*	*ī*	*ā*	*ē*	*e*	*ō*
〔'〕	ዐ	ዑ	ዒ	ዓ	ዔ	ዕ	ዖ
z	ዘ	ዙ	ዚ	ዛ	ዜ	ዝ	ዞ
j	ዠ	ዡ	ዢ	ዣ	ዤ	ዥ	ዦ
y	የ	ዩ	ዪ	ያ	ዬ	ይ	ዮ
d	ደ	ዱ	ዲ	ዳ	ዴ	ድ	ዶ
j	ጀ	ጁ	ጂ	ጃ	ጄ	ጅ	ጆ
g	ገ	ጉ	ጊ	ጋ	ጌ	ግ	ጎ
t	ጠ	ጡ	ጢ	ጣ	ጤ	ጥ	ጦ
chh	ጨ	ጩ	ጪ	ጫ	ጬ	ጭ	ጮ
p	ጰ	ጱ	ጲ	ጳ	ጴ	ጵ	ጶ
ts	ጸ	ጹ	ጺ	ጻ	ጼ	ጽ	ጾ
ts	ፀ	ፁ	ፂ	ፃ	ፄ	ፅ	ፆ
f	ፈ	ፉ	ፊ	ፋ	ፌ	ፍ	ፎ
p	ፐ	ፑ	ፒ	ፓ	ፔ	ፕ	ፖ
ku	ቈ		ቊ	ቋ	ቌ	ቍ	
hu	ኈ		ኊ	ኋ	ኌ	ኍ	
ku	ኰ		ኲ	ኳ	ኴ	ኵ	
gu	ጐ		ጒ	ጓ	ጔ	ጕ	

የኢ. ሠ. ፓ. አ. ኮ. ተልዕኮ ይሳካል !

አዲስ ዘመን

የኢትዮጵያ ሠርቶ አደሮች ፓርቲ ሕልውና ያገኛል !

« ኢትዮጵያ ትቅደም »

የደርግ ጠቅላላ ጉባኤ ተደረገ

ሊቀ መንበሩ ለካምፑቺያ መሪየደስታ መልእክት ላኩ

በሰላም ለመኖር ፍትሕና ርትዕን ተግባራዊ ማድረግ ያሻል ተባለ

የጭነትመኪናዎችንሽያጭ የሚመለከት ውል ተፈረመ

በውጭ ለሚገኙ ኢትዮጵያውያን አብዮታዊ ቅስቀሳ ይደረጋል

የወዳጅነት ኮሚቴ ለካምፑቺያ ሕዝብ መልእክት ላከ

የነፃዪቱ ጀርመን ወጣቶች ድርጅት የምርት ግን መጣ

የማስታወቂያ ሚ/ር የዜና ማሰራጫ ኃላፊዎች ሰሚናር ተጀመረ

የዲ.የመን ስፖርት ልዑካን ጉብኝት ፍሬያማ መሆኑ ተገለጠ

An Ethiopian newspaper published in Amharic. Its title is አዲስ ዘመን *adīs zaman.*

HIEROGLYPHICS. Ancient Egyptian ideograms established in the 31st century B.C. One of the oldest writing systems. (Wallis)

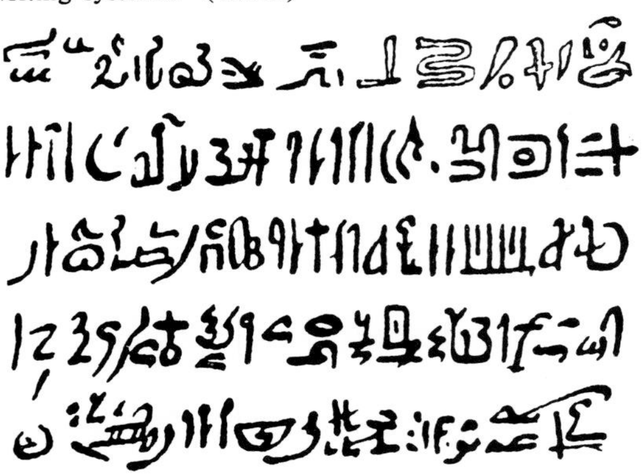

HIERATICS. A cursive style of hieroglyphic used by priests in the ancient Egyptian Empire. (Gilyarevsky)

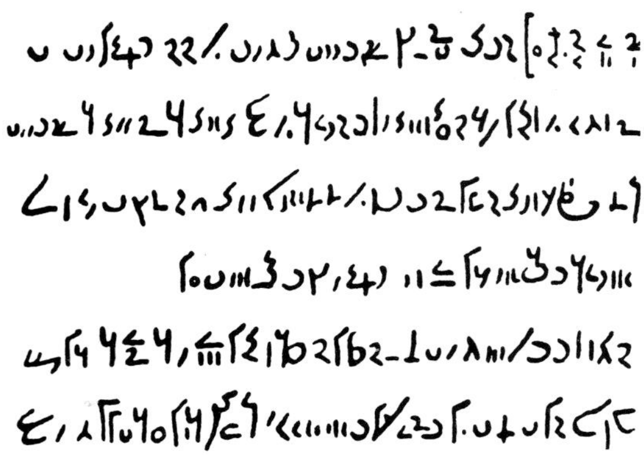

DEMOTIC. A more cursive style than Hieratic, used by the common people of the ancient Egyptian Empire. (Gilyarevsky)

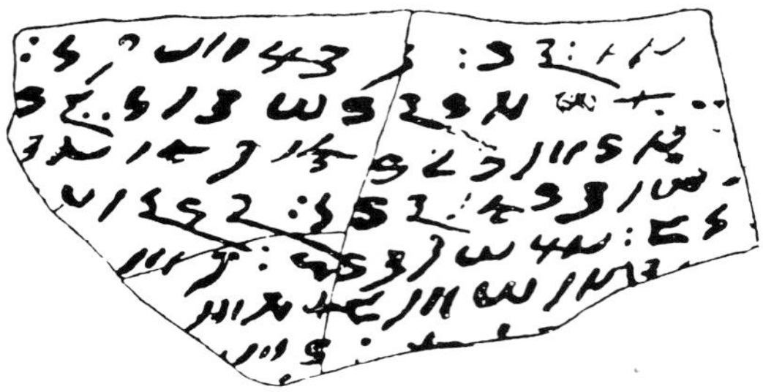

MEROITIC SCRIPT. The writing of the Nubian kingdom in the south of Egypt about the 8th century B.C. This form is one of two Meroitic scripts. (Diringer)

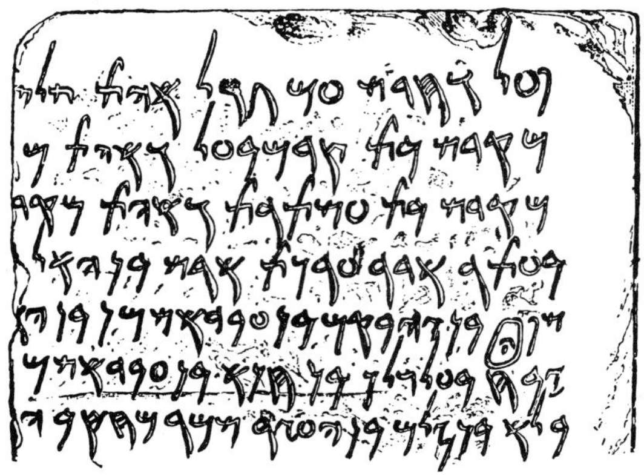

PUNIC SCRIPT. The writing of Carthage, which competed with ancient Rome. It is close to Phoenician script. (Diringer)

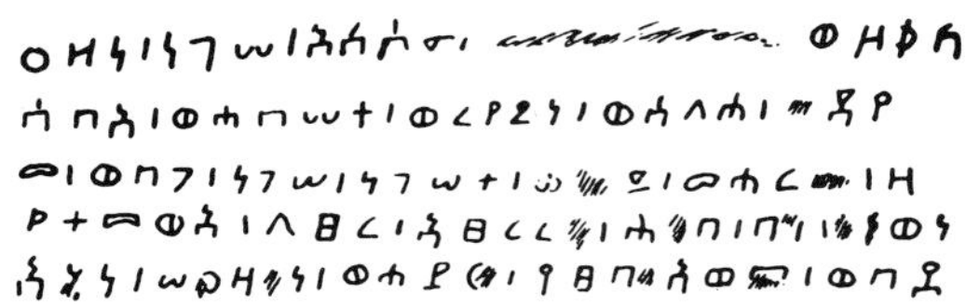

GE'EZ SCRIPT. The writing of the ancient Ethiopian Empire. It was the basis of Amharic script. (Jensen)

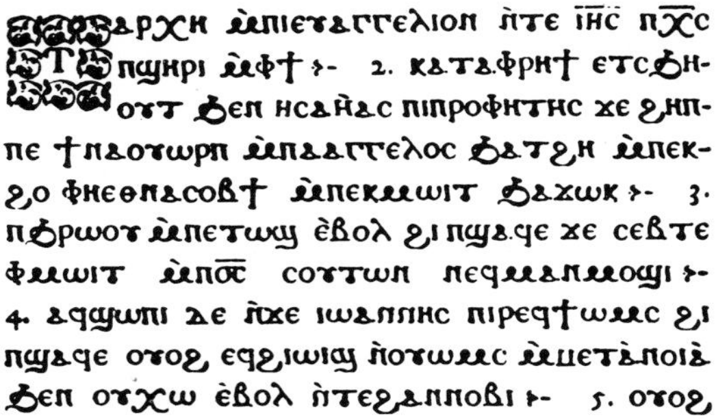

Coptic script. The writing of Egyptian Christians. It was based on Greek and Meroitic scripts. From the 2nd century. (Nida)

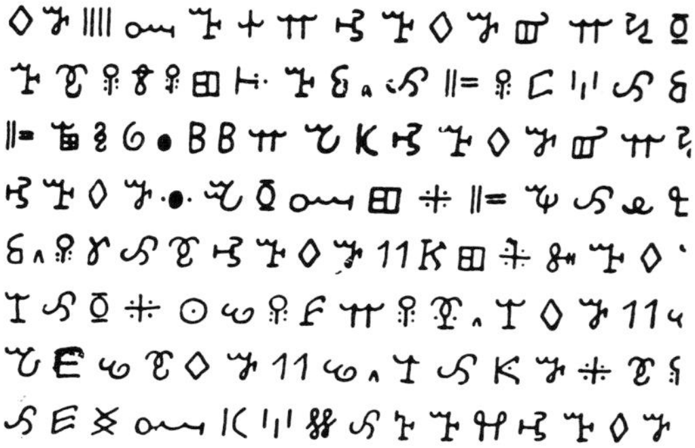

Vai script. A syllabary from Liberia in western Africa. It was invented about the end of the 19th century. (Jensen)

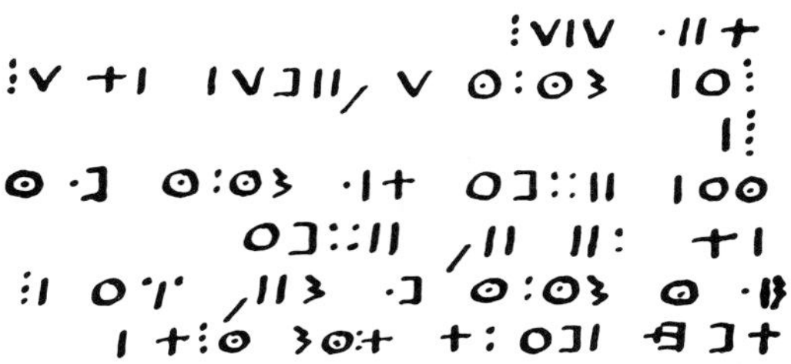

Tifinagh script. A descendant of the ancient North African scripts. Used now by nomadic Berbers in the Sahara Desert. (Nida)

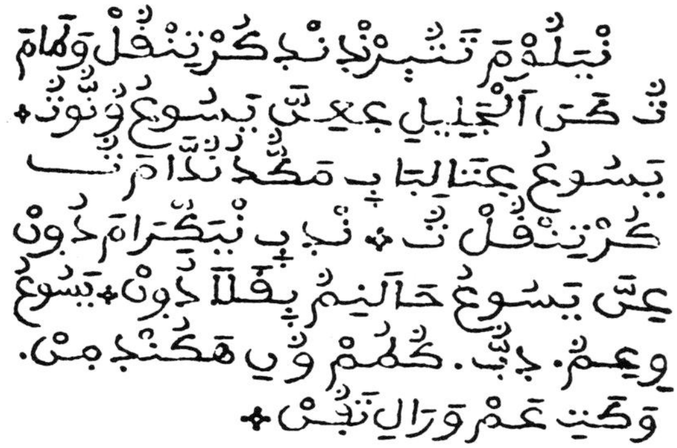

Maghreb script. The African styles of Arabic script differ somewhat from Arabic in their forms and diacritical signs. (Nida)

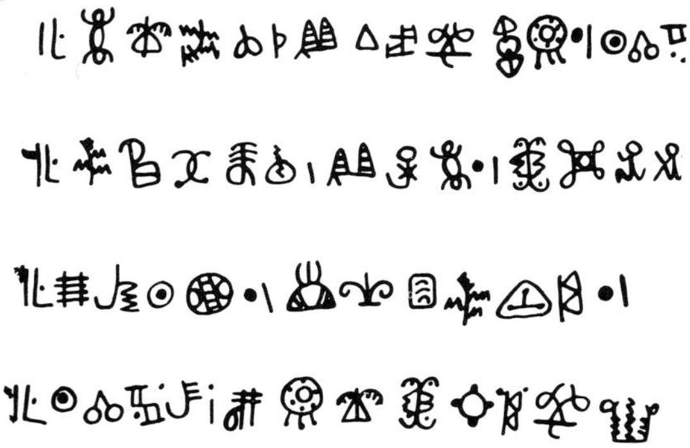

Bamum script. Ideograms invented by a Bamum king in western Cameroon early in the 20th century. Now extinct. (Jensen)

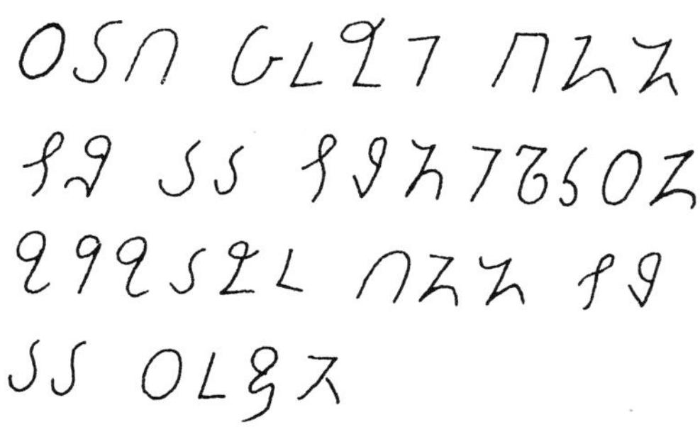

Somalian script (Osmanya script). The writing for the Somalian language. It is under trial adoption by the Somalian government. (Jensen)

8. SCRIPTS OF NORTH AND SOUTH AMERICA

The writing situation on the American continents is unique, since there was no contact with the Old World before the 15th century. Of the scripts used before the European invasion, only the Mayan ideograms in Mexico and Guatemala and the Aztec pictograms in Mexico remain. Aymara ideograms found in Bolivia may possibly date prior to the 15th century, but Paucartambo pictograms in Peru seem to have originated after the introduction of Christianity. The Cree and Cherokee scripts in North America are syllabaries invented under the influence of the Latin alphabet in the 19th century. These scripts are shown on pages 109 and 110.

At present, all writing used in the Americas is in Latin script. The official spoken languages are English, French, Spanish, Danish, Portuguese, Dutch, Quechua, and Hindi. Though the vernacular languages of the American Indians are spoken, no daily newspaper is published in them.

ARGENTINA

Newspapers are published in Spanish, the official language, and a few in English and German.

BELIZE

Formerly, British Honduras. Newspapers are published in English.

BOLIVIA

Newspapers are published in Spanish, the official language.

BRAZIL [BRASIL]

Brazil is the only nation in the Americas whose national language is Portuguese. Newspapers are published in Portuguese, and there are some newspapers for immigrants in various languages.

CANADA

The official languages of Canada are English and French, in which newspapers are published.

CHILE

Newspapers are published in Spanish, the official language.

COLOMBIA

Newspapers are published in Spanish.

COSTA RICA

Newspapers are published in Spanish.

CUBA

Newspapers are published in English and in Spanish.

DOMINICAN REPUBLIC

[REPUBLICA DOMINICANA]

Most newspapers are in Spanish, but some are in English.

ECUADOR

Newspapers are published in Spanish, the official language.

A postage stamp of Ecuador.

EL SALVADOR (Salvador)

Newspapers are in Spanish, the official language.

FRENCH GUIANA

[GUYANE FRANÇAISE]

The official language is French.

GREENLAND [GRØNLAND]

Since Greenland is a part of Denmark, Danish is the official language.

GUATEMALA

Newspapers are in Spanish, the official language.

GUYANA

The official languages are English and Hindi.

HAITI

Though the official language is French, the Creole language (close to Spanish) is also used in daily conversation and some news in the French newspapers is written in it.

HONDURAS

Newspapers are published in Spanish.

JAMAICA

The official language is English, in which newspapers are published.

MEXICO

Existing in Mexico are Maya and Aztec (Central/American Indian), languages of Mexico's past glory, and many other Indian languages, but the official language is Spanish, which is used in all newspapers.

NICARAGUA

Newspapers are published in Spanish.

PANAMA

The official language is Spanish, but newspapers are also published in English.

PARAGUAY

The official languages are Spanish and Guarani (Southern/American Indian). Newspapers are published in Spanish.

PERU

The official languages are Spanish and Quechua (Southern/American Indian).

Quechua was an official language of the Inca Empire, and attained the status of an official language of Peru in 1974. The newspapers are, however, published in Spanish only.

SURINAM

Formerly, Dutch Guiana. The official languages are Dutch and English.

TRINIDAD TOBAGO

[TRINIDAD AND TOBAGO]

Newspapers are published in English, the official language.

UNITED STATES OF AMERICA

The official language is English. Almost all newspapers are in English, but for the many immigrants from all over the world there are newspapers published in various languages and scripts.

URUGUAY

Newspapers are published in Spanish, the official language.

VENEZUELA

The official language is Spanish. Newspapers are published in it and in English.

9. SCRIPTS OF OCEANIA

In Oceanian writing, mention should first be made of the Rongo-rongo ideograms of Easter Island; besides these there is only the Woleai syllabary in the Caroline Islands. The origins of both are unknown (see page 110). Indian scripts reached as far as Indonesia. Micronesia, Melanesia, Polynesia, New Guinea, and Australia had no writing systems. At present most of Oceania belongs to the English-language area except for a few French territories.

AUSTRALIA

Newspapers are all in English.

FIJI

Newspapers are published in English and in Fijian (Melanesian/Malayo-Polynesian). Fijian is written in Latin script without h, x, and z.

NAURU

The Nauru official languages are English and Nauru (Melanesian/Malayo-Polynesian), which is written in Latin script.

NEW ZEALAND

Newspapers are published in English, but not in the Maori language (Polynesian/Malayo-Polynesian).

PAPUA NEW GUINEA

The official language is English. The Pidgin language is also used.

SAMOA [SAMOA I SISIFO]

Newspapers are in English and in Samoan (Polynesian/Malayo-Polynesian). Samoa I Sisifo means Samoa of the West in Samoan, which is written in Latin script without b, c, d, h, j, k, q, w, x, y, and z.

A postage stamp of Samoa.

TONGA

The Tongan language (Polynesian/Malayo-Polynesian) is spoken, but newspapers are published in English.

Other Scripts in the Americas and Oceania

Maya hieroglyphics. From the ancient Mayan culture that prospered in Mexico and Guatemala. (Ishida)

Paucartambo script. Pictograms discovered in the Paucartambo valley in Peru. (Diringer)

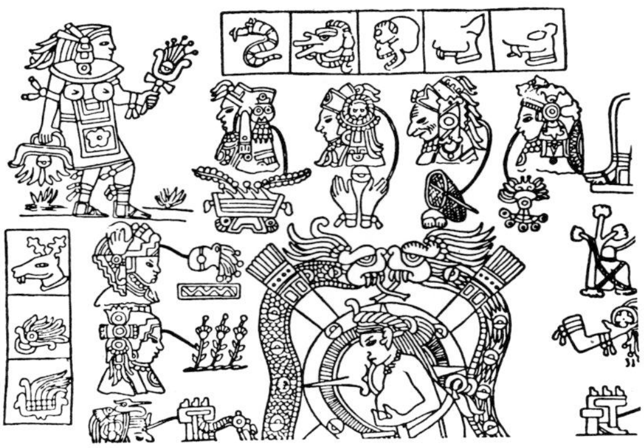

Aztec pictograms. From the Aztec Empire in Mexico that flourished before the Spanish invasion. (Gelb)

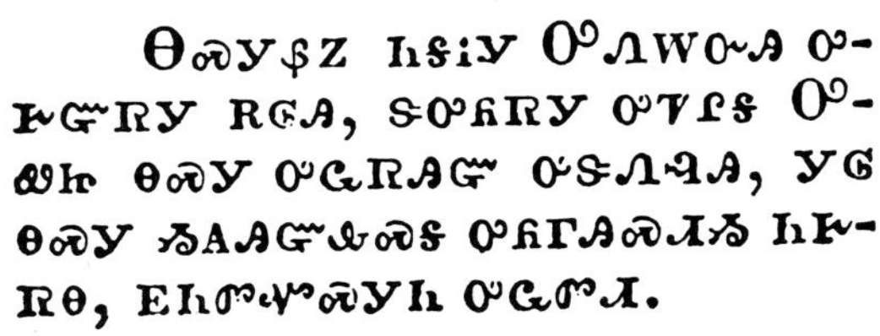

Cherokee script. A syllabary invented by a Cherokee Indian of North America in the beginning of the 19th century. (Nida)

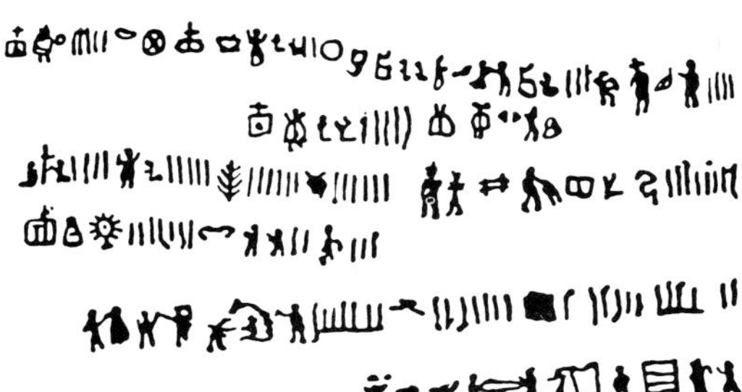

Aymara script. Antique pictograms of the Aymara tribe living around Lake Titicaca in South America. (Diringer)

Kauder script. Ideograms of the Micmac Indians who live near the mouth of the St. Lawrence River in North America. (Nida)

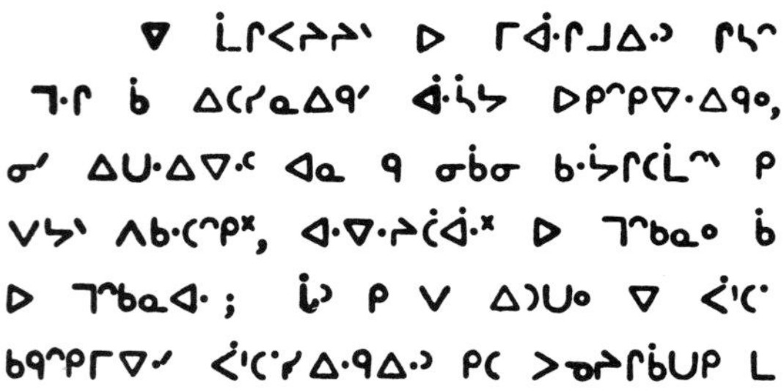

CREE SCRIPT (EVANS SYLLABIC SIGNS). A phonetic system invented for the Cree Indians by James Evans in the early 19th century. (Nida)

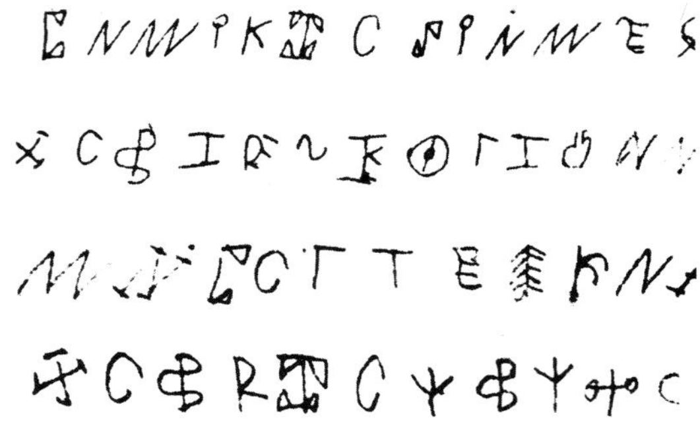

WOLEAI (CAROLINE) SCRIPT. The syllabary found on Woleai Island in the Caroline archipelago of Micronesia. (Diringer)

RONGO-RONGO SCRIPT (EASTER ISLAND SCRIPT). The mysterious ideograms from Easter Island in the southeastern Pacific. Undeciphered. (Diringer)

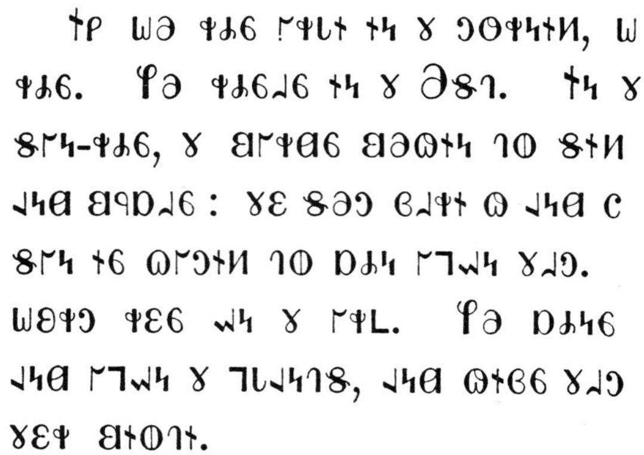

MORMON SCRIPT. The writing of Mormonism in North America. From the 19th century. (Author's collection)

APPENDIX 1. Kinds of Script

Scripts are classified into ideograms (pictograms, hieroglyphics, Chinese characters) and phonetic scripts.

An ideogram has a specific meaning in itself that has no relation to its pronunciation; for example, 山 represents a mountain though it is pronounced *shan* in Chinese and *yama* in Japanese, and "3" denotes "three" though it is pronounced *tatu* in Swahili and *trwa* in French.

In contrast to ideograms, the letters of a phonetic script have no specific meanings but show certain sounds; for example, "M" in Latin script, מ in Hebrew script, and Մ in Armenian script denote the *m* sound, while マ in Japanese script, म in Devanagari script, and 마 in Korean script denote the *ma* sound.

In this example, the former three are called phonemic scripts since they represent a single phoneme. The latter three are called syllabic scripts since they represent a syllable consisting of a consonant and a vowel. Letters representing a single vowel may consist of a single phoneme though they belong to a syllabary; イ in Japanese script and इ in Devanagari script indicate a single *i* sound, just as the "I" in Latin script represents a single *i* sound.

There are two syllabary systems. Japanese Kana script is the only example still in use today of what is called a pure syllabary, in which the shapes of the syllabics used have no relation to each other. For example, in Japanese the shapes of ミ *mi* and ム *mu* have no relation to the shape of マ *ma*. While pure syllabaries have become almost extinct, ones existing formerly were Archaemenid Persian cuneiform script (𐎶 *ma*, 𐎷 *mi*), Cretan Linear B (𐀔 *ma*, 𐀖 *mi*), Cherokee script (Ꮉ *ma*, Ꮊ *mi*), Lolo script (*ma*, *mi*), and several others.

The other syllabary system is considered a phonemic syllabary. Here, syllabics containing the same consonant are related to each other in shape; for example, 마 *ma*, 미 *mi*, and 무 *mu* in Korean script, and म *ma*, मि *mi*, and मु *mu* in Devanagari script.

Though this kind of syllabic is sometimes explained as a combination of two (or more) phonemes, it should be considered as one letter, because the ि of Devanagari or the ㅣ of Korean is never regarded as a separate letter, and because some syllabics can change the vowel by losing a part of the basic letter or simply by turning direction: for example, య *ya* → యి *yi* in Telugu script, and ᑌ *ta* → ᑎ *te* in Cree script.

Moreover, a syllabic consists not only of one consonant and one vowel, but sometimes of a conjunct consonant, a diphthong, or a final consonant: 만 *man* (in Korean), मै *mai*, म्र *mra* (in Devanagari). Eastern syllabaries, especially, tend to show one syllable by a single syllabic though the syllabic may comprise three or more phonemes, because in Oriental languages one syllable often makes one word; for example, *klyam* (to be sweet) in Lepcha script, and 병 *pyong* (illness) in Korean script.

APPENDIX 2. The Directions in Which Scripts Are Written

Scripts can be written in many directions. Simple explanations of these are given here based on the nine models (a) through (i).

Ancient Egyptian hieroglyphics were freely written in (a), (b), (d), or (e). Mirror-image letters were used, and sentences were read from the edge pointed at by the noses of the pictographic men or animals.

Ancient Phoenician and Aramaic scripts were written in (a) only; the descendants of these scripts, Arabic, Hebrew, Urdu, and others, are now written the same way.

Uighur script, a descendant of Aramaic script, turned ninety degrees from (a) to (h) in the medieval ages, when the Uighurs encountered Chinese culture (see page 97). As a result, its descendants, Mongolian and Manchu scripts, are written from top to bottom on vertical lines shifting from left to right as in (h).

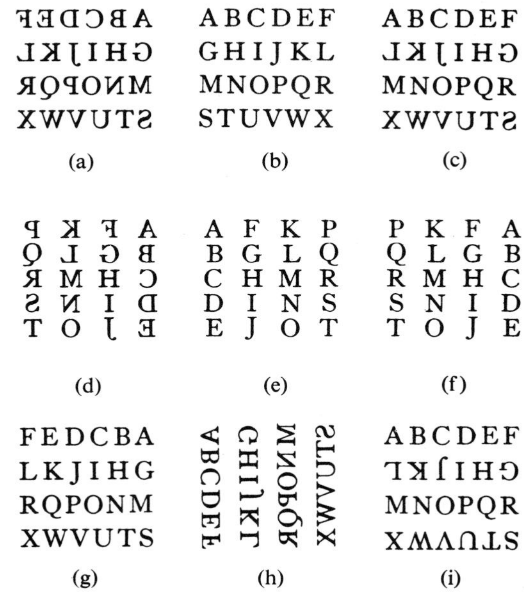

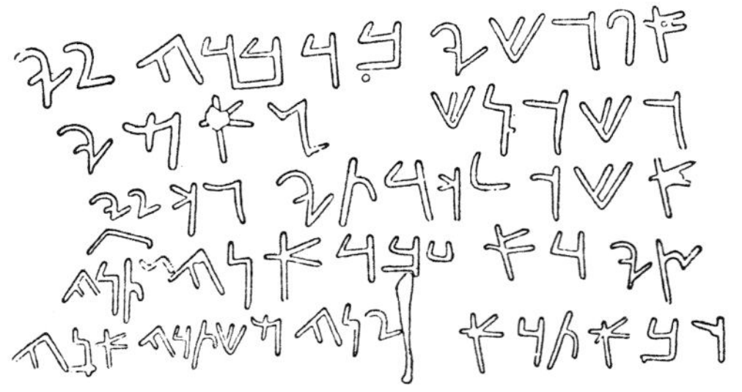

An Aramaic inscription, (a).

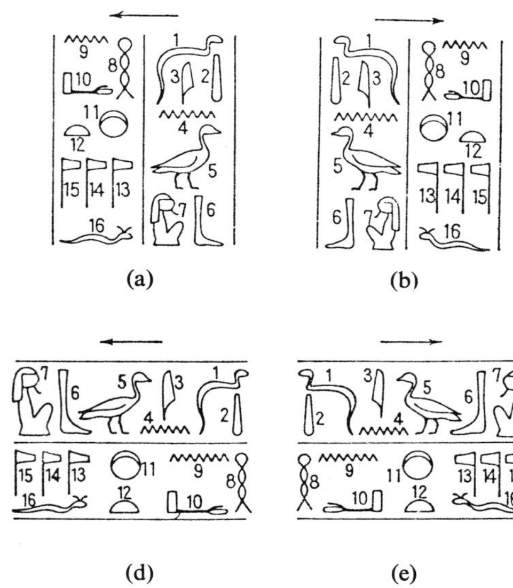

Egyptian hieroglyphics.

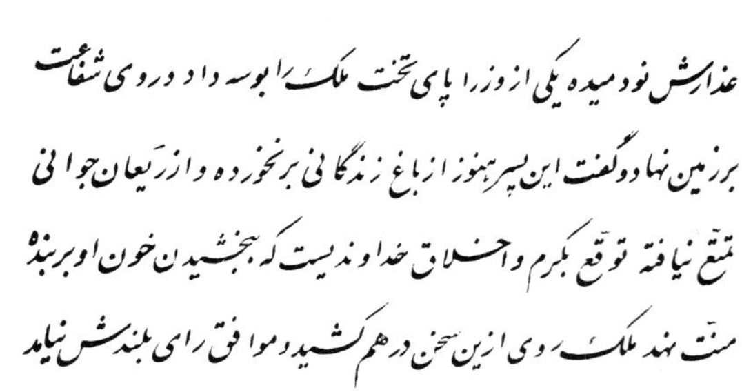

A Persian sentence in Arabic script, (a).

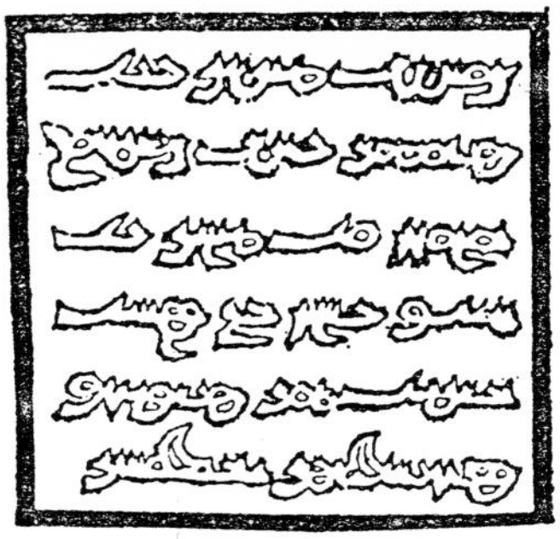

Uighur as read in Persia, (a).

Greek law written in boustrophedon, (c).

The same sentence of Uighur as read in China, (h).

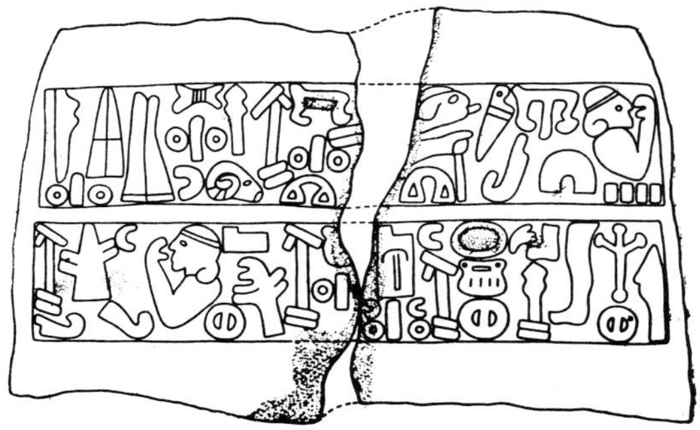

Hittite inscription, (c).

Ancient Greek script was written from right to left as in (a) or from left to right as in (b), each letter of the former being a mirror image. Sometimes, both types appeared on alternate lines, and this system, (c), was called boustrophedon. Ancient Hittite hieroglyphics were also written this way.

Greek script was gradually standardized to be read as (b), that is, from left to right on a horizontal line. Brahmi script in ancient India was also written in this way, but another ancient Indian script, Kharoṣhthi, was written in (a). The descendants of Greek and Brahmi script are now all written in (b). These include Latin, Russian, Armenian, Indian, Tibetan, Burman, Thai, Khmer, and many others. Even some Chinese, Japanese, and Korean sentences are written this way now.

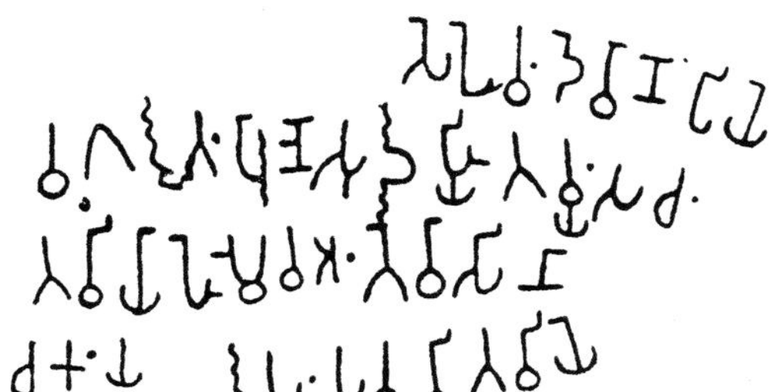

Brahmi inscription, (b).

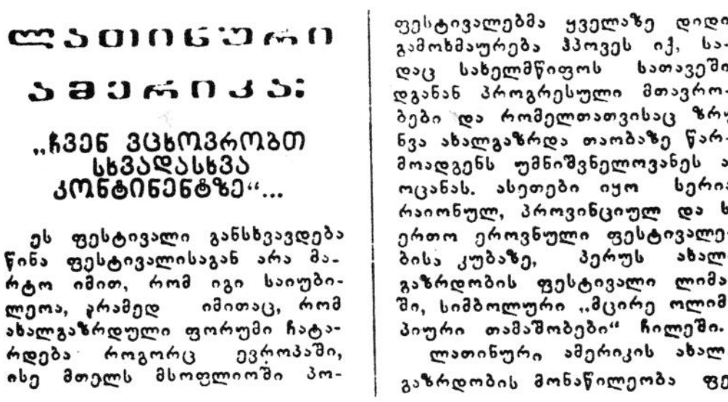

ლათინური ამერიკა:

„ჩვენ ვცხოვრობთ სხვადასხვა კონტინენტზე"...

ეს ფესტივალი განსხვავდება წინა ფესტივალისაგან არა მარტო იმით, რომ იგი საიუბილეოა, არამედ იმითაც, რომ ახალგაზრდული ფორუმი ჩატარდება როგორც ევროპაში, ისე მთელს მსოფლიოში პო-

ფესტივალებმა ყველაზე დიდი გამოხმაურება ჰპოვეს იქ, სადაც სახელმწიფოს სათავეში დგანან პროგრესული მთავრობები და რომელთათვისაც ზრუნვა ახალგაზრდა თაობაზე წარმოადგენს უმნიშვნელოვანეს ამოცანას. ასეთები იყო სერია რაიონულ, პროვინციულ და საერთო ეროვნული ფესტივალებისა კუბაზე, პერუს ახალგაზრდობის ფესტივალი ლიმაში, სიმბოლური „მცირე ოლიმპიური თამაშობები" ჩილეში.

ლათინური ამერიკის ახალგაზრდობის მონაწილეობა ფე-

Georgian newspaper, (b).

Since ancient times Chinese characters have been written from top to bottom on vertical lines shifting from right to left, and thus belong to (f). Various characters that were invented around China under the influence of Chinese characters have been written in the same way. These include Japanese, Korean, Hsihsia, Nuchen, and Khitan characters. The horizontal (f) is (g), in which each letter does not become a mirror image. Thus, a reader may become confused about the direction in which a sentence should be read. Script written in (g) is sometimes seen in Japan, Hongkong, and Taiwan.

The last is a strange type, (i), which has only been used for the Rongo-rongo script of Easter Island. Though the directions of the lines alternate from right to left as in (c), boustrophedon, each letter of the line read from the right is upside down rather than a mirror image. A reader of a Rongo-rongo document must have had to turn the wooden tablet on which Rongo-rongo was carved whenever he moved from one line to the next.

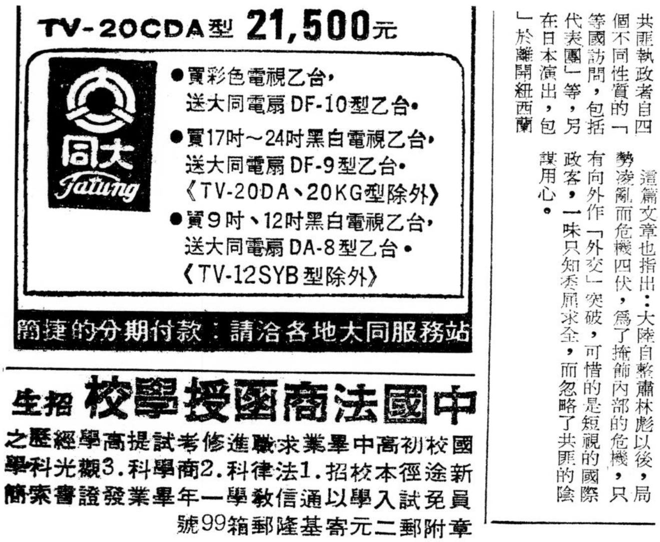

TV-20CDA型 21,500元

●買彩色電視乙台，
送大同電扇 DF-10型乙台。
●買17吋～24吋黑白電視乙台，
送大同電扇 DF-9型乙台。
《TV-20DA、20KG型除外》
●買9吋、12吋黑白電視乙台，
送大同電扇 DA-8型乙台。
《TV-12SYB型除外》

大同 Tatung

簡捷的分期付款：請洽各地大同服務站

生招 校學授函商法國中
之歷經學高提試考修進職求業畢中高初校國
學科光觀3.科學商2.科律法1.招校本徑途新
簡索書證發業畢年一學教信通以學入試免員
號99箱郵隆基寄元二郵附章

共匪執政者自四
個不同性質的「
等國訪問，包括
代表團」等，另
在日本演出，包
」於離開紐西蘭
這篇文章也指出：大陸自整肅林彪以後，局
勢凌亂而危機四伏，為了掩飾內部的危機，只
有向外作「外交」突破，可惜的是短視的國際
政客，一味只知委屈求全，而忽略了共匪的陰
謀用心。

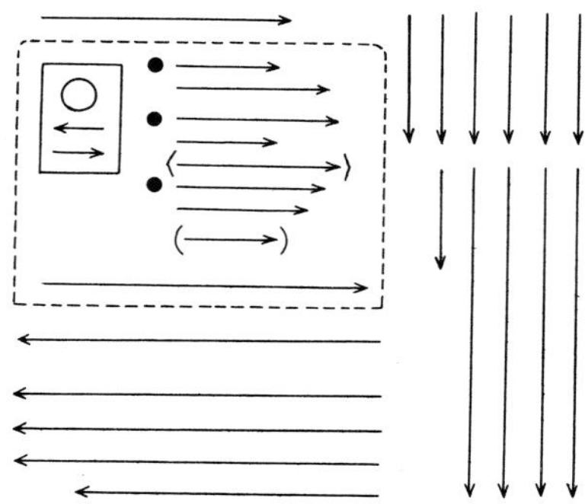

Part of a newspaper from Taiwan written in three directions, (b), (f), and (g).

A wooden tablet from Easter Island, (i).

GLOSSARY OF TERMS

alphabet: The set of phonemic letters used to write a language, usually arranged in a fixed order determined by custom.

Arabic figures: Conventionally, the numerical symbols 1, 2, 3, 4, 5, 6, 7, 8, 9, and 0. The numerals associated with the script used in the Arab world, however, are different from these.

aspirate sound: A consonant sound incorporating an *h* sound or rough breathing.

cerebral sound: A sound made with the tongue curled up so that its underside touches the palate. It is used especially in Asian and Indian languages.

Chinese characters: The group of ideograms used today in the writing systems of China, Japan, and Korea. Each character represents a meaning rather than a sound and may depict a real object in stylized form, be abstract, or combine realistic and abstract elements.

conjunct consonants: Consonants whose sounds blend together within a single syllable. In Indian scripts, these are written as a single letter.

cuneiform: The angular or wedge-shaped writing used in ancient Sumer, Babylon, and Persia.

dental sound: A consonant sound articulated with the blade or tip of the tongue against or near the upper front teeth.

diacritical mark: A mark placed near or through a phonetic character to change its sound.

diaeresis: In Greek script the mark placed over a vowel, especially the second of two adjacent vowels, to indicate that it is pronounced as a separate syllable.

diphthong: Two or more vowel sounds blended together within a single syllable.

final form: The form taken by a letter when it appears at the end of a word.

glottal stop: A sound produced by momentary closure of the space between the vocal chords, followed by an explosive release.

guttural sound: A sound produced in the throat.

hard consonant: In Russian, a consonant incorporating or followed by a *y* sound.

hard vowel: In Russian, a vowel preceded by a *y* sound or a *y*-like modification of a consonant.

hieroglyphic: The type of ideogram, representing a meaning rather than a sound, used in ancient Egypt. The term sometimes refers to Mayan writing. Hieroglyphics developed from pictures of real objects, but are more sophisticated than pictograms.

ideogram: In this book, any picture, stylized picture, or abstract symbol used in writing a language and representing a meaning rather than a sound. Thus, Chinese characters, hieroglyphics, and pictograms are all ideograms. Some texts treat them separately.

independent form: The form taken by a letter when it stands alone, apart from any word.

inherent vowel: A vowel sound which is unwritten but always pronounced with a consonant unless otherwise indicated. In the Indian scripts each consonant has an inherent *a*-vowel.

initial form: The form taken by a letter when it appears at the beginning of a word.

italic style: A way of writing Latin script so that the letters slant upward to the right, as opposed to upright roman style. *These words are in italics.*

labial sound: A sound produced with the participation of one or both lips.

Latin script: Writing using the alphabet a, b, c, etc. Based on older forms, it developed during the Roman Empire and is used today in most countries of Europe, the Americas, Africa, and Oceania, and some Asian nations.

ligature: A written character consisting of two or more letters combined into one or joined by a tie, such as [&], a combination of e and t.

medial form: The form taken by a letter when it appears in the middle of a word.

monosyllabic language: A language all or nearly all of whose words are single syllables.

palatal sound: A sound formed with the tongue touching or near the hard palate.

phoneme: The smallest unit of speech that distinguishes one utterance from another. The *p* sound of English "pin" and the *f* sound of English "fin" are two different phonemes.

phonemic script: A script each of whose letters represents the sound of one phoneme.

pictogram: The type of ideogram, representing a meaning rather than a sound, which depicts real objects.

pure syllabary: A syllabary in which the shapes of the syllabics bear no relation to each other. Japanese Kana script is the only example in use today.

roman style: A way of writing Latin script modeled on the upright letters of ancient Roman inscriptions, as opposed to slanting italic style. These words are in roman.

sibilant sound: A sound having, containing, or resembling *s* or *sh*.

simplified form: In this book, an abridged Chinese character of the type used today in the People's Republic of China. Original-form Chinese characters are used in Taiwan, and slightly simplified forms are used in Japan.

soft consonant: In Russian, a consonant neither incorporating nor followed by a *y* sound.

soft vowel: In Russian, a vowel preceded by neither a *y* sound nor a *y*-like modification of a consonant.

syllabary: A set of written characters each of which represents the sound of a single syllable but has no meaning.

tone: The pitch of a word. In some languages, like Chinese, the tone of each word is fixed, and a change in tone may produce a change in meaning.

vanishing-vowel sign: The mark placed above a consonant in Arabic script and some Indian scripts to indicate that no vowel follows.

vowel sign: A mark placed above, below, or to the side of a consonant to indicate the vowel sound that follows.

BIBLIOGRAPHY

Some of the books listed here served as sources for the script samples in the main text. Each caption in the main text indicates the source of the sample by the author's last name in parentheses.

Books in Western Languages

Andronov, M. S. *The Tamil Language.* Moscow, 1965.

———. *The Kannada Language.* Moscow, 1969.

Ballhorn, F. *Grammatography.* London, 1861.

Chinggaltai. *A Grammar of the Mongol Languages.* New York, 1963.

Das Gupta, B. B. *Oriya Self-Taught.* Calcutta, 1967.

Diringer, D. *The Alphabet: A Key to the History of Mankind.* London, 1968.

Fossey, M. C. *Notices sur les Caractéres Étrangers, Anciens et Modernes.* Paris, 1927.

Ganathe, N. S. R. *Learn Gujarati in 30 Days.* Madras, 1973.

Gardner, F. *Philippine Indic Studies.* San Antonio, 1943.

Gelb, I. J. *A Study of Writing.* Revised Edition. Chicago and London, 1963.

Gilyarevsky, R. S., and Grivnin, V. S. *Languages Identification Guide.* Moscow, 1970.

Grierson, B. A. *Linguistic Survey of India.* Vols. 1–11. Delhi, 1963–.

Gunasekara, A. M. *A Comprehensive Grammar of the Sinhalese Language.* Colombo, 1962.

Harrison, R. K. *Biblical Hebrew.* London, 1973.

Henning, W. B. *Acta Iranica* 14. Leiden, 1977.

Hood, M. S. F. "The Tartaria Tablets," *Antiquity* 41. London, 1967.

Hospitalier, J. J. *Grammaire Laotienne.* Paris, 1937.

Hudson, D. F. *Bengali.* Teach Yourself Books. London, 1965.

Huffman, F. E. *Cambodian System of Writing and Beginning Reader.* London, 1970.

Jaspan, M. A. *Redjang Ka-Ga-Nga Texts.* Canberra, 1964.

Jensen, H. *Die Schrift in Vergangenheit und Gegenwart.* Berlin, 1969.

Malov, S. E. *Pamyatniki Drevnetyurkskoy Pisimennosti* (Old documents of ancient Turkey). Moscow, 1951.

Meenaksi Amma, C. L. *Learn Malayalam in 30 Days.* Madras, 1973.

Nida, E. A. *The Book of a Thousand Tongues.* New York, 1972.

Ojha, P. G. K. *Universal Self-Hindi Teacher.* Delhi, 1973.

O'Neill, P. G. *Essential Kanji.* Tokyo, 1974.

Postma, A. *Treasure of a Minority.* Manila, 1972.

Rahman, A. *Teach Yourself Urdu in Two Months.* Karachi, 1975.

Rao, R. *Learn Kannada in 30 Days.* Madras, 1973.

Rock, J. F. *The Zhi Mä Funeral Ceremony of the Na-Khi of Southwest China.* Vienna, 1955.

Senapati, T. N. *Learn Bengali in 30 Days.* Madras, 1973.

Shackle, C. *Punjabi.* London, 1973.

Sivaramamurti, C. *Indian Epigraphy and South Indian Scripts.* Madras, 1966.

Sofroniw, S. A. *Modern Greek.* London, 1976.

Srinivasachari, K. *Learn Sanskrit in 30 Days.* Madras, 1974.
———. *Learn Telugu in 30 Days.* Madras, 1974.
U Tha Myat. *Pyu phat sa* (Pyu reader). Rangoon.
Wallis Budge, E. A. *Egyptian Language.* London, 1966.

BOOKS IN JAPANESE

Ceram, C. W. *Semai Tani, Kuroi Yama* (Narrow ravines and dark mountains). Tokyo, 1959.
Doblhofer, E. *Ushinawareta Moji no Kaidoku* (Deciphering lost scripts). Tokyo, 1963.
Harada, M. *Kiso Birumago* (Basic Burmese). Tokyo, 1966.
Ichikawa, S., Kozu, H., and Hattori, S. *Sekai Gengo Gaisetsu* (General outline of world languages). Two volumes. Tokyo, 1971.
Ishida, E. *Maya Bummei* (Mayan civilization). Tokyo, 1967.
Ishihama, J. *Chuo Ajiya Kodaigo Bunken* (Buddhist manuscripts and secular documents of the ancient central Asian languages). Kyoto, 1961.
Ito, Y. *Sekai no Rekishi 2: Kodai Oriento Bummei* (History of the world 2: ancient oriental cultures). Tokyo, 1960.
Kaizuka, S. *Kodai Yin Teikoku* (Ancient Yin Empire). Tokyo, 1957.
Kato, I. *Shokei-moji Nyumon* (A primer in hieroglyphics). Tokyo, 1962.
Kawakatsu, M. *Bonji Kowa* (A lecture on Sittan script). Kyoto, 1944.
Nishida, T. *Ikite-iru Shokei-moji* (Living hieroglyphics). Tokyo, 1966.
Ogawa, T. *Kodai Kyokai Surabugo Bumpo* (Ancient Slavic church grammar). Tokyo, 1971.
Ozawa, S. *Mongorugo Yonshukan* (Mongolian in four weeks). Tokyo, 1974.
Saito, S. *Girishago Nyumon* (A Greek primer). Tokyo, 1943.
Song, J. *Kiso Chosengo* (Basic Korean). Tokyo, 1959.
Sugi, I. *Kekkei-moji Nyumon* (A primer in cuneiform scripts). Tokyo, 1968.
Suzuki, H. *Echiopia Hyojungo Nyumon* (Standard Ethiopian primer). Tokyo, 1974.
Tamura, J. *Kei Ryo* (Tombs and mural paintings of Ch'ing-ling). Kyoto, 1952.
Teramoto, E. *Tibetto Bunten* (Tibetan grammar). Kyoto, 1940.
Togo, M. *Togo Roshiyago Koza* (Togo's course in Russian). Tokyo, 1967.
Tomita, T. *Taigo Kiso* (Basic Thai). Tokyo, 1957.
Yajima, H. *Moji no Rekishi* (History of writing). Tokyo, 1967.
Yamamoto, T. *Sekaishi Taikei 6: Indo, Higashi Ajiya* (An outline of world history 6: India, East Asia). Tokyo, 1959.
Yoshikawa, T. *Gendai Raosugo no On'in-soshiki to Moji-taikei* (The phonemic and writing systems of modern Lao). Osaka, 1968.

INDEX

Of Nations, Languages, and Writing Systems